Project Management in Health and Community Services

The new edition of this best-selling text presents the tools and techniques for effectively managing every kind of development and change in health and community services, while also balancing the needs of a range of stakeholders. It offers practical problem-solving strategies based on real-life scenarios.

A core competency for health and community service practitioners internationally, project management is a key challenge for both new and existing staff. This practitioner's guide uses project stories and examples to illustrate the core challenges that practitioners may face, including managing the project life cycle, project planning, execution and evaluation, risk management, handling change and building effective teams. Alongside new interviews with staff working across a range of sectors, this edition includes new content on career development and pathways as well as the growing integration of project methods into general management, and the impact of broader changes like digital innovation and transformation.

Written by highly experienced authors, and underpinned by the latest research, this enlightening and practical guide is an essential resource for anyone studying or working in health and community services.

Zhanming Liang is an Associate Dean of Research Education and Associate Professor in the School of Public Health, Medical and Veterinary Sciences, James Cook University. She is a leading researcher in management competency development in the health sector. As President of the Society for Health Administration Programs in Education she has played a key role in building capacity in health management workforce training and research in Asia Pacific. She received a La Trobe University Chancellor's Award in 2021 for her significant contribution to regional assistance during the COVID-19 pandemic.

Valerie Thiessen has a distinguished career as a project manager and academic. She holds qualifications in health information management, health services management and project management. Her experience includes roles in health information, health services management and consulting in both the private and public sectors in Australia and internationally. She has expertise in electronic health record and patient information system implementations, as well as specialty clinical systems and staff training for successful implementation.

Judith Dwyer is an adjunct Professor in the Flinders University College of Medicine and Public Health, and Deputy Chair of the Board of the Central Adelaide Local Health Network. She is a former CEO of Southern Health Care Network in Melbourne, and of Flinders Medical Centre in Adelaide. She was for several years a Research Program Leader for the Lowitja Institute, Australia's national Aboriginal health research institute. In 2014, she received the Sidney Sax Medal for her outstanding lifelong contribution to the Australian health system.

Project Management in Health and Community Services

A contemporary guide to practice

Fourth edition

Zhanming Liang, Valerie Thiessen and Judith Dwyer

Routledge
Taylor & Francis Group

LONDON AND NEW YORK

Designed cover image: shutterstock

First published 2025
by Routledge
4 Park Square, Milton Park, Abingdon, Oxon OX14 4RN

and by Routledge
605 Third Avenue, New York, NY 10158

Routledge is an imprint of the Taylor & Francis Group, an informa business

© 2025 Zhanming Liang, Valerie Thiessen and Judith Dwyer

British Library Cataloguing-in-Publication Data
A catalogue record for this book is available from the British Library

Library of Congress Cataloging-in-Publication Data
Names: Dwyer, Judith, 1951– author. | Liang, Zhanming, author. | Thiessen, Valerie, 1964– author.
Title: Project management in health and community services / Zhanming Liang, Valerie Thiessen, Judith Dwyer.
Description: Fourth edition. | Abingdon, Oxon ; New York, NY : Routledge, 2025. | Judith Dwyer's name appears first in previous editions. | Includes bibliographical references and index.
Identifiers: LCCN 2024032383 (print) | LCCN 2024032384 (ebook) | ISBN 9781032556758 (hardback) | ISBN 9781032556741 (paperback) | ISBN 9781003431701 (ebook)
Subjects: MESH: Community Health Services—organization & administration | Program Development—methods | Program Evaluation—methods
Classification: LCC RA427 (print) | LCC RA427 (ebook) | NLM WA 546.1 | DDC 351.0068/4—dc23/eng/20240916
LC record available at https://lccn.loc.gov/2024032383
LC ebook record available at https://lccn.loc.gov/2024032384

ISBN: 978-1-032-55675-8 (hbk)
ISBN: 978-1-032-55674-1 (pbk)
ISBN: 978-1-003-43170-1 (ebk)

DOI: 10.4324/9781003431701

Typeset in Sabon
by Apex CoVantage, LLC

Contents

CONTENTS

CONTENTS

Figures

Tables

TABLES

Templates

About the authors

Zhanming Liang is an Associate Dean of Research Education and Associate Professor in the School of Public Health, Medical and Veterinary Sciences, James Cook University. She is a leading researcher in management competency development in the health sector. As President of the Society for Health Administration Programs in Education she has played a key role in building capacity in health management workforce training and research in Asia Pacific. She received a La Trobe University Chancellor's Award in 2021 for her significant contribution to regional assistance during the COVID-19 pandemic.

Valerie Thiessen has a distinguished career as a project manager and academic. She holds qualifications in health information management, health services management and project management. Her experience includes roles in health information, health services management and consulting in both the private and public sectors in Australia and internationally. She has expertise in electronic health record and patient information system implementations, as well as specialty clinical systems and staff training for successful implementation.

Judith Dwyer is an adjunct Professor in the Flinders University College of Medicine and Public Health, and Deputy Chair of the Board of the Central Adelaide Local Health Network. She is a former CEO of Southern Health Care Network in Melbourne, and of Flinders Medical Centre in Adelaide.

She was for several years a Research Program Leader for the Lowitja Institute, Australia's national Aboriginal health research institute. In 2014, she received the Sidney Sax Medal for her outstanding lifelong contribution to the Australian health system.

Acknowledgments

We want to thank the many people who have contributed to our thinking and knowledge about project management, particularly the colleagues, students and friends who discussed their project work across the broad fields of health, community, aged and disability care, and their use of the principles and practices explained in this book. We would like to thank Paul Adcock, Janine Antcliffe, Kam Leung Chan, Ying Yee Chan, Rachel Campanella, Kate Dowson, Andrea Hutchinson, Tracey Hutt, Jackie McLeod, Rachel Meisner, San Le, Shawn Lin, Anuj Saraogi, Siegi Schmidmeier, Fiona Telford-Sharp, Lou Williamson and Nola Wyman for their generous assistance.

We are grateful to Lee Cheng Koh, our talented research officer, for technical help and good advice in the research for the book and the preparation of the manuscript. We also acknowledge our colleagues Professor Pauline Stanton and Dr Angelita Martini, who were co-authors of previous editions and made vital contributions to the thinking on which this book is based.

Finally, our thanks go to Russel George, editor and Madii Cherry-Moreton, editorial assistant at Routledge.

Glossary of terms

Benefits realisation (management) (BRM) A method of evaluating project success according to whether the intended benefits (financial or other) are achieved, often completed after the project itself is finished. BRM is used to identify, measure and track achievement of the desired benefits and is used most frequently in digital projects.

Best practice A method or technique that has consistently shown results superior to those achieved with other means and that may be used as a model or benchmark.

Business case Establishes the justification for an intended service or 'business' in operational and financial terms, and seeks to establish that the service as planned can be financially viable (or profitable) – a positive business case is one in which the revenue/benefits outweigh the costs.

Close/close-out The end of the fourth phase of the project cycle when project completion tasks and handover or transitioning from the project to the new method or state are completed.

Co-design Collaboration between agencies and consumers in the design of services or products; and when community or consumer representatives work with agencies as partners in planning and design.

Commissioning This term has two meanings: the process of ensuring that a new facility, piece of equipment or service is fully operational; and the process of contracting a team, vendor, company or consultant to conduct a project, service or other activity on the agency's behalf.

Contingency A potential problem or change in the project; an amount of money or other resource held within the project budget to cover elements of risk or uncertainty.

Control Ensuring that the project keeps to the agreed project scope, budget, schedule and quality.

Cost-benefit analysis Estimates (in monetary terms) the costs and the positive effects of an intervention or program.

Cost-effectiveness analysis Compares relative cost and outcomes (or effect) of two or more interventions with the effect expressed in non-monetary terms using 'natural units' such as cure rate or reduction in the incidence of a disease.

Cost-utility analysis Expresses outcomes in non-monetary units such as quality-adjusted life years (QALYs) so that comparisons of benefit can be made between alternative treatments or interventions.

Critical path The group of tasks that are interdependent and must happen in a certain sequence (called critical tasks). The longest sequence of critical tasks makes up the critical path which defines the project (minimum) timeframe.

Critical path method (CPM) or critical path analysis A method to identify and schedule all the critical tasks of a project, as well as their dependencies, to understand the minimum time required to complete a whole project.

Critical success factors (CSF) The important aspects of projects (and their contexts) that are known to affect the achievement of outcomes.

Deliverables Any outcomes or outputs required by the business to achieve a project or business goal such as goods, services, products, systems or documents.

Digital technology (or information and communication technology [ICT]) The utilisation, development or implementation of computing-based technologies including software, systems or applications.

Direct costs The costs incurred by and for the project that would not otherwise be incurred by the organisation.

Economic evaluation Analysis that estimates the relative value of alternative options.

Effectiveness The extent to which planned outcomes are achieved by a service or product in normal conditions (rather than in the laboratory or in trials). The answer to the question: 'Does it work in practice?'

Electronic medical record (EMR) The systematic collection of patient and care information stored in a digital format, replacing paper medical records. Also called electronic health record.

Escalate Take a problem or issue higher in the organisation for resolution; or implement the next level of action required to overcome an identified risk.

Evidence-based practice The design of care practice and decision-making based on evidence from research studies and other sources of reliable information (e.g. internal data).

Exclusions What is out of the project scope (what the project won't do).

Gantt chart A commonly used method of presenting the timelines and tasks of a project and charting actual progress. It plots activities (in rows) against the timeline (in columns), thus showing the relationships between them.

Gap analysis An assessment of inadequacies or missing aspects and potential capacity in the available service system.

Gateway review/process A project assurance method to improve the delivery of major projects. It involves short, sharp and confidential reviews conducted by reviewers not associated with the project at key stages of the project life cycle, also known as 'gates'.

Go/no go The time at which the organisation decides whether or not to proceed with the next stage of a project, or to accept/go live with a chosen system or model.

Go-live (also called cutover) The time at which a product, deliverable or outcome is put into practice.

Grey literature Research that is unpublished or not published in the peer-reviewed research literature, including government reports and policy documents.

Impact evaluation Measures achievement of the project's goals and objectives – that is, it focuses on the immediate results.

Indirect costs Costs that are not readily identified and attributed to a particular project. These costs may be necessary for the implementation and completion of the project but are 'built in' or shared with other activities within the organisation.

Information and communications technology (ICT) All devices, networking components, applications and systems that in combination allow people and organisations to interact in the digital world.

Kanban A project method and set of tools which feature visual signboards such as project dashboards, project overviews, task management, workflow and personal agenda boards.

Lessons learned Insights and knowledge gained by the project team throughout the project life cycle which could be useful in future project (or operational) design and practice.

Lessons learned log A tool for capturing project lessons learned that makes the information available to the project management team.

Literature review A process of finding, describing, summarising, evaluating and clarifying evidence found in the research and policy literature.

Milestones Markers of specific points along a project timeline that serve as an indication of progress and timeliness.

Needs analysis or needs assessment An activity to develop a comprehensive understanding of a problem or need in the community or population, in order to identify interventions or strategies that can solve the problem or address the need.

Network diagram A chart depicting each task and the time it requires e.g. days, with arrows to depict dependencies between tasks.

Objectives Statements of the steps or changes that need to be achieved in order to achieve the goal.

Outcome evaluation Measures the longer-term results or benefits of the project.

Phase A sequential section of the project life cycle i.e. initiation, planning, implementation and close. Each phase has one or more specific project objectives and related activities, and specified results, deliverables, processes, and milestones.

PMBOK (Project Management Body of Knowledge [C3]) A widely used comprehensive resource for project management which encapsulates generally accepted project management knowledge, practices and terminology.

PRINCE2 (PRojects IN Controlled Environments) A project management methodology with a structured set of components, techniques and processes designed for managing any type or size of project.

Probity (tender process integrity) The criteria for good conduct and decision-making in a tendering process: fairness, impartiality, transparency, security, confidentiality and compliance with legislative obligations and government policy.

Process evaluation Measures the effectiveness of the strategies and methods used in the project, and the skill of their execution.

Procurement The sourcing, negotiation, strategic selection and acquisition of goods and services.

Program A group of projects managed in a coordinated way; or a service, intervention or set of activities that aims to meet a health or social care need.

Program logic A method of planning and evaluating projects that specifies the links between the goals of a service or project and the inputs, processes, outputs and impacts/outcomes it will produce.

Project assurance A discipline that seeks to provide an independent and objective oversight of the likely future performance of major projects for those responsible for sanctioning, financing or insuring such undertakings.

Project brief or concept brief/proposal A short document that outlines the rationale, goals and scope of a project, prepared for the purposes of seeking approval for a project prior to development of a full plan. Basis for the project charter.

Project charter (also called project definition or project initiation document [PID]) A more detailed version of the project brief, the charter is the authorising document for a project, developed during the approval process.

Project life cycle A framework of the phases that a project must move through as it progresses from abstract idea to actual completion.

Project management The methods, skills, tools and techniques by which those responsible for a project make it happen and monitor and control the time, cost and quality of the project.

Project management office (PMO) A group or department within an agency that defines and maintains standards for project management within the organisation and offers guidance and assistance to projects.

Project manager The person responsible for managing the whole project, across the various departments and staff who may be needed.

Project plan(s) also called project management plan(s) The guidebook(s) for the team and stakeholders that details strategies, work program, scope and boundaries, deliverables, stakeholder engagement, communication, control, planning assumptions, approved budget and schedule.

Project portfolio(s) The collection(s) of projects being conducted by the organisation, or by major divisions within it.

Project portfolio management (PPM) A business management approach for the organisation to prioritise and select the right projects in line with its capacity to deliver and strategic intent.

Project sponsor The executive or senior manager who acts as the supervisor for the project manager and decision maker for major changes (alone or with others) and promotes and supports overall project delivery.

Proof of concept (POC) A small exercise to test the design idea or assumption and to demonstrate functionality of a proposed approach, concept or method prior to commencing full development.

Risk matrix A table used during risk assessment to define the level of risk by considering the probability or likelihood of an event or problem occurring against the severity of its consequences if it does.

Scope The reach and boundaries of the project – 'who, what, where, when and how' – within defined limits.

Scope creep Unmanaged changes to scope – usually expansion.

Scope statement Describes the reach of the project including limits and exclusions.

Sign-off Formal approval by the authorised person or group.

Soft project(s) Complex undertaking(s) aimed at intangible results.

Stage A distinct part of a large project with its own outputs or deliverables; stages are often separated by decision points.

Stakeholder Individuals, groups and organisations actively involved in the project, or whose interests may be affected as a result of the project, or who may exert influence over the project and its results.

Stakeholder analysis Identifying project stakeholder priorities, interests, expectations and allegiances with the aim of ensuring their engagement is constructive and productive.

Status report Advice to the steering committee, project sponsor and other stakeholders as to whether the project is on track to deliver the planned outcomes, and to highlight where their decision-making or direct help is needed.

Steering committee A formal committee of high-level project stakeholder representatives and/or experts, normally chaired by the project sponsor, that provides guidance on key issues, acts as the decision-making body for project changes, authorises acceptance of reports and deliverables, and acts as a sounding board for the project team.

Tender/tendering An offer submitted by interested bidders (organisations that apply or 'bid' to win the contract) to the agency commissioning the project (sometimes called the 'purchaser').

Tracking Monitoring the progress of the project against planned activities and milestones.

Variance(s) A measurable change from a known standard or baseline – the difference between what is expected and what is actually accomplished.

Work breakdown structure (WBS) A tool that the project team uses to plan the strategies, activities and tasks required to achieve the deliverables (and the goal) of the project. The WBS enables detailed planning of the work, budget and timeline required for the project.

Work package All scheduled activities and tasks (with milestones) required to complete a deliverable in a WBS.

Introduction

It is a pleasure to present the fourth edition of this book for new and old readers. Much has changed in the world of project management over the 20 years this book has been in print. In health and community care, projects and project management have changed radically. From being a management method mastered by a relatively small number of project managers, project management knowledge and skills are now embedded in the general management and strategies of organisations. This edition responds to growth in the volume, scope, complexity and urgency of the project work that organisations undertake – work that is vital in the modern era to strengthen and renew the mission, methods and service offerings of the health and community care sectors.

With this book we aim to assist managers, project practitioners and students with information and resources about project management based on how things really work in health and community care. Much of the most up-to-date thinking and resources for project management are now found on websites: of companies with products and services to sell, of government authorities and agencies with advice and guidance for project practitioners (particularly for practice improvement and digital solutions), and of peak project management organisations seeking to provide information and advice to members. There are also many project management research studies in academic and industry journals providing evidence on what works and what doesn't and aiming to take project management practices to a higher level. This edition of the book references many of the reputable websites as well as the journal literature and textbooks.

DOI: 10.4324/9781003431701-1

As has been our practice, this new edition is informed by two kinds of research. First, we systemically reviewed the recent literature to explore new evidence on projects and project management from around the world; then we interviewed 15 project directors and senior managers working in health and community care in Australia, Hong Kong (China), the UK and New Zealand to confirm current project management practices and gain insight into new and old challenges. Throughout the book we use quotes from the interviews to illustrate or explain key concepts and perspectives. Since position titles vary between organisations, and in order to preserve anonymity for our participants, we have used 'senior manager' as a blanket term to describe participants who hold executive or other senior level positions.

We attribute the success of the last three editions of the book to three characteristics. First, the book was developed specifically for professionals working in health and community care (and students on track to do so) by a team of practitioners and academics with broad expertise and experience in project management and evidence-based practice. Second, we use worked examples of methods, and real-world project stories, to illustrate the concepts and help readers see how project management methods are applied in practice in the complex world of health and community care. Finally, we acknowledge the importance of human factors in project work and write plainly about how these factors influence project design, practice and success.

In addition to research evidence from academic studies, we refer to high-quality websites where readers can find more detailed information on methods and access to technical resources. At the end of each chapter additional resources from websites, books and academic publications are listed.

How to use this book

The book can be read from start to finish for an experience of immersion in the world of projects and project management, highly recommended to those who are new to project management. Or parts can be used as a reference and guide by project managers at various stages of their careers and students of the health and community care professions, public health and management. Senior managers and those who decide which projects to approve and fund might use it to improve their decision-making as they endeavour to increase the impact of their organisations' project work.

Chapter 1 explains the basics and offers a list of critical project success factors. Chapter 2 addresses the context of health and community services, captures significant changes in the project management space in response to that changing context, and explains the characteristics and practices that assist organisations to be successful in their project work. Chapter 3 explains the project life cycle, gives an overview of the methods and tools of project management, and discusses career pathways in the field of project management. These three chapters establish the basis for the detailed guide to managing a project that is provided in the following chapters.

The rest of the book addresses the practice of project management, according to the phases of the project life cycle – initiation, planning, implementation and closure. The use of a broad range of methods, approaches and tools is explained, along with the challenge of making change happen through projects. Additional methods particular to health and community care, or used differently in the sector, like evaluation, literature reviews and needs assessment, are included. These chapters are designed to meet the needs of both the practising project manager and those entering the field. They are also important for those who manage groups of projects, plan project strategy for their organisations, or lead the planning and development effort.

We have included lots of headings and subheadings in each chapter to help the reader locate particular topics of interest, as well as understand the logical development of the material. Each chapter starts with an introduction to provide an overview and ends with a summary of the major points. Examples and useful checklists are highlighted within the text for easy reference.

There is a lot of technical language in the world of projects, which we seek to explain and demystify throughout. Terms that might be unfamiliar are explained in the glossary at the beginning of this book and shown in **bold** type the first time they appear in each chapter.

Writing the book was also a project, starting with the preparation and initiation phase, organising the needed resources, conducting the research, developing writing plans and delegating responsibilities. The project then went through multiple writing and revision stages. We are now at the satisfying moment of handover – the work has been done, celebrations have been held, and all the documentation is in order. For this project, the final evaluation will come later, and is in the hands of our readers.

CHAPTER 1

Why project management?

This chapter explains what projects are and why they are important and notes changing trends in the use of projects in health and community services. It describes the characteristics of projects and how they are designed and implemented to achieve defined goals within time, cost and quality constraints. We discuss the challenges facing **project management** in a time of rapid change and define project success from the perspectives of different stakeholders. The chapter ends with an explanation of **critical success factors** for projects in the sector.

DOI: 10.4324/9781003431701-2

What is a project?

A temporary endeavour undertaken to create a unique product, service or result.

(PMI, 2021, p. 4)

A project is a unique set of interrelated activities designed to produce a set of **deliverables** and achieve a defined goal within clearly defined time, cost and quality constraints (Westland, 2007). That is, a project has a beginning and an end, it requires resources and is often described as having a '3D' objective: to meet specifications (**scope** and quality), to finish on time and to be done within budget (see Figure 1.1). This is also called the project triangle. While these are the defining characteristics, each project is unique in its particular focus, scope, size, complexity and setting. Hence, project management is about applying relevant knowledge, skills, tools and techniques to a broad range of activities in order to meet the requirements of each particular project (Project Management Institute, 2021).

The development of project methods and tools

Project management is defined as the application of skills and the use of methods, tools and techniques that enable organisations to plan, manage and achieve one-off tasks or goals (Meredith et al., 2021). It offers a method for driving development processes and successfully implementing change. Successful project management enables organisations to remain relevant and competitive, and to continuously improve products, services and processes. Project management is also important in responding to a crisis – for example, in the development and deployment of disaster plans or in response to the COVID-19 pandemic.

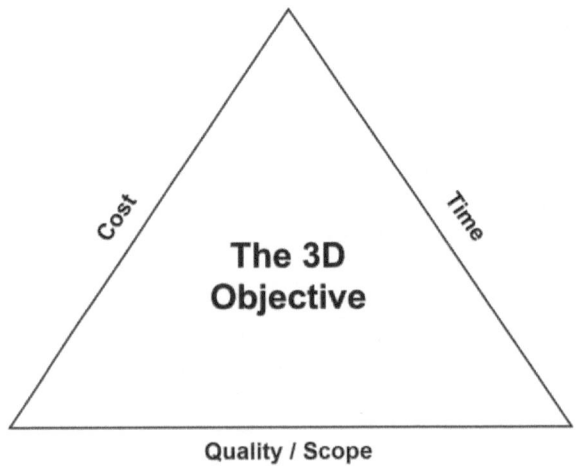

Figure 1.1 The project triangle

Project management tools first emerged in engineering in the early 1900s, with the projects simply being managed by the architects, engineers and builders themselves. From the 1950s, the role of **project manager** was initiated, and project management tools and techniques were systematically applied to engineering and spread to other fields, such as construction and defence activity (Cleland & Gareis, 2006). Since then, the rapid development of modern project management has seen it recognised as a distinct discipline, with two major worldwide professional organisations: the International Project Management Association (IPMA), established in 1967, and the Project Management Institute (PMI), in 1969. The PMI has published seven editions of the popular project management guidebook – *A Guide to the Project Management Body of Knowledge* (**PMBOK** Guide).

The temporary nature of a project indicates a definite beginning and end. The end is reached when the project's **objectives** have been achieved or when the project is terminated because its objectives cannot be met, or resources required by the project are no longer available, or because the need for the project no longer exists. However, while projects are temporary, their outcomes usually far outlast their end dates.

The growing importance of projects in health and community services has been clear over the past 20 years. Our research for this book has confirmed that getting things done through projects is now embedded in the normal ways that health and community service organisations manage their work and achieve needed change, though not always as comprehensively as in this senior manager's organisation:

> *I would say that 80 plus per cent of my job is now managing projects. The way we run the business is actually via a whole suite of projects, and a key role is program governance of the whole series of projects. . . . I think that's completely shifting the way I work. . . . It's basically, I'd say, yeah, it's project-based work.*
>
> *(Senior Manager, Home Care Service)*

General managers in health care now routinely need to be competent in project management (Sandhu & Liang, 2021; Zawada & Gągała, 2021). This shift can also be seen in the offering of formal and informal training in project management, and its inclusion in the curriculum of most postgraduate courses in health care management, public health and health promotion (Browmmeyer et al., 2021).

Project characteristics

Although each project is unique, they all have some common characteristics. Virtually all projects have a budget and all require resources to support project implementation. Projects also have a life cycle and defined deliverables that can be measured during or at the end of the project. More importantly, projects may enable changes that transform processes, performance and culture, and extend beyond the predetermined project outcomes (PMI, 2021; Pells, 2021). Projects are also opportunities to learn and create new knowledge and techniques to improve practice as well as future project design.

Projects have several characteristics that distinguish them from programs and services. First, each project is a *unique* and novel endeavour (Westland, 2007) so by definition, it hasn't been done before, at least not in its particular setting or circumstances. This is one of the reasons why the original project design is often modified during project implementation, and why monitoring to identify and respond to early warning signs is often critical to project success.

Second, depending on its type, size and focus, the project may require the *bringing together* of many different occupational groups, different parts of the organisation, and different functions and resources to achieve the objectives of the project. Project team dynamics can also be critical when a wide range of roles, skills and expertise is required by the project.

Third, the scope and targets set by a project are often *complex* and can require high levels of technical performance. Complexity can arise from the different perspectives of the various professions involved, the inexperience of the players, the number of interested parties, the geographic spread, the quantum of change or technical/solution complexity. For example, the selection and implementation of information systems are typically complex undertakings involving market testing, **procurement**, user testing, integration with other applications, preparing the workplace for the adoption of the new system and perhaps changes in staff roles, and developing staff skills to work with the new system. Project management is also relationship management, so the implementation challenges are not just technical but also bring in human factors, particularly if the new system or method is to be used effectively across different functional areas (Meng & Boyd, 2017). In a project such as this, **stakeholder** consultation and engagement and creating high user satisfaction are critical (Verbeke et al., 2015).

Fourth, managing a project also means managing a *dynamic* situation, as the unexpected is always happening (Furniss et al., 2018). When a new problem arises, it must be addressed immediately, because the project is limited by its timelines. In addition, changes and modifications may add significant costs to the project budget. For example, it is expensive to change the specifications of a new **information and communications technology (ICT)** system once design work is underway. It can be expensive in a different way to change the goals or scope of an organisational restructuring project. Senior management can dictate a change of direction to respond to changes in the internal or external environments, but doing so is likely to have consequences including reduced commitment and goodwill among those affected.

Fifth, projects can *vary in scope* from something as simple as implementing the use of a new type of catheter to a complex undertaking such as introducing a new model of care. Projects may impact and be visible to the whole organisation and wider community (i.e. glamorous and exciting) or they may be hidden away in a small team or department (i.e. committed people doing innovative work).

Finally, managing projects can be similar to managing *high-risk* businesses (PMI, 2021; Swarnakar et al., 2022). Projects are often used to trial new ideas, so there is a lot of uncertainty and some unknowns. For large complex projects, estimation of time and cost is as much an art as a science, based more on the experience of the project manager and expertise in the organisation than sophisticated modelling. Projects can also be at risk from external factors such as political intervention, financial trouble, changes of policy direction and funding cuts.

The project life cycle

Although projects are highly varied in almost every characteristic, they all move through common phases – from initiation to closing, via planning/preparation and implementation phases. Figure 1.2 shows a model of the **project life cycle** in these four phases. Thinking about the phases in a project life cycle is useful both for seeing the whole picture and for planning and managing each phase. But it would be a mistake to think that having an idea, conceptualising the idea into a project, and successfully completing the project is a linear process. Projects generally don't go exactly as

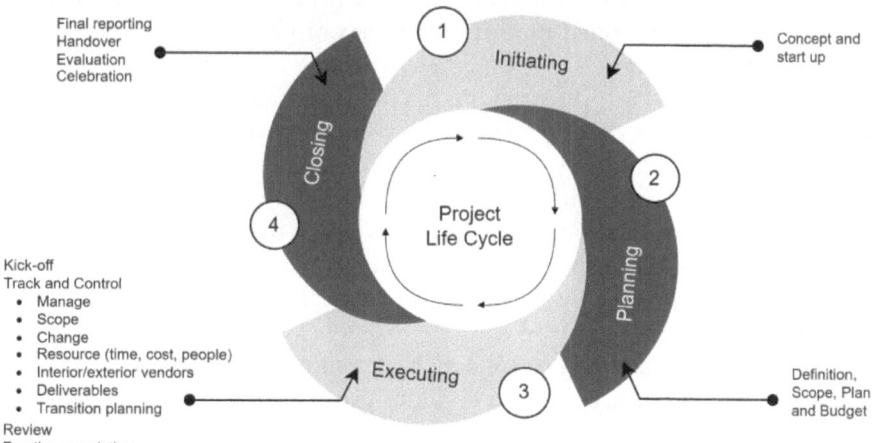

Figure 1.2 The project life cycle

planned, and project managers have a critical role in monitoring progress, identifying problems or variations, modifying the plan and taking action accordingly.

Planning and managing the project in phases is useful to identify key project **milestones** (i.e. markers of specific points along a project timeline) or decision points and to guide the development of sequences of tasks. However, the phases are not really separate – rather, they tend to overlap and may not have clear boundaries. Even when the team is using a project management method with formal approval steps, there may not be an obvious point where they can say 'the initiation phase is complete; we are now starting the planning phase'. Projects can also go backwards – for example, problems in the project planning or implementation can force a rethink of the original concept and/or a redesign of the project. There are also activities that continue throughout the project, such as stakeholder management, change management, evaluation activities, risk management and monitoring of progress. The project life cycle is addressed in more detail in Chapter 3.

Projects in health and community services

The use of project management methods in human services came to prominence in the 1970s and 1980s when local government authorities and community health centres began defining much of their community development and health promotion work as projects, and developed in-house templates and protocols to plan and manage their work. Government and hospitals had already been using project management methods for capital and **digital** (or ICT) projects for many years, and widespread application of these methods to their core business began largely in the 1990s. The introduction of continuous quality improvement methods and process re-engineering also provided important sources of project thinking and project skill development.

Since we started our research on this field more than 20 years ago, there has been large-scale development in the volume, purposes, scope and complexity of projects.

The literature also confirms an increase in published research on project management in health and community services in the past five years, with a focus on project management competencies, project evaluation and project success factors. Project management is also increasingly used in the field of research.

Government departments are active in **commissioning** health and community service organisations to conduct projects that test new ideas and develop new services. They also aim to encourage innovation, quality improvement and the move into new models of care or modes of service delivery (such as services that reduce the demand for hospital admission).

In health and community services, project management methods are used for five major purposes:

1. to develop new services, programs or technologies
2. to improve existing services, care processes, work practices or service delivery models
3. to implement new organisational structures or systems, including those made possible by advances in digital health and care systems
4. to construct, acquire and/or commission new facilities, equipment and systems
5. to design and conduct research projects, such as evidence reviews, needs studies and service planning.

The first three of these purposes are fundamentally about the management of change and basic organisational strategy where change management principles will also apply. In projects that are about changing the roles and practices of staff, it is critical for project managers to understand the impact of projects on staff and to engage those who will be affected early at the design phase of the project life cycle (Alghanmi et al., 2022; Crooks et al., 2018).

Project story: early staff engagement

A residential aged care service developed and implemented a clinical governance framework across the organisation to guide quality care provision and continuous improvement. They had intended that the framework would be focused on staff and consumers and would support the provision of consistently good care. However, high compliance from staff was not achieved as staff perceived the clinical governance activities as 'extra work' without practical meaning.

The executive team realised that designing, implementing and monitoring a clinical governance system for genuine staff and consumer benefits requires specific knowledge and skills. In the absence of effective staff and consumer engagement and a clear implementation pathway skilfully conducted, the potential of the board and executive commitment to good clinical governance was not likely to be realised in practice.

The executive recommitted to a clinical governance 're-set' to make clinical governance more meaningful and useful to staff, with a focus on supporting their engagement in creating consistently good care. Broad consultation among staff to assist with defining quality of care and identifying changes that made sense to them was undertaken as the fundamental first step.

Changes in project management practices and environment

With growing project management expertise and increasing scope and complexity in projects in the sector has come the emergence of more specialised personnel and growing skill and confidence among project staff. It can be easier to employ suitably skilled and experienced project staff, although workforce is still often a problem.

The health and community services sector and its operating environment have also been changing, and the recent large-scale, often system-wide, transformation has inevitably changed the landscape of project management. For example, the rising importance of innovation and the adoption of digital technology such as telehealth and remote patient monitoring (RPM) (Tabacof et al., 2022) in the health sector has contributed to increasing project complexity and scope. Our interviews with senior project directors, senior managers and policy makers confirmed that technologies have enabled them to do things differently and more effectively, while at the same time adding complexity to project design and implementation.

> *That's been a big change. And then, of course, that means that . . . you're managing a very, very complex program. It's not a project, it's a program of multiple projects all working together.*
> *(Senior Manager, Digital Health)*

Moreover, the COVID-19 pandemic has provided opportunities to change many aspects of 'business as usual' in the sector, including in its project work. For example, the use of remote communication platforms like Microsoft Teams and Zoom to support project activities and communication was often mentioned in our interviews.

The more common use of cloud-based applications such as OneDrive enables the sharing of project resources across the team more conveniently and securely. This flexible virtual environment also creates better opportunities for project staff and managers to participate in off-site training and in formal education programs (Muller et al., 2021).

Project management challenges

Like any method, project management can be well or badly suited to its chosen use and can be well or badly used. Properly used, it enhances the organisation's ability to innovate and grow, brings discipline to the processes of change, and enables organisations to focus more strongly on their purpose and the outcomes they need to achieve.

While the use of project management methods and tools is important to project success, many were designed and tested in general industry. They may not give adequate attention to the complexities of multiple stakeholders, multiple agendas and the politics of change that so often underlie project failure in health and community services. Nor do they address the problems that arise in sectors so dominated by skilled professional labour and often so closely linked to the processes and complexities of government and public policy. Furthermore, the tools themselves may be too rigid to use when many projects in the sector require a high level of flexibility.

In our attempt to provide insights into the effective use of projects in health and community care, we believe it is important to proceed from an understanding of the typical project management problems encountered there.

One of the strongest themes in the literature and our interviews is the fact that projects are usually about making changes, and change management methods are needed. However, change is difficult in the complex and politicised environment of health and community services, with multiple empowered stakeholders and other conditions that can support successful resistance to change. Projects are also often initiated as a response to opportunities, leaving inadequate time for preparation and proper planning, potentially further enabling resistance.

Projects flounder and sometimes fail because they are trying to achieve things that are at odds with the team or organisational culture, or which require unwelcome change in work practices, power relationships or ways of working together; or simply because they are too big to 'chew'.

> Organisations don't want to invest in the change management piece. So, you can build this amazing Residential Aged Care facility, you can co-design it, . . . but unless you step the staff through the change piece and what that means for them . . . it doesn't work.
> (Project Manager, Consulting)

For large-scale projects, organisation readiness will need to be assessed, and the organisation may need to take steps to be prepared for the changes. Stakeholder buy-in needs to be built, and skilful management throughout the implementation process remains important (Zawada & Gągała, 2021).

Another challenge is how to develop and sustain the organisation's project capacity – keeping good project managers and embedding the skills of project management as part of the organisation's know-how. Project teams also need a good understanding of the internal and external environment including economic, social and environmental aspects (Martens & Carvalho, 2016).

While there is an increasing general level of knowledge and skill in project work, organisations do still struggle to appoint competent project managers and teams. It still happens that staff members who lack experience in project work are asked to take on projects without adequate preparation.

As one of our project directors put it: 'it was assumed that staff members know how to lead and manage projects'. Some organisations are developing methods for identifying those with skills and building their capacity in leading and managing projects. Others are treating project competence as a general requirement for many roles.

Last, but not least, one important challenge is sustaining project benefits and changes. Often, the purpose of testing new ideas through successful completion of projects is to implement ongoing programs or services. The potential benefits can prove difficult to sustain if little thought has been given to how results might be integrated, or what level of resources and support will be needed to sustain them.

Considering the unique challenges to project management discussed above, the question is: are these issues indicators of weaknesses in the project management method or simply due to ongoing characteristics in the health and community care sectors? In a sense, projects are simply segments of the ongoing, complicated and sometimes messy business of the organisations in which they sit, with a somewhat artificial line drawn around them and some special rules and resources applied. The theoretical model of the project gives it a clear, uncontested goal, a set of technical requirements that must be fulfilled to meet the goal, and a set of methods and tools for doing so. In theory, the results are then handed back to grateful operating units, which use them to achieve transformational change (Shao et al., 2012) and move forward to a brighter, more effective and more competitive future.

In reality, no project exists in isolation (PMI, 2021), and organisations work with complex goals and contested structures, policies and methods. Internal projects must deal with stakeholders who are in effect both the subjects and the objects of change – that is, the change makers and the changed. Thus, the project team may need to change the roles, mindsets or privileges of the very people who must endorse the project's goals and outcomes. Effective engagement and maintaining stakeholder interest and commitment is always a challenge (Meng & Boyd, 2017; Verbeke et al., 2015). In addition, projects may bring their own bureaucracy and, paradoxically, project teams can be resistant to change in the project itself while also advocating the use of projects to pursue organisational change. Finally, if the methods of project management are not built on an adequate research and theory base, their claims to universal application cannot be justified.

Turning the question around, it may be that some of the traditional approaches to general management are more correctly seen as the problem. In the context of changes in project methods and complexity, the increasing adoption of technology and innovation, and the changing broader environment for health and community services, more agile and timely action and decision-making are required, and traditional decision-making through many committees and management layers in large organisations is perhaps just no longer workable (Escoffery et al., 2019; Prybutok, 2018; Australian Institute of Project Management, 2022). In these circumstances, a focus on more effective methods of delegating authority to the project sponsor and manager could help.

Project success

The definition of a project suggests that the criteria of project success are limited to meeting cost, schedule and performance targets. In reality the picture is more complex – many projects go over time and budget but are still judged to be successful by participants for a variety of other reasons, such as positive changes arising from the way the project was managed, the flow-on of positive changes more broadly in the organisation, or insights that can be used to improve future project design and practice.

Table 1.1 gives examples of how project success may be defined from three important perspectives: those of **project sponsors** (this may include senior management of the organisation), project managers and key stakeholders (including consumers).

Researchers have found that projects often have unexpected side effects. Some are beneficial to the organisation – for example, an increase in business, sales or opportunities; gaining new knowledge and understanding; or improving reputation and increasing influence. However, undesirable effects also occur, such as organisational conflicts and problems with staff, clients, contractors and/or suppliers, as well as technical limitations and impacts on patient or client care. Projects may generate unplanned increases in demand for other services exceeding the current service capacity. For example, health promotion projects may lead to increases in demand for screening, diagnosis and care – possibly a good outcome from a health perspective, but also possibly leading to long waitlists and increased staff workload.

Unsuccessful projects may prove that the intended models or approaches will not work or will not produce the intended benefits. And in reality, even successful projects may not lead to further actions or result in new services or program development. Therefore, while the classic criteria of time, budget and quality are important, no set rules can be used to assess project success, and it cannot be judged without reference to the views of those who are involved and affected.

Critical success factors

Many authors have sought to determine the critical success factors (CSF) for achieving desired project outcomes, on the basis of studies of project

Table 1.1 Defining project success from different perspectives

Perspectives	How project success may be defined
Project sponsor	■ Will the expected benefits be achieved? ■ Have the potential long-term gains been maximised? ■ Have we funded the right people to do the job, and have we got the best return for the financial investment? ■ Has the project contributed to the achievement of organisational objectives and to our partner relationships? ■ Are the project users/customers satisfied with what they received? ■ Has the leadership of the organisation enabled project success? ■ Are there new opportunities as a result of the completion of the project?
Project manager	■ Was the project completed on schedule and within budget? ■ Have all activities been completed and all outputs delivered as planned? ■ Have changes been managed according to sponsors' expectations along the way? ■ Have any detrimental effects, risks or issues been minimised? ■ Has the project team stayed motivated and focused? ■ Have the key stakeholders been well engaged? ■ Have all the necessary project records been kept for reporting and future use? ■ Has the importance of the project been recognised by the project sponsor and stakeholders?
Stakeholders	■ Have we received the best services/products possible? ■ Have the benefits been maximised? ■ Are the benefits sustainable for the long term? ■ Have my needs and expectations been heard/met as well as possible? ■ Are the overall outcomes of the project satisfactory? ■ Have our contributions to the project been recognised?

success, since the 1960s. The most significant early study on critical success factors (Pinto & Slevin, 1988) identified ten factors that determine success regardless of project type, and these were further tested and mainly reinforced by a number of subsequent studies (Andersen et al., 2006; Crooks et al., 2018; Fortune & White, 2006; Hassan et al., 2017; Kautsar & Budi,

2020; Mishra et al., 2011; Osei-Kyei & Chan, 2017; Swarnakar et al., 2022; Yalegama et al., 2016). They are:

1. communication
2. client consultation (engagement of stakeholders)
3. client acceptance (**sign-off**)
4. people management
5. project mission (clear goals and direction)
6. project planning
7. monitoring and feedback
8. top management support
9. technical tasks (having the needed technology and expertise)
10. troubleshooting.

Of all the factors, project quality, strong leadership (with clear vision and goals) and effective communication have been consistently highlighted. Our review of literature in the past ten years identified 22 articles presenting research evidence on critical project success factors. These studies are mostly focused on projects in digital health, health promotion, organisational process improvement and quality improvement. Considering the evidence from these papers and our interviews, there have been some shifts in the critical success factors in the past ten years. Table 1.2 details the five main categories and the specific factors that were important.

The critical success factors listed are focused on individual project, team and organisation levels. In Chapter 2 we also address large scale projects initiated at the organisation, system or regional level, and consider the organisational capabilities that best enable organisations to be successful across their **project portfolios**.

Table 1.2 Project critical success factors

Categories	Factors
Project design and planning	■ Clear and specific goals, objectives and deliverables suited to local context and aligned with the organisation's strategic intent ■ Realistic allocation of time and resources ■ Adoption barriers identified and addressed early ■ Evaluation design focused on measuring concrete benefits including financial ■ Design for quick wins and early stage implementation ■ Design for simplified process

(Continued)

Table 1.2 (Continued)

Categories	Factors
Project team performance	■ Project manager with strong 'people leadership' and communication skills ■ Setting clear performance measures ■ Producing deliverables and generating value ■ Bridging understanding between e.g. clinicians and ICT staff ■ Working collaboratively across disciplines, with effective communication within the team and with stakeholders ■ Having both project and content knowledge among the team ■ Building authentic working relationships and team cohesiveness
Leadership and governance	■ Senior management engagement, and alignment of projects with organisational vision and strategy ■ Communicating project goals and impact to staff ■ Strengthening organisational culture and systems to enable innovation ■ Project sponsor/leaders understanding of organisation politics and the complex project environment ■ Promoting transparency of progress and results across the organisation
Change management	■ Early and sustained stakeholder engagement in project design, structures and processes ■ Creating positive stakeholder experience ■ Training for staff in new ways of working, use of new methods and systems ■ Project intelligence – integrating information from all areas
Organisation support and readiness	■ Climate of acceptance of continuous improvement, evidence-based care and evidence-informed policies ■ Alignment of project goals and methods with enduring values and culture of the organisation ■ Implementation capability

Summary

- Projects are a way of achieving specific goals within clearly defined time, cost and quality constraints. Each project is unique and projects vary in scope and complexity.
- There is a wealth of methods and tools available to support this work.
- Managing a project is not a simple linear process, but rather has a life cycle of four phases: initiation, planning, implementation and closure.
- Project management is increasingly seen as a core general management competency.
- Health and community service organisations encounter some particular challenges in achieving the anticipated value from their project work and in managing their project portfolios.
- Project success involves more than achieving the project's intended outcomes within the time and cost allowed: it is also influenced by the broader interests of the organisation and its internal and external stakeholders and by unintended effects.
- The determinants of project success have been extensively studied since the 1960s. The newly emerged evidence and the research conducted by the authors of the book confirmed five categories of factors that are critical to achieving project success.

Readings and resources

Association for Project Management: www.apm.org.uk

Australian Institute of Project Management: https://aipm.com.au/

Project Management Association of Canada: www.pmac-ampc.ca

Project Management Institute (2021). *A guide to the Project Management Body of Knowledge (PMBOK guide) and the standard for project management* (7 ed.). Newton Square.

Project Management Institute: www.pmi.org

The Australian Institute of Project Management: www.aipm.com.au

References

AlGhanmi, N., AlJumah, S., Larabi-Marie-Sainte, S., & Alsaber, L. (2022, March 28–29). *Organizational culture and its impact on the success of virtual software development projects* [Conference paper]. 2022 Fifth International Conference of Women in Data Science at Prince Sultan University, Riyadh, Saudi Arabia.

Andersen, E. S., Birchall, D., Jessen, S. A., & Money, A. H. (2006). Exploring project success. *Baltic Journal of Management, 1*(2), 127–147. http://doi.org/10.1108/17465260610663854

Australian Institute of Project Management. (2022). *The state of project management in Australia 2022: Leading projects through volatility.* https://info.aipm.com.au/

hubfs/Reports%20and%20major%20content%20assets/The%20State%20 of%20PM%202022%20Report%20FINAL.pdf

Brommeyer, M., Mackay, M., Liang, Z., Schaper, L., & Balan, P. (2021). A proposed approach to investigate whether postgraduate health care management education in Australian universities facilitates the development of informatics competencies. *Studies in Health Technology and Informatics*, 15(284), 93–97. https://doi.org/10.3233/SHTI210677

Cleland, D. I., & Gareis, R. (2006). *Global project management handbook: Planning, organizing, and controlling international projects* (2 ed.). McGraw-Hill.

Crooks, C. V., Exner-Cortens, D., Siebold, W., Moore, K., Grassgreen, L., Owen, P., Rausch, A., & Rosier, M. (2018). The role of relationships in collaborative partnership success: Lessons from the Alaska Fourth R project. *Evaluation and Program Planning*, 67, 97–104. https://doi.org/10.1016/j.evalprogplan.2017.12.007

Escoffery, C., Riehman, K., Watson, L., Priess, A. S., Borne, M. F., Halpin, S. N., Rhiness, C., Wiggins, E., & Kegler, M. C. (2019). Facilitators and barriers to the implementation of the HPV VACs (Vaccinate Adolescents Against Cancers) program: A consolidated framework for implementation research analysis. *Preventing Chronic Disease*, 16, E85. https://doi.org/10.5888/pcd16.180406

Fortune, J., & White, D. (2006). Framing of project critical success factors by a systems model. *International Journal of Project Management*, 24(1), 53–65. https://doi.org/10.1016/j.ijproman.2005.07.004

Furniss, D., Curzon, P., & Blandford, A. (2018). Exploring organisational competences in human factors and UX project work: Managing careers, project tactics and organisational strategy. *Ergonomics*, 61(6), 739–761. https://doi.org /10.1080/00140139.2017.1405081

Hassan, M. M., Bashir, S., & Abbas, S. M. (2017). The impact of project managers' personality on project success in NGOs: The mediating role of transformational leadership. *Project Management Journal*, 48(2), 74–87. https://doi.org/10.1177/875 697281704800206

Kautsar, F., & Budi, I. (2020). *Analysis of success factors in the implementation of ERP system in state owned enterprise case study PT. XYZ*. 6th International Conference on Science and Technology (ICST), Yogyakarta, Indonesia, pp. 01–06.

Martens, M. L., & Carvalho, M. M. (2016). Sustainability and success variables in the project management context: An expert panel. *Project Management Journal*, 47(6), 24–43. https://doi.org/10.1177/875697281604700603

Meng, X., & Boyd, P. (2017). The role of the project manager in relationship management. *International Journal of Project Management*, 35(5), 717–728. https://doi.org/10.1016/j.ijproman.2017.03.001

Meredith, J. R., Shafer, S. M., & Mantel, S. J. (2021). *Project management: A managerial approach* (11 ed.). Wiley.

Mishra, P., Dangayach, G. S., & Mittal, M. L. (2011). An empirical study on identification of critical success factors in project based organizations. *Global Business and Management Research*, 3(3&4), 356–368.

Müller, S. D., Wehner, D. L., Konzag, H., Vesterby, M. & Høybye, M. T. (2021). The paradox of project success despite lack of the "My Pathway" telehealth platform usage. *Health Informatics Journal*, 27(1). https://doi.org/10.1177/1460458220976734

Osei-Kyei, R., & Chan, A. P. C. (2017). Comparative analysis of the success criteria for public–private partnership projects in Ghana and Hong Kong. *Project Management Journal*, 48(4), 80–92. https://doi.org/10.1177/875697281704800407

Pells, D. L. (2021). Project management needs a higher purpose. *PM World Journal*, *X*(I). https://pmworldlibrary.net/wp-content/uploads/2021/01/pmwj101-Jan2021-Pells-project-management-needs-a-higher-purpose-editorial-January-complete2.pdf

Pinto, J. K., & Slevin, D. P. (1988). Critical success factors across the project life cycle. *Project Management Journal*, *19*(3), 67–75.

Project Management Institute. (2021). *A guide to the Project Management Body of Knowledge (PMBOK guide) and the standard for project management* (7 ed.). Newton Square.

Prybutok, G. L. (2018). Ninety to nothing: A PDSA quality improvement project. *International Journal of Health Care Quality Assurance*, *31*(4), 361–372. https://doi.org/10.1108/ijhcqa-06-2017-0093

Sandhu, M. V., & Liang, Z. (2021). Competency assessment of project managers of a national NGO in India. *Journal of Health Management*, *23*(3), 558–574. https://doi.org/10.1177/09720634211035248

Shao, J., Müller, R., & Turner, J. R. (2012). Measuring program success. *Project Management Journal*, *43*(1), 37–49. https://doi.org/10.1002/pmj.20286

Swarnakar, V., Bagherian, A., & Singh, A. R. (2022). Modeling critical success factors for sustainable LSS implementation in hospitals: An empirical study. *International Journal of Quality & Reliability Management*, *39*(5), 1249. https://doi.org/10.1108/IJQRM-04-2021-0099

Tabacof, L., Baker, T. S., Durbin, J. R, Desai, V., Zeng, Q., Sahasrabudhe, A., Herrara, J. E., & Putrino, D. (2022). Telehealth treatment for nonspecific low back pain: A review of the current state in mobile health. *PM&R, 14*(9), 1086–1098. https://doi.org/10.1002/pmrj.12738

Verbeke, F., Karara, G., & Nyssen, M. (2015). Human factors predicting failure and success in hospital information system implementations in Sub-Saharan Africa. *Studies in Health Technology & Informatics*, *216*, 482–486.

Westland, J. (2007). *The project management life cycle: A complete step-by-step methodology for initiating, planning, executing and closing the project.* Kogan Page.

Yalegama, S., Chileshe, N., & Ma, T. (2016). Critical success factors for community-driven development projects: A Sri Lankan community perspective. *International Journal of Project Management*, *34*(4), 643–659. https://doi.org/10.1016/j.ijproman.2016.02.006

Zawada, M., & Gągała, D. (2021). An analysis of certification processes for good clinical practice and project management competencies. *Journal of Economics and Management*, *43*(1), 179–205. https://doi.org/10.22367/jem.2021.43.09

Projects in context

The industry and the organisation

In this chapter, we explain aspects of the industry environment and the organisational factors that influence project work in health and community care, and the organisational capabilities that support project success. We then address the organisational task of governing and managing the **project portfolio** and propose criteria for choosing and shaping projects that can be adapted by leaders and managers to help them make decisions about what projects to do.

DOI: 10.4324/9781003431701-3

The industry and organisational environment

Projects never stand alone but are embedded in organisations and influenced by their industry environments as well as the prevailing economic, social and policy context. In health and community services, aspects of the economic, demographic, technological, social, cultural, legal and political environments influence decision-making and have direct impacts on how services are designed and delivered. Within the organisation's management capability, the strength of governance practice, organisational culture, workforce development and the interests of stakeholders affect strategic direction and performance. Figure 2.1 details the factors at the organisation and system levels that shape projects and support or hinder their success.

Increasingly complex projects, which involve significant uncertainty and volatility, have become a constant in the current environment across all

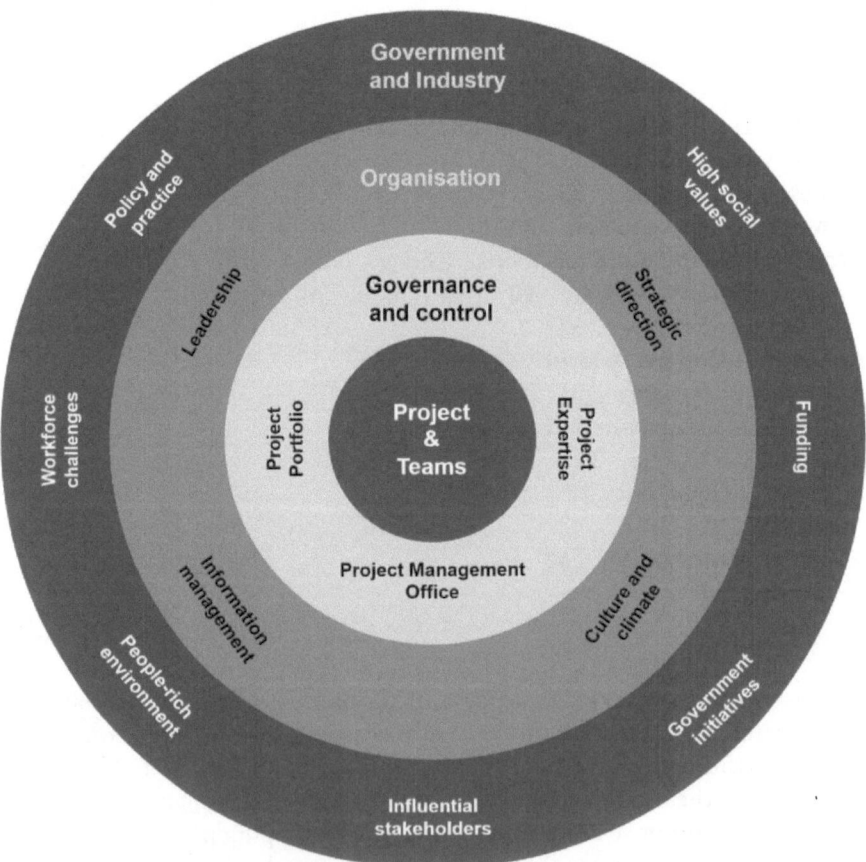

Figure 2.1 Project environments

industries, including health and community care. The 2022 annual survey of members of the Australian Institute of Project Management found that projects undertaken in all Australian industries are increasingly complex undertakings (Australian Institute of Project Management & KPMG, 2022) with some characteristics that are familiar in health and community care projects. For example, some project parameters are difficult to define at the outset, and projects are affected by intricate interfaces with internal and external stakeholders, political influences and updated legislation and regulations. The other common factor is the continuing importance of **digital** transformation. The survey report also highlights the 'disruptive forces' that are increasingly impacting on project performance including labour shortages, supply chain disruption, resource scarcity, spiralling costs, cyber threats, the pace of change, and the impact of environmental, social and governance (ESG) strategies.

> Project professionals and organisations must evolve to thrive in complexity.
>
> *(AIPM & KPMG, 2022, p. 15)*

Our research participants also report that large, complex and transformative projects are becoming commonplace with increased project complexity being driven by:

- projects being more likely to have a digital component that may involve legacy systems, systems integration, multiple vendors, solution infrastructure and storage, software and applications development, testing and upgrades
- **information and communications technology** (ICT) considerations including increasing volume of data, data analytics, decision support, device **procurement** and deployment, privacy and security, cybersecurity, safety and even artificial intelligence (AI)
- larger transformation projects that may offer increased benefits but require huge change management programs, intense and ongoing **stakeholder** engagement, skilled leadership at all levels, rigorous scrutiny via gateways, audit and **project assurance** processes; and significantly increased risk.

> *The big projects you're getting involved with, . . . they do appear to be more complex over time because of the amount of data you're either dealing with or the legacy systems you're managing, or the complex integration that's required. So, I think, yeah, things . . . are getting more and more complex.*
>
> *(Senior Manager, Health Service)*

Government departments have also developed their approaches to their role as system leaders for health and community services, creating incentives and restrictions on the way government-funded organisations and the whole industry operate and innovate. They fund large numbers of projects each year, and they conduct or commission projects as part of fulfilling their own responsibilities. Much of the work of staff in government departments can be defined as projects, and they, too, can experience difficulties managing their project portfolios.

The industry: complex, regulated and dynamic

The project challenges outlined in Chapter 1 are not unique to health and community services, but they do have particular causes and effects. For readers without direct experience of working in health or community care, the following information explains some important background.

Government regulation and funding: The health and community care industry, in both public and private sectors, is highly regulated – and at least partly funded – by government and so is subject to the impact of changes in government policy and ways of doing business. While this situation creates opportunities for growth, it restricts strategic choices and limits flexibility, particularly for organisations in the public sector, to set their own directions. It also requires leaders to find compromises between the demands of government and the needs or priorities of their own organisation.

Dynamic change in policy and practice: The industry is dynamic, and much of it is constantly engaged in change and development. For example, the introduction of national insurance schemes for people with disabilities has fundamentally reshaped the way disability services are funded, structured and delivered. This means that there is always a need to find better ways of working, and it can enable staff to muster great energy and commitment. However, it can also lead to important staff groups pulling in different and sometimes contradictory directions. Leaders are subjected to increasing demands for service development and the allocation of new resources, while budgets are always constrained. Staff get 'change fatigue', and project effort can be spread too thin.

People-rich environment: This is a people-rich industry, with many tertiary-educated staff who are used to exercising professional independence and are organised into powerful professional and trade union groups. Leaders are accustomed to standing on contested ground, with some sections of the workforce agitating for change and others (those with something to lose) digging in or refusing to engage. This means that stakeholder engagement is both critical and challenging.

High social values: The critical social role of the industry means that politicians, the media and the community have strong views about services and standards. This can result in both high motivation for change and stakeholder resistance to it from outside as well as inside the organisation. This reality impacts on the initiatives organisations seek to implement through projects, and on the ways that projects are managed, and highlights the importance of community and consumer engagement.

These characteristics of the industry can impact directly on the way projects are done (and how well they work), through three main factors addressed below: the influence of governments on the project agenda; the funding and resourcing of projects; and the challenges of stakeholder management.

The role of government

Governments and other funders have a major impact on the project portfolios of health and community services. While this is true in both the private and public sectors, it is more acute for government-funded agencies. Since the late 20th century, governments have taken up an active role as purchasers or commissioners of particular services (rather than passive subsidisers of provider organisations). They have also increasingly used project funding as a strategy for encouraging change in practice and models of care. Direct government funding **programs** for improvement and innovation projects enabled cash-strapped agencies to invest in updating their services, to bring in new approaches more suited to current needs and technologies, and to enhance their capacity to analyse service data.

> *We would have projects as low as half of a million dollars to as high as a couple of $100 million. Some of those projects would be within the year and the others would be spanning across multiple years. . . . We would have at any point in time between 40–50 initiatives through to over 100 initiatives within the year.*
>
> *(Senior Manager, Health Department)*

Over time, some government departments have changed their approach towards tighter specification, using regulation and performance standards, particularly for public health and community services. Leaders (including those in government health departments) face tighter constraints in their choice of projects and increasing requirements to respond to policy and funding changes – for example, adoption of digital technology; use of activity and performance-based funding; and greater emphasis on coordination of care across agencies and the resulting requirement for working in partnerships and alliances.

The response of governments to the COVID-19 pandemic is perhaps the most dramatic example of the broad social impacts of government emergency powers, policy and funding. In their responses, project methods were used by all agencies to drive the needed changes. This combination of direction, resources and hard project work rapidly transformed care systems, at large scale. Health and community care organisations were critical both as government implementation partners but also with smaller-scale local innovations to enable continuity of care in extraordinary circumstances.

There is also an increased presence of national government–owned organisations that are effectively project based (i.e. structured primarily to deliver a set of projects commissioned by government), such as the Australian Digital Health Agency, established in 2016 with a mission of 'creating a collaborative environment to accelerate adoption and use of innovative digital services and technologies' (Australian Digital Health Agency, 2023).

The Agency's projects cover a broad spectrum of activity including eHealth standards, telehealth, electronic prescription, My Health Record, health identifiers, information exchange, health terminologies and software development. Given the nature of the work, development needs to be driven centrally, and so the projects tend to be shared nationally with state and territory health authorities and/or be contracted out to major suppliers. The health services are largely recipients rather than drivers of this project agenda, although hospital and health services staff are involved as stakeholders.

Regardless of the methods governments use, government policy and funding is and will rightly remain a strong influence on project agendas. But health and community service providers have a different set of responsibilities, and different imperatives. They must attend to the capacity of the organisation, to the coordinated delivery of the right services to meet client/patient needs, and to the shaping of a coherent strategy to achieve the agency's purpose, all within usually tight budget constraints.

Resourcing projects

Competition for project resources among and within organisations is widespread and important. In many organisations, lack of funds is commonly the basis on which project proposals fail to get approval, and this means both cost per se and the strength of the **business case** – that is, the potential for the project results to generate a positive financial impact that justifies the costs and effort.

For private sector organisations, the direct need to generate a financial return on investment imposes discipline on decisions to authorise projects, while also enabling leaders to support promising projects. In the public sector, cost saving and cost neutrality (i.e. an alternative way of doing things should cost no more than is currently being spent) are important considerations in decision-making. However, there is usually less capacity to balance costs with enhanced revenue, which means that it can be very hard to find resources even for important and valuable projects. This is an enduring feature of the industry, and one that underlies several reasons for project failure, including inadequate staffing and budgets, and unrealistic timing.

Managing stakeholders

One of the most difficult challenges in **project management** in the sector is engaging and managing the many stakeholders: the people and groups (within and outside the organisation) who are affected by the project, who can influence its design and conduct, and who usually have diverse and competing agendas.

For many projects, internal groups – staff, volunteers, clinical and other professional groups, and the departments or units affected by the project – are the main stakeholders. But there are also external stakeholders for many projects, including agencies that are partners in a new approach to care, consumer representatives who participate in **co-design**, experts who are part of a steering or advisory committee, and perhaps project funders or suppliers (e.g. of information systems or equipment). Different professional and trade union organisations (and their internal representatives and members) may have their own sectoral interests that go beyond the **scope** of the project. Stakeholders can stymie change and derail projects, sometimes deliberately, but sometimes because adherence to their own agendas does not allow them to see any alternatives.

As important project funders, government departments are also stakeholders. They can be important supporters and allies in a project, but their roles also bring risks. As participants in our research reported, government agencies can alter their policy directions at inconvenient times, including well into a **project life cycle,** due to a change in government or a change of leadership, or because more important priorities come along. Governments are also influenced by public opinion and political lobbying, and a project that has potential for unpopularity is vulnerable if strong community or political opposition is mobilised against it.

Consumers are increasingly recognised as another important stakeholder group, with several of our research participants highlighting the valuable contributions of those with lived experience. There are several ways of effectively engaging and working with consumers which are progressively becoming standard practice for many organisations. While some professional staff are challenged by this shift in roles (i.e. from being 'in charge' to engaging with consumers as equals in considering problems and solutions), others welcome the useful contributions consumers can make. Managing stakeholders is dealt with in depth in Chapters 5 and 8.

Project capability in organisations

While important environmental and industry factors have a strong impact on projects, organisational capability can make a critical difference. There is growing project maturity in many organisations, evident in project management (and team) skills, the number and complexity of projects undertaken, significant organisational investments in the development of competencies and skills, and the widespread use of project methodologies (Gomes et al., 2016).

Our interviews also confirmed that health and community care organisations and the relevant government departments have adopted or adapted specific project management methods such as **PRINCE2** or others borrowed from quality improvement or approaches from other industries including digital and construction. They are also engaging with national project management institutes and sharing project approaches and results at industry conferences and workshops.

The health and community services field is large and diverse, but there are common factors at the level of the organisation that influence project success: organisational strategy, leadership, culture (and climate), the governance of project work and approaches to the management of people. Leaders need to recognise these underlying influences and anticipate and manage their potential positive or negative impact on projects.

Organisational strategy

Although projects 'stand alone' with their specific goals and **objectives**, they need to align with the organisation's strategic goals and be an integrated part of the organisation (PMI, 2021). Our research participants indicated that detailed strategic planning is routine and that any proposed project is evaluated against identified strategic priorities. When this is the case, projects are likely to benefit from both strong leadership and stakeholder support, and a sense of the importance of their success to the success of the organisation.

> We can usually do one to two big technology projects at a time. Infrastructure projects, we might run about five. But then we've got Engineering projects as well. So, we know exactly what we can run now . . . we look at our asset management plans, we look at our strategic plan, we look at the external government plan and we put it all together, effectively. And if it's not contributing to our strategic goal, it doesn't get done.
>
> (Senior Manager, Hospital)

However, organisational strategies need to be supported by staff and other stakeholders. Internal politics is an ongoing reality – the interests of individuals, units and teams within the organisation will not always align with the organisation's broader interests or strategies, and the result is a leadership problem. Neither leaders nor projects can change this reality – part of what is sometimes called the 'shadow side' of organisations (Egan, 1994) – but there are strategies for managing it. Strategic plans can be designed to recognise and better align the interests of important internal stakeholders with those of the organisation as a whole. Leaders can act to channel 'political' activity out of the corridors and into structured priority-setting processes. We return to this difficult question in Chapter 8.

Culture and climate

Organisation culture is a much-discussed but ill-defined concept, which makes intuitive sense to most people who have worked in organisations but is hard to study and perhaps even harder to change. By culture, we mean the unwritten values and rules that are understood and endorsed by the staff (or important subgroups) and therefore govern 'how things are done around here' (Schein, 1995, Fosslien & Duffy, 2020).

Organisations with a culture that supports project success have three key characteristics: they have an ability to handle change; they have the ability to incorporate new knowledge – that is, to learn; and there is a broad awareness among staff of the project method and how it can be used. These characteristics, particularly the first two, are generally seen as highly desirable aspects of culture.

Organisational leaders cannot change culture at will, but they can understand and encourage those aspects of the culture that support innovation, willingness to learn and the development of shared project capability (O'Kelly & Maxwell, 2001). Suda (2007) provides a useful categorisation of four core axes of culture – collaboration, **control**, cultivation and competence – that each have their strengths and weaknesses. For example, an organisation that has a strong control culture (where the emphasis is on ensuring certainty, predictability, safety, accuracy and dependability) may have strengths such as planning and building robust systems, policies and procedures but also weaknesses including an impersonal and very intense work environment.

Perhaps the business culture that produced modern project management is more pragmatic, with more concrete goals and more direct methods of pursuing them, than is the health and community services culture. Ideals like 'quality, access, equity' are more complex and abstract than business slogans like 'faster, better, cheaper'.

The concept of team or organisational climate is perhaps more directly amenable to leadership attention. If culture is defined as 'how we do things around here', climate is 'how it feels to work here'.

> A climate can be locally created by what leaders do, what circumstances apply, and what environments afford. A culture can evolve only out of mutual experience and shared learning.
>
> *(Wilkinson, n.d.)*

Typically, in a positive team climate, staff can answer yes to questions like: Are staff free to innovate? Can staff get on with their work without asking for permissions and guidance from the manager? Are goals high but attainable? Do staff know what is expected? Is good work recognised in a tangible way? Is there a sense of belonging to a winning team with shared goals? While it can be hard to put your finger on why some teams work well, staff generally know when they are in a good team climate, and that much more can be achieved under these conditions (Fosslien & Duffy, 2020).

Climate can be changed relatively quickly and profoundly by strong leadership. There is good evidence (e.g. in the foundational study by Edmondson [1999] conducted in hospital surgical units) that a team climate in which the leader enables staff to feel safe in questioning accepted ways of doing things creates the conditions for success in innovation.

While team commitment is positive, the related idealism that is often part of health and community services culture can be a source of resistance to change. The 'missionary organisation' (originally described by Mintzberg, 1991) is one that pursues values-based goals (e.g. relieving suffering or reducing inequality) and attracts staff who are personally driven by those goals. Their commitment, however, may lead them to resist what they perceive as incorrect interpretations of the mission. When this tendency is linked to self-interest (e.g. a proposed change to a model of service that will require inconvenient changes in patterns of work), it can be a powerful force. Any attempt to change the way that things are done can be seen as an attack on the fundamental values and philosophies of the organisation, and as a threat to service quality and commitment to consumers.

The idea of enhancing culture and climate may seem like a forlorn hope to embattled **project managers** and organisation leaders. Culture change may be difficult and sometimes painful, as the following project story illustrates, but attention to culture is useful for two reasons. First, even difficult and slow changes have to begin somewhere, and projects can make a significant contribution. Second, the savvy project manager needs to see the culture clearly, and work with the positive aspects and around the barriers they can't change. While climate and culture are connected and feed off each other, climate is often based on events, people's reactions and incidents between people, and therefore it can often change pretty quickly (Wilkinson, n.d.).

Project story: culture eats strategy, almost

The board of a charity focused on a childhood chronic condition had realised that they were failing to reach population groups that needed them the most (with higher incidence of the condition and a greater burden of illness and disability). A manager with a strong background in working with disadvantaged communities had recently been appointed to the health care team and had been tasked with leading a reform project that aimed to achieve a greater focus and reach among those with the highest needs for support services.

He established a project steering committee, chaired by the CEO, and prepared a proposal for overhauling the way the health care team fulfilled its responsibilities, including tailoring its programs to single-parent families, to those with lower literacy skills, and to people living in rural and regional areas, including Indigenous communities. He also proposed a change in the style of the organisation's publications and visual imagery to make them more inclusive and accessible. Other senior staff and particularly the CEO started to get nervous when they realised that the shift had implications beyond just the health care team.

Some of the existing health care team members were also uncomfortable, and one resigned as soon as she realised what the changes would mean for her job. The team manager took the opportunity to recruit a young educator who had transferable skills brought from experience in international development work.

The project proceeded, and gradually the team united behind the new manager and accepted the new challenges. Early outreach efforts to the target community organisations seemed to go well, and staff were gaining new insights into working with people of diverse backgrounds as partners as well as clients.

The board received positive progress reports and were strongly committed to the change, but the CEO was increasingly ambivalent about the project, could not relate to the new approach, and was uncomfortable interacting with members of the target communities. The team manager started to get really worried when the CEO asked him to divert some funding, which had been acquired specifically to cover the cost of new resources for clients, to cover a shortfall in another area of the agency's budget.

The team manager decided that he couldn't cross that line and challenged the CEO on the ethics of his request. Things went downhill fast from there, and the upshot was a complaint about bullying, and finally a case in the industrial tribunal. It was too late for the manager, whose health was suffering, and he accepted a payout and left the organisation in a fairly bruised condition.

The board realised that the changes they sought were going to require a more careful and thorough approach, because significant aspects of the organisation's culture were going to have to change. They secured the resignation of the CEO and set about recruiting a person with values and experience that aligned to the organisation's new strategic direction. They also recruited a few new board members (younger and more culturally diverse) to strengthen the base on which to build a different future for the organisation.

Leadership at every level

Among all the important project success factors, support from senior management (or management buy-in) and effective leadership are viewed as critical (Tabassi et al., 2017; Swarnakar et al., 2022). Effective leadership encourages ideas, empowers staff to achieve goals and engages them in decision-making to create a sense of belonging and shared ownership and responsibilities (West et al., 2019; Liang et al., 2020). Leadership is also important to ensure staff 'own' projects and understand how they fit into the overall direction of the organisation, as well as to marshal needed resources and support. And it is a project management truism that if you haven't got high-level endorsement and championing, it is very hard to make even a great project idea work (Ellahi et al., 2022; Escoffery, 2019; Swarnakar et al., 2022).

Leadership in project management includes effective planning, inspiring team members, and making decisions that guide actions in the implementation of a project plan. There is a paradoxical requirement for leaders: they need to both generate commitment and simultaneously impose discipline on project activity – a task that is challenging for all of the reasons outlined earlier in this chapter. This task applies at every level of the organisation, from the board of directors to project team members.

Project governance and control

Organisations need to govern their project management practices and standards and decisions about their project portfolios. There is now a stronger reliance on the discipline imposed by formal processes of development and approval, as well as greater emphasis on linking projects to the strategic or operational plan.

Faced with an increasing number of projects being undertaken at any one time, many large organisations have established a **project management office** (PMO) to enable consistent use of project methods and monitoring and reporting of project activities.

> A PMO is a group or department within a business or government agency or enterprise that defines and maintains standards for project management within the organisation. The PMO strives to standardise and introduce economies of repetition in the execution of projects.
>
> *(Project management office, 2024)*

PMOs can be the central resource across the organisation, or they can be established to support a division in large organisations. Some projects, such as the implementation of **Electronic Medical Records** (**EMR**) and capital infrastructure projects, can require a dedicated PMO to adequately support project activities. This is because of their size and complexity, with multiple interdependent projects or **stages** within one large envelope, and significant reporting and audit requirements.

PMOs emerged as a prominent point of discussion in academic literature in the early 1990s (Aubry et al., 2010) and PMOs are increasingly common in many industries. Their contribution to strengthening organisational capability and control of cost, quality and risk have been well recognised (Pirotti et al., 2022; PMI, 2023).

The roles of a PMO vary according to the organisation's needs, and they are classified by the Project Management Institute (PMI, 2023) as:

1. *supportive*: playing a supportive role to projects including providing templates, **best practice** examples and training etc.
2. *controlling*: providing support, tools and governance to meet compliance requirements
3. *directive*: directly managing projects.

Potential functions of the PMO

1. monitoring and controlling project performance including centralised reporting
2. development of project management competencies and methods
3. supporting the management of large complex projects or project programs
4. strategic management of the project portfolio
5. organisational learning
6. executing specialised tasks for project managers
7. managing project customer interfaces (with vendors, government etc.).

Source: Aubry et al. (2010)

Organisations that establish and deploy PMOs need to ensure that centralised PMO functions do not become top heavy or fall into the 'trap of bureaucracy' as they can fuel an 'argument . . . that the PMO is an office of useless work and low value-added procedures' (Ramos, 2016). This means more emphasis on the PMO's role as a resource hub with less emphasis on the role of policing paperwork and project management standards.

People management and project skills

Health and community care organisations can build their project capacity through attention to the people side of organisations in three ways: finding and keeping good project managers; embedding the skills of project management as part of the organisation's knowledge; and investing in continuous project management competency development across the organisation. This is explored further in Chapter 3.

Participants in our research confirmed that managers in health and community services are expected to have strong project management skills and be prepared to take on the project management role when required. However, not all staff are ready to take on project work and may need mentoring, support and skill development.

Recruiting project managers either as consultants or as temporary employees can work well but is not always a satisfactory solution – consultants can be expensive, and they might not fit well with the organisation's culture. Those we interviewed reinforced the importance of both insider knowledge of the organisation and content knowledge of the project's focus area.

It may be more strategic to identify and keep good project managers within the organisation. Skills that are seen as valuable for project management such as communication, negotiation, facilitation, and change and conflict management are valuable for all managers.

> *A good project manager also leverages off expertise within the team and the organisation, and not just independently thinking that they know the answer to every particular task. And I think [team members] feel more valued for the fact that . . . [the project manager] is actually reaching out and asking for support and assistance from the rest of the team.*
>
> (Senior Manager, Health Network)

The temporary nature of projects, and particularly the timing of project funding, also means that organisations need to focus on embedding the learning and skills gained through their projects, and on retaining corporate knowledge. This can be difficult if project managers are contract staff who take the learning and corporate memory with them when their contracts end, a problem that can be addressed at least partly by the PMO.

In the rest of this book, we turn to the models and methods of project management that are the immediate influences on project success, and that are supported or constrained by the industry and organisational factors outlined above. But first, we want to apply the industry and organisational analysis to the question of project strategy: the decisions organisations make about what project opportunities to pursue, and how they manage their overall project effort – the organisation's 'project portfolio' is the sum of these choices.

The project portfolio

Organisations need to make decisions about what project opportunities to pursue, and how they manage their overall project effort. **Project portfolio management** (PPM) is a business management approach for the organisation to prioritise and select the right projects in line with its capacity to deliver and its strategic intent. In a resource constrained environment, enterprises are challenged to invest in the best combinations of projects while maintaining business as usual and optimising return on investment (Petro et al., 2020; Ershadi et al., 2020).

Health and community service agencies are increasingly taking such an active approach to managing their project portfolios, and many have established practices for developing project proposals, setting criteria for their approval, ranking proposals against one another, selecting those to be approved (whether for internal funding or to be included in bids for external funding), and resourcing and coordinating the resultant activities. In larger organisations, these processes are generally applied to sets of potential projects that are seen to be truly competing with one another for endorsement and resources within a division or program (such as quality improvement or buying new equipment) rather than at the level of the organisation as a whole. Some organisations support bottom-up project proposals to resource teams to work on business process or quality improvement:

> So, we ran the shark tank like the TV show, where we had a panel of 'investors' who had money, and we got people to submit ideas first, and so we shortlisted six groups to come forward and present live to the panel, and the panel would quiz them on their ideas and their project, and had a checklist for what they'd invest in based on 'Does it meet the organisation's strategy?', and it could be different elements within that – financial sustainability, quality, innovation, partnership, sustainability measure, so a whole range of criteria. And then the judges with the money had the option to decide which projects they think they would invest their money in.
>
> (Senior Manager, Home Care Service)

Some smaller organisations have a single system for ranking and approving projects, ensuring coherence and manageability through a comprehensive annual priority-setting process.

It takes time to develop open, predictable, rational methods for prioritising projects, but experience indicates it is worthwhile. A decision-making framework that determines roles, boundaries, responsibilities and authorities in accordance with the organisation's hierarchy is needed. Robust tools and techniques to analyse performance data and act as a decision support system might also be required (Ko & Kim, 2019). The criteria for adopting projects into a portfolio will be unique to each organisation, and probably to the program or business area, and will change over time. Alignment with the organisation's strategic intent, and the feasibility of delivering the promised benefits are often espoused as the major criteria, but decisions can always be influenced by other agendas, or simply by a rush of enthusiasm or a response to external funding opportunities. Having explicit criteria, and a rigorous process for applying them, is a safeguard against the influence of organisational politics or an excess of zeal, but not a guarantee.

Project assessment

In the light of the project success factors explained in Chapter 1, and the environmental and organisational factors outlined above, we suggest that answers to the following eight questions could guide decision-making by both organisations and intending project proponents about the value of a project proposal to the organisation.

1 Will this project help to achieve our strategic goals, directly or indirectly?

This is the most fundamental criterion, but it is more useful for this purpose when strategic goals are more specific. If the strategic directions statement or business plan is not specific enough, it can provide the basis for a modified statement of strategic priorities for projects in the organisation, borrowing legitimacy from the main statement while making it more readily useful for project portfolio management.

There might be times when organisations decide to take on projects that do not fit clearly within their strategic directions, with good reason – for example, to explore a particular care process to see if it is something the organisation should be doing and whether it will fit with other aspects of the service. The strategic goals of the funders are also important, and sometimes it is worth being flexible on the alignment question in order to participate in important initiatives of governments and other funders. If this is the case, it is vital to be clear about why you are doing it and what you will do if it does or does not work out.

2 Does it fit with our culture and values, or what we want them to be – really?

We have emphasised the importance of aligning the project portfolio with the organisation's strategic plans and directions, but we have also noted the difficulties human service organisations often experience in moving in a coordinated way. Culture clash is a powerful source of some of these difficulties. As the saying goes: 'Culture eats strategy for lunch'.

It is worthwhile to check that the project fits with the culture and values in two ways, and to understand if any realignment is needed. First, does the project, its goals and methods, sit well with the values we aspire to? And second, will this project encounter strong resistance because it cuts across some of the strongly held values and practices or the unwritten ground rules of the organisation?

If the answer to the second question is 'yes', then decisions must be made as to whether the project offers a good opportunity to challenge these values and practices, and how this might be done. The other option is to look for ways of avoiding the point where the clash of values occurs. It may be, however, that the culture problem is so strong that the project is doomed to failure and should not be taken on.

3 Is there a leader for this project, a sponsor who will make sure it delivers?
Lack of leadership causes problems at two levels. The first is the level of the project team, but here we are focusing on the second: someone in a leadership position who is prepared to sponsor or champion this project, to be the person who will provide influence and access to needed resources when the team requires it. 'Top management support' is often cited in the project management literature as a make-or-break factor. But the level and type of support that is needed will vary widely depending on the project and the organisation's structure and style.

4 Have the important stakeholders been identified,
   and how can they be engaged?
All projects have stakeholders, and sometimes, external partnerships are needed. The challenge is to recognise the need for engagement or partnerships in the early stages and to manage them well. Organisations that are more engaged with their environments and their communities, and which have established more robust relationships, are better placed both to see the implications and to move quickly to respond to them.

5 Do we have, or can we readily get, the skills to succeed with this project?
Again, we are referring not only to project management skills, but also to the core competencies of the organisation. Do we have the basic technological know-how to support this project and its results? Are we in a position to work well with the intended client group, and with the key funders and regulators? This criterion can also be used for consideration of the human resource questions – will this project provide good opportunities for the development of project skills and for career development?

6 Can we handle the resource requirements in a timely manner?
This question is not simply about accurate estimation and securing the direct funding requirements of the project. The question here is about the capability of the organisation to mobilise the skills, staffing and management attention required to support effective project management.

7 If it succeeds, are the benefits worth the effort,
   and are the results sustainable?
The project proposal will specify the intended benefits, and perhaps whether and when they will be able to be measured, but is the return worth the effort? Sustainability is a related important challenge, and one that is often deferred. 'We won't know until we get there' may often be true, and sometimes you need to demonstrate a successful approach in order to generate the conditions

for acceptance and resourcing. But organisations should include consideration of this kind of project risk in their planning and decision-making.

8 Will this project contribute to our organisational learning and competence?
Related to the theme of sustainability is the question of the potential for projects to contribute to the development of the organisation, its core competencies and organisational learning.

Summary
- The health and community services industry is strongly regulated but also dynamic and constantly changing, which makes project management challenging.
- There is a trend to increasing project size and complexity, with a common feature being digital transformation and complex change to models of care and service delivery.
- Factors in both the external and internal environments shape project practice in health and community services including the role of government as regulators and funders, the extent to which projects are used as part of ongoing change and the influence of multiple empowered stakeholder groups.
- Government departments are deeply involved in project work, and face challenges in reconciling the project management approach with the complexities of government policy and bureaucracy. Governments are also an important influence on project agendas.
- There are five key factors that shape the capability of organisations to succeed in project management: strategic direction, leadership, supportive culture and climate, governance of the project portfolio and good people management (including building and maintaining project skills).
- With increasing numbers of projects being undertaken, larger organisations are establishing project management offices (PMOs) that aim to support and standardise project work across the organisation and bolster the capacity to deliver initiatives with strategic value.
- Eight general criteria for assessing projects as part of project portfolio management, that can be tailored to each organisation, are suggested for use in guiding decisions about which projects to conduct.

Readings and resources
On 'reading' organisational culture and climate
N2Growth. (2020, January 13). Stef du Plessis on culture & unwritten ground rules [Video]. YouTube. https://www.youtube.com/watch?v=ygqKWK kceYk

On engaging consumers

Australian Commission on Safety and Quality in Health Care. (n.d.). *Partnering with consumers standard.* https://www.safetyandquality. gov.au/standards/nsqhs-standards/partnering-consumers-standard

Wiles, L. K., Kay, D., Luker, J. A., Worley, A., Austin, J., Ball, A., Bevan, A., Cousins, M., Dalton, S., Hodges, E., Horvat, L., Kerrins, E., Marker, J., McKinnon, M., McMillan, P., Pinero de Plaza, M. A., Smith, J., Yeung, D., & Hillier, S. L. (2022). Consumer engagement in health care policy, research and services: A systematic review and meta-analysis of methods and effects. *PLoS One, 17*(1), e0261808. https://doi.org/10.1371/ journal.pone.0261808

On co-design

Australian Healthcare and Hospitals Association, & Consumers Forum of Australia. (2018). *Experience based co-design: A toolkit for Australia.* https://chf.org.au/experience-based-co-design-toolkit

Agency for Clinical Innovation. (n.d.). *Ways of working together in co-design.* New South Wales, Australia. https://aci.health.nsw.gov.au/projects/co-design/working-together

On investment in eHealth

Australian Digital Health Agency. (n.d.). *Connecting Australia to a healthier future.* https://www.digitalhealth.gov.au/

On project management methods and tools

Axelos. (2017). *Managing successful projects with PRINCE2* (7 ed.). The Stationery Office.

Project Management Institute. (2021). *A guide to the Project Management Body of Knowledge (PMBOK guide) and the standard for project management* (7 ed.). Newton Square.

On the PMO

Dietrich, P., Artto, K. A., & Kujala, J. (2010, July 14). *Strategic priorities and PMO functions in project-based firms* [Paper presentation]. PMI® Research Conference: Defining the Future of Project Management, Washington, DC, United States.

Project Manager. (n.d.). *Project management office.* https://www.project-manager.com/guides/pmo

On the project environment and complexity

Australian Institute of Project Management. (2022). *The state of project management in Australia 2022: Leading projects through volatility.* https://info.aipm.com.au/hubfs/Reports%20and%20major%20content%20assets/The%20State%20of%20PM%202022%20Report%20FINAL.pdf

References

Aubry, M., Hobbs, B., Müller, R., & Blomquist, T. (2010). Identifying forces driving PMO changes. *Project Management Journal, 41*(4), 30–45. https://doi.org/10.1002/pmj.20191

Australian Digital Health Agency. (2023). *The national digital health strategy 2023–2028.* Retrieved January 21, 2024 from www.digitalhealth.gov.au/national-digital-health-strategy

Australian Institute of Project Management & KPMG. (2022). *The state of project management in Australia 2022: Leading projects through volatility.* https://info.aipm.com.au/hubfs/Reports%20and%20major%20content%20assets/The%20State%20of%20PM%202022%20Report%20FINAL.pdf

Edmondson, A. C. (1999). Psychological safety and learning behavior in work teams. *Administrative Science Quarterly, 44*(2), 350–383. https://doi.org/10.2307/2666999

Egan, G. (1994). *Working the shadow side: A guide to positive behind-the-scenes management.* Jossey-Bass.

Ellahi, A., Rehman, M., Javed, Y., Sultan, F., & Rehman, H. M. (2022). Impact of servant leadership on project success through mediating role of team motivation and effectiveness: A case of software industry. *Sage Open, 12*(3), 21582440221122747. https://doi.org/10.1177/21582440221122747

Ershadi, M., Jefferies, M., Davis, P., & Mojtahedi, M. (2020). Towards successful establishment of a project portfolio management system: Business process management approach. *Journal of Modern Project Management, 8*(1), 22–41.

Escoffery, C., Riehman, K., Watson, L., Priess, A. S., Borne, M. F., Halpin, S. N., Rhiness, C., Wiggins, E., & Kegler, M. C. (2019). Facilitators and barriers to the implementation of the HPV VACs (Vaccinate Adolescents Against Cancers) program: A consolidated framework for implementation research analysis. *Preventing Chronic Disease, 16*, E85. https://doi.org/10.5888/pcd16.180406

Fosslien, L., & Duffy, M. W. (2020, October 26). *Write down your team's unwritten rules.* Retrieved January 05, 2024 from https://hbr.org/2020/10/write-down-your-teams-unwritten-rules

Gomes, J., Romão, M., & Carvalho, H. (2016). Successful IS/IT projects in healthcare: Pretesting a questionnaire. *Procedia Computer Science, 100*, 375–382. https://doi.org/10.1016/j.procs.2016.09.172

Ko, J. H., & Kim, D. (2019). The effects of maturity of project portfolio management and business alignment on PMO efficiency. *Sustainability, 11*(1), 238. https://doi.org/10.3390/su11010238

Liang, Z., Howard, P., Wang, J., & Xu, M. (2020). A call for leadership and management competency development for directors of medical services – evidence from the Chinese public hospital system. *International Journal of Environmental Research and Public Health, 17*(18), 6913.

Mintzberg, H., & Quinn, J. B. (1991). Ideology and the missionary organisation. In J. Lampel & J. B. Ghoshal (Eds.), *The strategy process: Concepts, contexts and cases* (2 ed.). Prentice Hall.

O'Kelly, S. W., & Maxwell, R. (2001). Implementing clinical governance. Medical training should include project management. *British Medical Journal, 323*(7315), 753. https://doi.org/10.1136/bmj.322.7299.1413

Petro, Y., Ojiako, U., Williams, T., & Marshall, A. (2020). Organizational ambidexterity: Using project portfolio management to support project-level ambidexterity. *Production Planning and Control, 31*(4), 287–307. https://doi. org/10.1080/09537287.2019.1630683

Pirotti, A., Rahim, F. A. M., & Zakaria, N. (2022). Implementation of project management standards and project success: The mediating role of the project management office. *Journal of Engineering, Project and Production Management, 12*(1), 39–46. https://doi.org/https://ssrn.com/abstract=3923768

Project Management Institute. (2021). *A guide to the Project Management Body of Knowledge (PMBOK guide) and the standard for project management* (7 ed.). Newton Square.

Project Management Institute. (2023). *Which PMO is right for your organization?* Retrieved December 13, 2023 from www.pmi.org/learning/publications/pm-network/digital-exclusives/which-pmo-is-right-for-your-organization

Project Management Office. (2024, January 30). In *Wikipedia*. https://en.wikipedia. org/wiki/Project_management_office

Ramos, H. (2016, January 04). The trap of bureaucracy. *Project Management*. Retrieved January 08, 2024 from www.projectmanagement.com/blog-post/ 17353/the-trap-of-bureaucracy#_=_

Schein, E. H. (1995). *Organizational culture and leadership* (3 ed.). Jossey-Bass.

Suda, L. V. (2007). *The meaning and importance of culture for project success* [Conference paper]. PMI Global Congress 2007–EMEA, Budapest, Hungary. www. pmi.org/learning/library/meaning-importance-culture-project-success-7361

Swarnakar, V., Bagherian, A., & Singh, A. R. (2022). Modeling critical success factors for sustainable LSS implementation in hospitals: An empirical study. *International Journal of Quality & Reliability Management, 39*(5), 1249. https://doi.org/10.1108/IJQRM-04-2021-0099

Tabassi, A. A., Roufechaei, K. M., Bakar, A. H. A., & Yusof, N. A. (2017). Linking team condition and team performance: A transformational leadership approach. *Project Management Journal, 48*(2), 22–38. https://doi.org/10.1177/ 875697281704800203

West, D. J., Liang, Z., & Krcmery, V. (2019). Principles of effective leadership. In C. Michael, B. Ramirez, D. J. West & W. E. Aaronson (Eds.), *The global healthcare: Competencies, concepts, and skills* (pp. 165–210). Health Administration Press.

Wilkinson, D. (n.d.). The difference between organisational culture and climate and why it matters. *Oxford Review Briefings*. https://oxford-review.com/blog-research-difference-culture-climate/

CHAPTER 3

Project management methods, tools and careers

In this chapter we explain the foundations of **project management** as a method, explore popular project management methods and tools, and outline the development of careers in project management in the industry as well as where to find good sources of information and resources.

As project management practice in health and community care has matured, and organisations have undertaken large, innovative and often transformational projects, project management methods, skills and practices have become trusted ways of getting things done. Nimble adaptation and quick project turnarounds are routinely expected, and there has been a general uplift in project management skills, experience and confidence as well as the wide adoption and customisation of project management frameworks, methods and tools.

At the same time, general management practices have evolved and methods such as team huddles have been widely adopted by managers, changing both the style and rhythm of normal operations and the way projects are managed.

For newcomers, it can seem that project management has a language all of its own. In the literature there are lots of acronyms – like CPM (**critical path method**) and WBS (**work breakdown structure**) – and technical terms such as **Gantt chart**, 'close-out', 'go-live', 'benefits realisation', 'project scope' and 'deliverables'. The use of project terminology can be confusing – it is not necessarily consistent, and sometimes the terms are simply alternative labels for the activities that managers do as part of their daily work: setting goals and targets, deciding on strategy, working out tasks and responsibilities, and undertaking quality improvement activities. However, the terms are helpful and are widely used in practice and in project management literature. The glossary at the beginning of the book defines some common project management terms (they are in bold type the first time they are used in each chapter).

The project life cycle

The **project life cycle** is a fundamental concept used by **project managers** to successfully guide their projects from start to finish (Australian Institute of Project Management, 2022c). It explains the normal progression of projects to completion.

The project life cycle model assists project teams to plan and monitor progress: it provides a useful structure for managing and monitoring, and acts as a roadmap so that all involved know what to do when and what to expect (AIPM, 2022c).

The project life cycle is not usually a simple linear process. Instead, there may be two or more cycles of planning, implementation, evaluation and variation. Thus, the project life cycle is often used to refocus and reframe activities, and project management then includes a reflective learning process as well as enabling decision points or gateways along the way.

Different project management frameworks use various terms to describe the project life cycle and it is often presented as five or more **phases**. In this book, we use a model with four phases. The first phase, *initiate*, will usually involve some initial concept development and scoping depending on the project's genesis – which could arise from identification of a problem or opportunity, a strategic goal, a legal or regulatory requirement or perhaps a government imperative. It is common for organisations to have a process for documenting, reviewing and sifting these ideas before any more detailed work is done, for example, using a concept brief (sometimes called 'a project-on-a-page').

Those that pass this test and get any necessary management support enter the second phase, *plan*. This involves exploration and analysis focused initially on clarifying the goals; then on defining the **scope** (how big is it?); and finally on preparing a plan for how and when and by whom the project will be done, what resources are required and how success will be judged. The results of this stage are generally captured in a project plan, which may go through more than one version with checking and adjustments as details are added. Larger projects may also require a detailed **business case** to be developed and approved (see Chapter 7) in order to progress to the implementation phase.

The third phase, which commences when the project plan is approved, is to *implement* (also called execution or launch phase). This is where the work happens, and all involved need to work together to get the tasks of the project completed. Managing this phase requires that the project's progress is tracked and corrected if needed, and that the tendency to drift into extra work or to change the original aims is also managed (sometimes through accepting change, sometimes by sticking to the plan). Implementation also includes ensuring that the costs don't blow out, that the defined deliverables are in fact produced, and that the needed data and information are collected and recorded.

The fourth phase is *close* (also called close-out), when the process of handover, or transitioning from the project to the new method or state, is completed. In this phase, final reports are submitted; all project documentation is completed and handed over; a review or evaluation of the project's success and the learnings is completed; and final communications are made, celebrations are held and thanks expressed.

Although these phases are presented sequentially, during the actual project several of the phases may occur concurrently or repeatedly (in projects with more than one stage, or as plans need to change). Information system projects and those involving software development will likely incorporate phases according to the system development life cycle (SDLC). The SDLC is a term used in systems engineering, information systems and software engineering to describe a process for planning, creating, testing and deploying an information system. The SDLC is not a method per se, but rather a description of the phases in the life cycle of a software application. These phases (broadly speaking) are investigation, analysis, design, build, test, implement, and maintenance and support (Systems development life cycle,

2024), but may differ according to the system development methods being used, such as Waterfall, Agile or Scrum. The 'project life cycle encompasses all the activities of the project, while the systems development life cycle focuses on realizing the product requirements' (Taylor, 2004, p. 39). The use of repeated cycles of the project management method is diagrammatically represented in Figure 1.2 in Chapter 1.

Project phases versus stages

As well as having a life cycle, projects may be divided into more than one **stage** to make a large or complex project more manageable, particularly where the outcomes of one stage may change the nature of the work in subsequent stages.

> ## Phases and stages
>
> The terms *project phase* and *project stage* are sometimes used interchangeably and in multiple contexts. For the purposes of this text, we have used the following definitions:
>
> *Project phase*: A phase of the project life cycle (e.g. initiation, planning). Each phase has one or more specific project **objectives** and related activities, and specified results, deliverables, processes and **milestones**.
>
> *Project stage*: Large or complex projects may proceed in stages, with 'mini-life cycles' within each stage. Stages may each have their own outputs or deliverables, and are often separated by decision points (e.g. design stage, testing stage).

Defining project stages and their outputs enables progressive decisions to be made about whether or not to move on to the next stage, with these decision points commonly known as gateways. Gateways might also require a decision about which of two or more options will be implemented in the next stage. A gateway would normally include a requirement for '**sign-off**' (formal acceptance by the client or sponsor of the project) before the next stage could proceed.

For example, a project that aims to acquire and implement a new information system for registering clients of a mental health service will have at least one '**go/no go**' decision point – that is, the time at which the organisation decides whether to accept the chosen system. Work before and after that point can be seen as two cycles (initiate, plan, implement and close) within the larger project or, in other words, as two separate stages. Other stages might also be required – for example, after technical installation and testing, it may be useful to manage the remaining implementation work as a separate stage of the project. There may be significant aspects of the **commissioning** process that require new planning, execution and closure (such as the conduct of staff training, the transfer of existing data and 'go-live' commissioning), which were unable to be planned extensively before the system was tested.

As this example illustrates, some projects may not continue after the completion of a stage perhaps because they were found not to be feasible; or they were not able to be completed within acceptable timeframes; or funding was not available; or the project simply didn't rate enough priority for the organisation by the time a gateway process was reached.

The number of stages and the activities or deliverables in each stage depend entirely on the project and are also influenced by the industry or sector context.

While all projects involve the principal phases described above, certain phases might contain a greater number of steps than others depending on the nature and size of the project. Capital development or projects involving the **procurement** and implementation of information systems such as an **electronic medical record (EMR)** can have a more complex life cycle than other projects – including several stages – but they still use the same tools and techniques to achieve project success. This does not necessarily mean that other types of projects are any less complex to manage. While each project is different, the lists of key tasks of each phase developed by the Australian Institute of Project Management are common to most projects, and they are available at https://aipm.com.au/blog/using-project-life-cycles-for-your-projects-success/.

Differentiating projects and programs

In the health and community sectors, there is a need to distinguish projects from **programs** or services. Projects are one-off activities with an end result (which may include trialling and refining a program or service). A program, on the other hand, is usually a service, intervention or set of activities that aims to meet a health or social care need. It may be ongoing or have a defined operating period; it may also be a grouping of related services or interventions. For example, a community health service may plan to implement a new diabetes management program and use project methods to pilot and then implement the program. After the project ends and the program is in use, program management techniques help ensure that it remains effective and is delivered efficiently on a 'business as usual' basis. There are some real similarities between program and project methods, but it is useful to make the distinction.

The other use of the term 'program management' in the project management literature is to mean a group of projects managed in a coordinated way to obtain benefits not available from managing them individually (PMI, 2021, p. 20). Program management is also used in a more general sense, to include both projects and ongoing business activities. For example, Roberts (2011, p. 14) refers to a program as:

> a management vehicle for progressing, coordinating and implementing an organisation's strategy, specifically by linking together an often complex combination of business activities and new projects, all of which are focused on the delivery of a defined business objective.

Project management methods and tools

The last decade has seen an upsurge in the development, sophistication and accessibility of project management approaches, methods and tools. Project management resources, including methodologies, tools and templates, are more readily available online and often free. This growth has been driven by the changing complexity and needs of projects, but also step-changes such as the crisis of the COVID-19 pandemic with its need for rapid change and implementation. It could also be argued that there has been a democratisation in the use of project management resources both within organisations and within projects themselves with growing expertise amongst health and community workers.

Previously, health and community services mainly looked to **PRINCE2** and **PMBOK,** and these frameworks continue to be widely referenced as project management guiding principles. They were perhaps once viewed as the standard and adherence to them was often mandated by the organisation, the project funding body or the government, mostly to ensure consistent project management practices. The project management practitioners we interviewed advised that health organisations undertaking projects are now rapidly learning from experience. They adapt and customise a range of project management methods and tools from diverse sources such as continuous quality improvement, general management, communications and software development disciplines.

Project management methods

A project management method is a set of principles and practices that can be used to help conceptualise and understand the tasks of managing a project and how and when to use project management tools and techniques in effective, disciplined and reliable ways. Using such methods does not guarantee successful outcomes, but success is less likely without them.

Project management methods are often adapted for different industries and for specific circumstances (Teamwork, n.d.), and this is certainly true in health and community care. **Co-design,** quality improvement, risk management, change management and benefits realisation models and frameworks are regularly deployed in health and community care projects.

There are thousands of project management methods available, each with their own approaches, principles, tools, templates and sometimes software applications. Many organisations also use their own in-house tools and methods or a hybrid of adapted, in-house and standard methods. The use of customised in-house approaches is common, for reasons of conformity with the organisation's established practices and ways of thinking, and to simplify the task. For example, some organisations use the Plan, Do, Study, Act cycle popular in quality improvement for planning and designing relevant projects.

While certain principles and methods are necessary for project success, in most instances there is no one best way, and no single recipe for success. Project management approaches commonly used in health and community services include those based on PRINCE2 (Axelos, 2017), Lean Thinking (used for redesigning or 'transforming' the processes of health care [Kovacevic et al., 2016]) and PMBOK (PMI, 2021).

There are many other methods in project management literature, but they can vary in their relevance and applicability for the health and community care sectors. In the eHealth field, vendors often bring their own project management methods or implementation/service delivery models. Project managers are also not limited to a single method for a project. It might make more sense to use a different approach for a systems integration phase as opposed to managing the project Gantt (schedule).

There is also some variation in practice in different settings. Some government departments and authorities have adopted PRINCE2, often with local modifications, and use it as a framework or set of guiding principles for project management. Which model or framework is used can also depend on the source of funding. If the project involves a **tender** process or a consultancy, some standardised methods used by government may be stipulated as part of the funding arrangement, including methods of contracting, **tendering** and procurement, and rules of **probity**. For example, the Victorian government Department of Treasury and Finance (DT&F) requires the use of the technique known as the Investment Logic Map as part of its business case template for some publicly funded projects (DT&F, 2018).

PRINCE2

PRINCE2 (PRojects IN Controlled Environments) is a structured set of components, techniques and processes designed for managing any type or size of project (Axelos, 2017). Originally developed for use in **information and communications technology (ICT)**, it has been mandated in the UK public sector and is widely used (and perhaps often simplified) elsewhere.

The PRINCE2 method is an adaptable process-based model for the management of projects and includes principles, themes, templates and tools.

PRINCE2 provides an overview of project management theory, as well as practical methods for thinking about how the project fits into the organisation, how to go about planning and initiating the project, and managing the stages of the project. The PRINCE2 package also includes templates that can be used as is or adapted – for example, a **project brief**, quality plan, business case, communications plan, risk log and end of project report.

A guide to the Project Management Body of Knowledge (PMBOK Guide)
Published by the US-based Project Management Institute (PMI), *A Guide to the Project Management Body of Knowledge* is a widely used set of standard terminology and **best practice** guidance that encapsulates generally accepted project management knowledge and practices, based on the American Standard for Project Management (PMI, 2021, p. 3). The project management principles described in the PMBOK Guide are management of project integration, scope, schedule, cost, quality, resources, communications, risk, procurement and stakeholders. Rather than being a recipe book for successful project management, this publication is an excellent resource explaining theories and principles of project management, project processes and phases, and relevant tools and techniques.

The Agile approach
The Agile approach uses short development cycles called 'sprints' to focus on continuous improvement in the development of a product or service (Alexander, 2018). It is designed as an alternative to traditionally planned projects and is often used in software development projects. The intention is to release and test new solutions, and then use customer feedback for continuous improvement. The method incorporates a range of tools and approaches, including sprints, daily standup (meetings) and scrum teams (tightly focused small teams committed to the achievement of sprints). Advocates argue that the Agile approach fosters rapid system development, innovation and team collaboration. More information is available at www.atlassian.com/agile. Other forms of the Agile method that are commonly used in software projects include Scrum, **Kanban**, Scrumban, eXtreme Programming (XP), Adaptive Project Framework (AFP), and Rapid Application Development (RAD).

Other project methods
Table 3.1, while not exhaustive, describes other project methods that may be relevant to health and community care projects.

Table 3.1 Other project methods

Waterfall methodology	a modern version of traditional approaches to project management which retains the linear stepwise design, and emphasises the need to complete each major step before starting the next one. The Waterfall stages are often described as requirements, analysis, design, construction, testing, and then deployment and maintenance.
Lean thinking	has its origins in manufacturing and aims to maximise value and minimise waste (by removing unnecessary tasks, handovers and waits in business or care processes) to create more efficient workflows.
Critical path method (also known as critical path analysis)	a way of identifying and scheduling all of the critical project tasks, as well as their dependencies (see Chapter 7). The longest sequence of critical tasks becomes the critical path and defines the timeframe for the project. An extension of this method is also known as critical chain project management.
New product introduction (NPI) or development (NPD)	is used in projects to define, develop and launch new (or improved) products.
Six Sigma	a method for improving business processes with the aims of achieving quality and reliability in the outputs. There are several versions, linking the approach to Agile and Lean, for example. It is used for both improving existing processes and creating new ones. It may be less suitable for health and community service settings, where standardisation of processes is not always the goal.
Kanban	crosses the line between a method and a tool. The features of Kanban (meaning *signboard* or *billboard* in Japanese) include visual project dashboards, project overviews, task management, workflow, personal agenda boards, Gantt-style timelines, time tracking and reports. Kanban is increasingly described as 'light project management' or 'task management'. See https://www.atlassian.com/agile/kanban.

Source: Adapted from Teamwork (n.d.).

The method or the tool?

There is a difference between a project method and a tool. The *method* is the practice of the activity; the *tool* is the mechanism by which it is achieved. For example, monitoring the project schedule is an important method of ensuring timeliness, and the Gantt chart is a useful tool for the task. It is easy to get carried away with an impressive array of tools, but it is important not to lose sight of the underlying method and also to choose the correct tools for success.

Some authors and managers believe that there is a technique or tool to cover any project management situation. Others firmly believe that a good manager is also a good project manager and that special tools and techniques are less important. The balance is probably somewhere in the middle, in that formal project management methods and tools are necessary and have intrinsic value but cannot of themselves ensure project success.

For project managers it is important to know when and how to use tools and techniques. Many tools will be ineffective, regardless of where they come from, unless they are supported by strong management practices including effective negotiation, communication, leadership, use of alliances and networks, and change management methods.

Selecting the right project management methods for your project

The right project management methods can elevate a project and help the project manager to get the best out of the team and the best results for the organisation. No two projects are alike, and so selecting the methods to use to manage each project can be tricky.

The following are some key considerations that might assist in selecting methods for projects:

- Are there existing methods in use in the organisation (or in previous projects) that could be effectively used and with which the team has experience?
- Are existing methods fit for purpose?
- What methods are suitable given the type, size and complexity of the project or activity?
- Can the project budget cover a new method? Consider software, certification, training and resource costs.
- Is the method collaborative, flexible, scalable and easy to use?
- Does the project involve a vendor who brings a built-in method? What parts of the project will that method cover?

Project management tools

Project management tools are used to assist project teams to achieve specific tasks. Many organisations have their own standard tools and templates for project proposals, plans, communication, risk management and status and variation reporting, and some have implemented software to facilitate some project management processes.

Traditionally, project-specific tools including Gantt charts, computerised scheduling and **tracking** tools such as Microsoft Project have been widely used in healthcare settings. Over the past decade, however, organisations have deployed enterprise-wide work management and collaboration platforms such as Google Workspace or Teams, which enable shared workspaces, document management and virtual communication, and their use has naturally extended into the project management space.

There is also a multitude of purpose-specific tools for managing risk, quality improvement, defects, process/workflow documentation, resource management, change management and **project assurance**. Project managers often have the flexibility to mix and match the best tools and adapt them to the project at hand.

Digital project tools and technologies

A wide range of project management software packages and applications are readily available to assist in the management of projects and in the establishment of an organisation-wide project management information system. The potential pitfalls in buying and using project management software include:

- The purchased software may never be used, or is only used by a small number of people, for example in the **project management office (PMO)**.
- The software may be used for limited functions – for example, scheduling, timekeeping, high-level reporting or budgeting.
- Overly sophisticated software may be too large and unwieldy to be useful for most projects.
- Detailed training may be required to use the software effectively.
- The software may not be a good fit for the project at hand.
- The project manager may become too involved in the software, to the detriment of the project.

Microsoft Project is a commonly used project management product which enables the use of Gantt and critical path charts, milestones, project baselines, resource allocation and a work breakdown structure. It is important, when evaluating project management software, to have a good idea of which tools would assist in the management of individual projects, and whether there is a need for a management system for multiple projects. Project management software, as with any other ICT application, needs to be thoroughly evaluated in relation to the organisation's existing systems, software infrastructure and projects.

Fortunately, project managers now have a choice of modern software applications that may be easily accessed and adapted for use at potentially low cost or free for a small number of users. Some of these applications may already be in use in the organisation for another purpose, for example Jira as a software development or bug tracking platform. To choose the best application(s) for your project, the following are some key considerations:

- license requirement: enterprise, PC based, software as a service, number of users
- suitability for the devices the application or software will be deployed on
- software budget, implementation budget
- project complexity, size of team and number of users
- scalability requirements
- the required functional features and specifications, for example dashboards, reporting, scheduling, resource management, task management, workflow redesign or templates
- the method being used by the organisation or by key vendors, for example Agile or Kanban
- alignment with vendor software tools and need to integrate with existing platforms already in use in the organisation
- ease of use, existing expertise and the need for additional training.

The following are some commonly available proprietary applications each with a variety of work management features such as scheduling, task management, visual dashboarding, workflows, tracking, reporting, resource management, collaboration and analytics (https://project-management. com/category/software-reviews/). Some of these applications are aligned with a specific project management method such as Agile or Kanban and others have features that can be adapted for managing projects. Please note that this list is not exhaustive, and that the software market is dynamic and often subject to change (adapted from https://thedigitalprojectmanager. com/tools/best-project-management-software/).

- monday.com https//monday.com/
- Microsoft Project https://www.microsoft.com/en-au/microsoft-365/ project/project-management-software
- GanttPRO https://ganttpro.com/
- GoodDay https://www.goodday.work/
- ClickUp https://clickup.com/
- Trello by Atlassian https://trello.com/home.html
- Jira Work Management https://www.atlassian.com/software/jira
- Wrike https://www.wrike.com/vad/
- Asana https://asana.com/

- Smartsheet https://www.smartsheet.com/project-management
- Basecamp https://basecamp.com/
- Kantata https://www.kantata.com/product/project-management-software
- Zoho Projects https://www.zoho.com/projects/
- Businessmap (formerly Kanbanzie): https://businessmap.io/
- Celoxis https://www.celoxis.com/
- Hive https://hive.com/
- Hub planner https://hubplanner.com/

COVID and project management 'lite'

The COVID-19 pandemic impacted all aspects of health and community services – organisations, the workforce, the delivery of care and how projects are conducted both during the pandemic's height and on an ongoing basis. The sheer volume and scale of project imperatives, often with extremely short turnaround times, were unlike what most organisations had ever experienced. Many of these projects were driven by government and public health policy and were funded accordingly.

Some of the project goals and scope were familiar but many were outside the normal experience and responsibilities of organisations and staff. Examples of pandemic projects in the health sector included:

- *establishment of COVID clinics and services*: testing, assessment, respiratory, quarantine and vaccination
- *processes, workflows and protocols*: personal protective equipment (PPE) including donning/doffing, utilisation, spotters, individual fit checking of masks, cleaning, contact tracing, isolation, security, visitor and access protocols, hand sanitising, COVID-positive pathways and vaccinations for staff, patients and the community
- *rapid stand-up and set-down of clinical and client services*: ward/bed, clinic, residential, aged care, outreach and telemedicine services
- *COVID research and data collection projects*
- *other projects*: workforce rostering, surge workforce recruitment, reporting, training; communications and hotlines, procurement and supply management, technology and applications (e.g. QR codes, online and virtual meeting software, booking systems).

In response to government and organisational priorities what would have previously taken weeks or months was now often to be delivered in days. Many projects were undertaken in an atmosphere of uncertainty, with shifting requirements and a depleted workforce. In order to make things happen project teams were required to be innovative, agile, flexible and dynamic. Our research participants reported that the following techniques were used:

- Time constraints usually meant that formal project documentation was minimised. Teams were briefed and formed quickly, met often (huddles, standups, walking meetings and online), used work collaboration platforms such as Teams to draft up simple schedules, action lists and workflows and for streamlined reporting and fostered a Kanban (visual) project culture.
- Communication technologies and platforms were cherry-picked to enable rapid information sharing including social media, online chat and smartphone capabilities. Project activities, goals and decisions were recorded on glass walls (then photographed) or shared using virtual whiteboards and applications.
- A wide variety of staff stepped up to manage and participate in project teams as it was 'all hands on deck' to get things done. Many project management skills were acquired on the job.
- Uncertainty and risk were managed as much as possible; however, planning activities were often abbreviated. Timeframes did not support extensive testing and trialling. Proactive decision-making and ongoing problem-solving were required to work through issues on the fly.
- Hard deadlines meant that innovative, 'crash-through' and non-standard implementation approaches and were deployed through necessity, as were Agile and Lean methods.
- Project teams worked closely with government at all levels as well as partnering with other organisations and industries. Staff from sporting facilities and airlines were employed to organise rapid standups of clinics. Testing centres were set up at racecourses and in car parks, there were hospitals in hotels, aged care homes were staffed by acute service providers and command structures, and experts were borrowed from military organisations.

Overall there was a significant upsurge in project management skill and capacity. Many of the methods, technologies and processes deployed for the pandemic response are now embedded in everyday project management practice together with the benefits of long-lasting relationships formed during that time. Positive impacts of COVID-19 were also reported by project managers responding to a Project Management Institute (PMI) survey conducted mid-pandemic. Respondents reported that there had been an increased investment in technology to support remote work and virtual teams, a significant rise in staff accessing online training and increased opportunities for networking and partnerships (Hafed, n.d.).

Project management skills and careers

Achieving good project outcomes depends on good project managers, and having the right people in this role is critical. While project management has a set of methods, the art lies in understanding what the project must achieve, and in being responsive to contingencies, open and flexible, intuitive and able to deal with crises. Of equal importance is the persistence to keep the project moving on.

Project management skills

Projects vary enormously in size and complexity, and the workforce involved can be large and sophisticated, or a single person. At small scale, a single project officer takes on the functions of both manager and team, frequently sharing the role of project manager with the person they report to. They usually need to negotiate with other staff for contributions of time, energy and support (and this is true for almost all projects in one way or another). So, even sole operators of projects need to pay attention to coordinating the work of others and motivating their (virtual) team.

At large scale (consider, for example, the project of building and commissioning new facilities or the implementation of an EMR), project managers may have both an in-house team and a large number of external consultants, vendors and suppliers to manage. Clearly, the knowledge, skills and experience required for success will vary along the continuum of scale and complexity, but also according to the substance of the project.

Opinions differ about the importance of content knowledge for the project manager – that is, does it matter whether the manager has expert knowledge in the project's area of focus? For example, in a project that will amalgamate two pathology services, how important is it that the project manager has a scientific background or hands-on experience of pathology services? For a project implementing a new diabetes service, does the project manager need a clinical or allied health background? How important are general project management skills and experience in these settings versus an understanding of the business?

Our experience indicates that content knowledge is a distinct advantage, and that working familiarity with the culture of the organisation and the professional groups within it is essential. But project management skills are also essential. Our experts inform us that an in-depth understanding of health or community care cultures, contexts, organisations, systems and stakeholders is essential for a project manager while some technical project management skills can be acquired on the job with the right mentoring and support.

Our conclusion is that content knowledge should be defined fairly broadly. For example, for a project that will develop a clinical service, knowing the clinical environment and its culture and dynamics is important, but you don't need to be a clinician. For an ICT project, you need to understand the ICT environment, information systems (including knowledge of the software development life cycle) and technical concepts, but you don't have to be an expert programmer. On the other hand, where a potential project manager has great content knowledge and general management skills, but lacks project experience, some training, mentoring and support might bridge the gap. In large organisations, this expertise is sometimes available from the project management office (PMO), the project director, or an executive with responsibility for strategy and innovation (and whose job involves significant project leadership).

When it comes to selection criteria and choosing the best person, the general principles for defining the required knowledge and skills for any job apply. Knowledge and skills should be specified in terms of competence or ability required rather than particular qualifications or backgrounds. Careful definition of the requirements, so that there is a balance between strong content knowledge and project management experience and ability, is also important. General skills and knowledge requirements include some or all of the following:

- *leadership ability*: in particular, creates and shares the vision for project success, and motivates the team and stakeholders.
- *discipline and drive*: demonstrates application to the task, takes responsibility, is decisive, has the ability to work effectively at both strategic and detail levels.
- *excellent communication and interpersonal skills*: talks to the right people, influences others, builds consensus, makes the project visible, negotiates, lobbies for the project, can manage conflict, can appropriately **escalate** issues.
- *initiative and organisation*: works independently, meets deadlines and ensures follow-through.
- *technical project management skills*: has know-how and experience.
- *local knowledge*: knows the working environment and has the ability to adapt tools and methods to suit.
- *analytical and reflective*: keeps their eye on the ball, understands risks, can read situations, is flexible and responsive.

What makes a good project manager

Great project managers are like Swiss army knives, with a multitude of technical capabilities and leadership qualities ready to deploy in any situation.

(AIPM, 2022b)

Traditionally, the value of project managers was judged on their certifications and their skills in implementing different methodologies (Patra, 2023). However, now there is an overwhelming amount of information, tips and advice available online about what makes a good project manager and the skills, traits or experience they need to be successful.

Most commentators agree that project managers need a complex combination of technical, business and interpersonal skills (Pratt & Alexander, 2023). Sometimes authors resort to naming tasks rather than skills, such as the Australian Institute of Project Management (AIPM) listing of planning, scheduling, budgeting, risk management and contract management, along with the 'soft skills' of communication, leadership, motivation and networking (AIPM, 2022a).

Others argue that project managers need just about every work capacity: to serve as a strategic business partner, possess extraordinary organisational skills, be flexible, have extreme awareness of resource capacity and utilisation, have highly tuned **stakeholder** management skills, understand who has authority, have a knack for picking the right tools, be somewhat clairvoyant, credit others, motivate others, be fully vested in success, accept accountability, communicate effectively, build community and rapport, prepare the team for the journey, establish themselves as leaders, serve as change agents, possess an even-keeled demeanour and work comfortably in the grey (Pratt & Alexander, 2023).

Our research participants highlighted the skills and attributes that they prioritise. A senior manager noted that 'leadership and personal skills are rated highly, sometimes surpassing knowledge, experience and training'. Others emphasised emotional intelligence, leadership and interpersonal skills, as well as experience in the industry and its organisations. Subject matter expertise together with an understanding of the impact of the project on the organisation were valued, as well as technical project management skills. There was a shared view that the technical skills were more amenable to being developed as needed, with the right support.

> If [project management training] is their only toolkit, then they completely miss on the engagement and communication. . . . I would rather they be really good at the soft skills.
>
> (Project Director, Health Network)

> Deliver on time matters, doing what you say by that time matters . . . that culture of accountability.
>
> (Senior Manager, Health Department)

> Focus on the relationship stuff first . . . go out there and understand and build those relationships, and then you can do the other stuff.
>
> (Senior Manager, Health Department)

Assertive enough . . . to be able to delegate and keep others accountable.
(Senior Manager, Health Network)

The Project Management Institute boils it down to three categories in their updated Talent Triangle: Ways of Working (technical PM skills), Power Skills (leadership, soft skills) and Business Acumen (strategic and business management). The soft skills are prominent in their Pulse of the Profession 2023 report which ranks 'communication, problem-solving, collaborative leadership and strategic thinking as most important in helping project professionals fulfill organizational objectives' (PMI, n.d.).

So, it seems that project managers need all the things that we look for in management roles everywhere. In health and community care, there is perhaps more emphasis on the need to know and understand our particular business and its culture, a kind of knowledge that is seen to rely on experience in the industry.

For practicing project managers, embracing lifelong learning seems to be essential (AIPM, 2022a) in a complex, uncertain and dynamic industry. Securing recognition of skills and experience via certification and professional networking is a good idea.

And finally, even a great project manager will struggle in a dysfunctional organisation, with poor governance, culture or leadership, or where the project is widely considered to lack merit. As Marker (2021) writes, 'You can hire the most successful PM available but they will not succeed if the company does not have the right conditions in place'.

All of these skills, attributes, experience and knowledge add up to a tall order when it comes to finding a suitable project manager. And much of what is required of a project manager is only gained through experience – of projects, of workplaces and of people. Finding good project managers, especially those with the skills to deal with complex or large projects, is not easy.

Of course, no matter how experienced, competent, enthusiastic and intelligent the person chosen for the job of project manager may be, they cannot expect to operate effectively without support and cooperation from senior management, staff engaged in the project and the organisation at large. Good project managers are not made or developed overnight. However, experienced line managers will already have many of the skills and attributes outlined above, and the skills of project management can be learned.

For small and medium-sized projects, we have seen some evidence that the strategy of developing promising project staff internally has greater long-term benefits than the option of buying in project management skills, including the retention of people and knowledge. Some organisations take a long-term view, and work to develop a project management culture or to encourage project management thinking throughout their organisations which may extend to the development of a critical mass of project managers. They also invest in both formal training and informal learning opportunities for key members of their staff.

Project management careers

In the wider health and community services industry, there is evidence of increasing demand for project managers and project officers. A scan of employment advertisements shows that there are many opportunities at all levels and in all areas of health and community services for fixed-term project positions for those with industry experience and qualifications. Contract and project-based employment arrangements increasingly suit employers.

There is also an emerging career structure for project managers, although as usual, it may not be a linear path and encompasses many potential roles from project team member to leader, or from technical expert to corporate Project Director and many more. Larger organisations are establishing PMOs and appointing senior project managers to positions that require them to plan, acquire funding and coordinate a set of major projects. Experienced health and community services project managers are also recruited by consulting firms and vendors to jobs that offer increasingly complex project management tasks and team leadership and management roles. In specialised areas such as EMR projects, project directors and managers are often able to move from one project to the next, deepening their technical and professional knowledge and their standing in the field.

There are many pathways to becoming a project manager in health and community care. A common route is to work as a team member or project officer on a project which provides project experience, and then progress into portfolio or project management roles that enable the development of both technical and **soft project** management skills. The transition from clinical roles such as nursing and allied health (including health information management) into project management is now quite common, as is the transfer of both clinical and managerial skills and career progression within the organisation. Practitioners often build their careers on achieving success from small local projects, then progressing to more senior roles in larger projects while undertaking professional development activities. It is not uncommon for project staff to move from project to project, or equally to move between project, clinical and operational roles both within and outside the organisation. Experience is one requirement; professional development and formal qualifications generally follow for those who decide to specialise.

Project management courses and professional development

Courses, training and professional development in project management are offered by universities, project management organisations, consulting firms, technical and adult education facilities, registered training organisations and project management software providers. Project management education is available by distance education, online, on-site and face-to-face, and there are a few courses tailored to the health and community services sectors. There is no single recognised qualification in project management in the industry. This is mainly due to the fact that the majority of project managers gain project management skills and experience on the job. But it is also due to the wide range of projects that are undertaken – from building hospitals to implementing new models of care for fields as various as community aged care to child protection.

Certificate, diploma and master's level courses in project management are available through universities and further education facilities and provide the relevant skills, as well as the credentialling that assists in career development. Most Master of Public Health and Health Administration/Management programs in Australia include project management as one of their core subjects. We suggest that those looking for training consult their employers, their professional associations or experienced project managers for advice. The relevant national project management institute is also likely to be helpful, for example, the Australian Institute of Project Management website (www.aipm.com.au/home) offers both training and up-to-date listings of project management courses. We have also observed the value to career development of other activities, including networking and documenting project successes in in-house or industry publications, and presenting at professional conferences or workshops.

Project management resources

In this section, we present a short guide to finding project management resources that can both assist project staff to skill-up quickly and assist students of project management to find their way around the literature. These resources, many of them available free online, include project management websites, professional organisations, blogs, journals and textbooks.

Project management organisations and websites

There is a growing number of project management organisations with helpful websites containing a multitude of resources. However, none of them is health or community care specific; many of the blog posts are written on behalf of software vendors; and many articles are not peer-reviewed or moderated. Some websites are dedicated to project management education, training, accreditation and professional certification in project management, while others offer membership, services, software, events, webinars, articles, case studies, blogs and tools. Table 3.2 details

Table 3.2 Project management peak bodies and organisations

Organisation and website	Country	Services and resources
Australian Institute of Project Management (AIPM) www.aipm.com.au	Peak body in Australia	Professional development – certification, achievement awards, networking Events and education – workshops, webinars, master classes, conferences Publications – blogs, guides and reports
Association for Project Management (APM) www.apm.org.uk	Peak body in the UK	Professional development – chartered membership, qualifications, tracker, research, networking, mentor program Events and education – learning portal, webinars, conferences Publications – podcast, journal, APM Body of Knowledge
Project Management Institute (PMI) www.pmi.org	Peak body in the USA	Professional development – certifications, research, networking Events and education – academic programs, online courses, webinars, conferences, PMI study hall Publications – standards, podcast, journal, practice guides, blogs, tools, business solutions
International Project Management Association (IPMA) www.ipma.world	Federation of leading PM associations in each country	Professional development – certification, global awards, research, members hub Events and education – courses, programs, special interest groups, conferences Publications – standards, resources
Project Management Institute China (PMI China) www.pmichina.org	China division of PMI	See PMI above

some of the key project management organisations in their countries of origin or beyond. Table 3.3 provides details of other useful websites.

Project management textbooks

A number of practical and useful project management textbooks are available, featuring varying amounts of jargon and technical complexity.

Table 3.3 Other useful websites

Website	Resources
Project Manager www.projectmanager.com	Templates, Ultimate Guides (e.g. Gantt, WBS, Critical Path), blogs, training videos (e.g. how to write a scope of work), books, articles
TeamGantt Project Management Resources www.teamgantt.com/resources	Blog, podcast, newsletter, classes, guides, video tutorials, tools and templates
Project Management.com www.ProjectManagement.com	Webinars, templates, articles, education, downloads, events, blogs and discussion forums
Teamwork.com www.teamwork.com/ project-management-guide	Guides, blog, webinars, books and tools

There are not many texts that explore project management in health and community services (hence the need for this book). The following are suggested as good all-round project management texts (mostly available as eBooks) that project managers and students might find useful when investigating project management theory or when initiating or managing a project:

- Heagney, J. (2022). *Fundamentals of project management* (6 ed.). HarperCollins Leadership.
- Kerzner, H. (2022). *Project management case studies* (6 ed.). Wiley.
- Meredith, J. R., Shafer, S. M., & Mantel, S. J. (2021). *Project management: A managerial approach* (11 ed.). Wiley.
- PRINCE2 official guides and textbooks at www.prince2.com/aus
- Project Management Institute. (2021). *A guide to the Project Management Body of Knowledge (PMBOK Guide) and the standard for project management* (7 ed.). Newton Square.
- Project Management Institute Inc.: Various textbooks on global standards grouped into 'Foundational standards', 'Practice standards and frameworks' and 'Standards extensions': www.pmi.org/pmbok-guide-standards
- Verzuh, E. (2020). *The fast forward MBA in project management: The comprehensive, easy-to-read handbook for beginners and pros* (6 ed.). Wiley.

Project management journals

The leading journals dedicated to project management theory and practice are:

- The *International Journal of Managing Projects in Business* (IJMPB) publishes articles on the theory, research and practice of all aspects of project management, with a focus on multidisciplinary approaches based in social science. www.emeraldgrouppublishing.com/journal/ijmpb
- The *International Journal of Project Management* (Elsevier) is associated with the UK Association for Project Management (APM) and publishes research on project management in all relevant disciplines, conference reports and book reviews. www.journals.elsevier.com/international-journal-of-project-management
- *Project Management Journal* (Sage) is the academic and research journal of the USA Project Management Institute and publishes papers on research, techniques, theories, and applications in project management. https://journals.sagepub.com/description/PMX

Most professional and management journals also carry articles about project management in their specific areas from time to time. These include *Australian Health Review, Harvard Business Review, Health Care Management Review, Health Services Journal, Journal of Health Care Management*, and *Journal of Health Organization and Management*. The *Health Information Management Journal (HIMJ)* also has regular articles examining EMR and clinical system implementation projects.

Summary
- An understanding of the frameworks of project management is essential for anyone doing projects in health and community services.
- Project management has a unique language, but many of the principles are familiar to experienced managers.
- The project life cycle is a foundational model for thinking about and managing the phases of a project. It can also assist project staff to refocus and reframe the project if necessary.
- There are a large number of project management frameworks, models, methods and tools that are of assistance in understanding project management concepts and theories. However, no single approach or method can guarantee project success.
- Project management software can be useful – and there are many good applications available with a variety of functions and features – but it does not substitute for leadership and sound management.

- There is debate about what makes a good project manager, and whether content knowledge and industry experience are more important, or project management skills and qualifications. There is more consensus that the 'soft skills' of people management, communication and leadership are essential.
- Skilled project managers are in demand, and project management career pathways are developing as well as opportunities for professional development via qualifications and credentialling, networking and presentation of project results to peers at conferences and workshops.
- There are many valuable resources available to assist project managers and team members, including online resources, project management organisations, journals, seminars, textbooks and courses.

References

Alexander, M. (2018). *Agile project management: A comprehensive guide*. www.cio.com/article/3156998/agile-development/agile-project-management-a-beginners-guide.html

Australian Institute of Project Management. (2022a, April 08). *The 9 essential project management skills you need to be successful in 2022*. https://aipm.com.au/blog/project-management-skills/

Australian Institute of Project Management. (2022b, August 02). *How to be a great project manager*. https://aipm.com.au/blog/how-to-be-a-great-project-manager

Australian Institute of Project Management. (2022c, May 31). *Using project life cycles for your project's success*. https://aipm.com.au/blog/using-project-life-cycles-for-your-projects-success

Axelos. (2017). *Managing successful projects with PRINCE2* (7 ed.). The Stationery Office.

Department of Treasury and Finance of Victoria. (2018). *Applications of the investment management standard*. www.dtf.vic.gov.au/investment-management-standard/applications-investment-management-standard

Hafed, A. (n.d.). Positive impact of the COVID-19 crisis on project management. *Project Management Institute*. Retrieved January 15, 2024 from www.pmi.org/chapters/luxembourg/stay-current/newsletter/positive-impact-of-the-covid-19-crisis--on-project-management

Kovacevic, M., Jovicic, M., Djapan, M., & Zivanovic-Makuzic, I. (2016). Lean thinking in health care: Review of implementation results. *International Journal for Quality Research*, 10(1), 219–230.

Marker, A. (2021, October 12). Project governance: How little processes can have big impacts. *Smartsheet*. Retrieved March 13, 2024 from www.smartsheet.com/project-governance

Patra, A. (2023, January 23). *12 Project management trends emerging in 2023*. www.replicon.com/blog/project-management-trends/

Pratt, M., & Alexander, M. (2023, October 12). *20 Traits of highly effective project managers*. Retrieved January 16, 2024 from www.cio.com/article/276269/project-management-six-attributes-of-successful-project-managers.html

Project Management Institute. (2021). *A guide to the Project Management Body of Knowledge (PMBOK guide) and the standard for project management* (7 ed.). Newton Square.

Project Management Institute. (n.d.). *Power skills: Redefining project success.* Retrieved January 01, 2024 from www.pmi.org/learning/thought-leadership/pulse/power-skills-redefining-project-success

Roberts, P. (2011). *Effective project management.* Kogan Page.

Systems Development Life Cycle. (2024, February 22). In *Wikipedia.* https://en.wikipedia.org/wiki/Systems_development_life_cycle

Taylor, J. (2004). *Managing information technology projects: Applying project management strategies to software, hardware, and integration initiatives.* PHI Learning.

Teamwork. (n.d.). *Project management methodologies.* www.teamwork.com/project-management-guide/project-management-methodologies/

The initiation phase

From concept to proposal

DOI: 10.4324/9781003431701-5

In this chapter, we explain the first **phase** of the **project life cycle:** the project initiation phase. This is when the project concept or idea is broadly defined and developed into a **project brief,** and early support is secured. We start with the question of where ideas for projects come from and who the likely participants are. The chapter then explains the key steps to be taken in developing an idea into a project proposal that can be used to seek support, funding and approval, and later guide the development of a project plan. Some specialised approaches to establishing the feasibility or merit of projects in health and community care, which are sometimes needed in the initiation phase, are also explained. We conclude with a discussion of submitting applications in response to tendered projects or funding rounds and contracting projects to consultants.

Why projects are initiated

Projects generally arise when an organisation or team needs to solve a problem or take up an opportunity. Project ideas are often the answer to the question of what to do in response to changes in policies or funding **programs,** the need to relocate a service or develop new facilities or infrastructure, changes in legislation, or the need for new clinical guidelines or care protocols. Crises can also be the catalyst for projects that implement needed changes, as happened with the COVID-19 pandemic. The ideas might come from leaders or arise more informally in conversations with colleagues at team meetings, case conferences, networking forums, or from seminars or conference presentations. Sometimes projects emerge simply because someone thinks of a better way of doing something (or reads a success story from elsewhere) and lobbies decision makers to test it out. One of our participants described their practice:

> *I often think lots of people have . . . great ideas, they just don't have the sponsorship within the organisation to get them up or to be heard. And so, as a leader that's something I'm conscious of, listening to people. Because all the best ideas are from the frontline or the managers who know how to do things better.*
> *(Senior Manager, Home Care Services)*

When the leadership group identifies problems that need a project-based solution and then commissions project work, this top-down approach has the advantage of senior management support and therefore better access to resources. However, if the project requires change in the processes of service delivery, it may still be difficult to get staff further down the hierarchy to own and support it (known in **project management** language as 'buy-in').

It is also common that organisations commit to large and complex projects as a response to government directives and legislative requirements or as a response to government funding opportunities and strategic focus. For example, in recent years, national governments in many countries have invested in supporting digital transformation in the health system, and in developing aged and disability care and mental health services. Such opportunities have seen a growing number of large-scale technological and infrastructure development projects across the industry (Scott et al., 2020).

Management activities, such as strategic planning or preparation for accreditation surveys also often give rise to projects. For example, quality and safety improvement has been a core focus of healthcare organisations in recent decades, shaped in response to quality and safety principles and driven by accreditation requirements such as the implementation of the National Safety and Quality Health Service Standards in Australia (Australian Commission on Safety and Quality in Health Care, 2017).

Wherever project ideas come from, their progress will depend on things like their fit with organisational strategic priorities or directions, the commitment of individual champions and sometimes serendipity and good timing. The project initiation phase is the critical first step when project ideas are tested and refined.

Who participates in project initiation?

There is always someone who leads the initiation process. This person can be a staff member who is the 'idea owner', or a member of the executive who is the potential **project sponsor**. Often in practice, the idea owner and the potential project sponsor become the project champions and play a critical role in seeing the project through initiation. For some projects the idea owner drives the ideas, expressing their benefits and alignment with the organisation's vision and purpose, as well as informally garnering support. The role of the project sponsor in the initiation phase includes understanding the organisation's relationships, vested interests and stakeholders, and the potential impact of the project, as well as securing resources (LeRouge et al., 2014).

The other important potential contributor who may be identified early in the initiation phase is the **project manager**, who can bring project leadership skills and contextual knowledge and may have the confidence of important stakeholders. If appointed during this phase the project manager can lead the development of the project brief and other key initiation activities.

Representatives of stakeholders also need to be involved in contributing to the conceptualisation of the project to develop necessary support and head off potential opposition. Potential project funders may also need to be consulted as an important step of securing resources in money or in-kind.

Project initiation tasks/activities

The five steps below are essential to successful initiation of a project:

1. consolidate the reasons behind developing the proposed project
2. broadly define the project – the goals, key actions, estimated length and tentative budget
3. develop a draft project brief for presenting the project idea to key stakeholders and potential sponsors/funders
4. identify key stakeholders and the project sponsor, and conduct consultation and engagement; talk with known or potential funders
5. finalise the project brief and present it for consideration by decision makers.

Step 1: consolidate reasons

Articulating the reasons why the project is needed is an important foundation for clarifying the goals. 'Why would we do this?' is a different question from 'What will the project achieve?' A problem statement is a concise description of the problem(s) or opportunity that the project will aim to address. It briefly sets out the background and context for the project and can identify the gap between the current state and the desired future state. In short, the problem statement draws people's attention to why the proposed project is important. As an example, the following problem statement addresses frequent falls by residents in a group of aged care homes.

Problem statement: falls at ABC Care Homes

Falling affects elders at various levels, and a fall can seriously harm a frail elder. The fear of falling can lead them to reduce their daily activity levels, with a potentially profound effect on their functioning and quality of life. Falls that result in minor or no injury are often neglected before serious harms such as a fracture to the limbs or joints or a traumatic brain injury, and even death, occur. Therefore, taking measures to reduce the incidence and severity of falls and to manage hazards and risk factors is a key preventative measure.

In the past three years, ABC Care Homes' residents have suffered an increasing number of falls and increased incidence and severity of harm and complications. The consequences for residents are accompanied by a reputational problem for ABC, increased insurance costs and heightened scrutiny from the government agency in charge of accrediting aged care homes in our city. Action needs to be taken.

Even when the project is an opportunity that has been offered by a benefactor, a partner organisation, corporate headquarters or government funders, the rationale for the project still needs to be articulated in the project proposal, to address the question of why the organisation or unit should take up this opportunity at this time.

Step 2: define the project: goals, strategies, scope, budget and timing
> *The fantastic thing about working on projects, is everyone's goals are aligned. And that's why it's great . . . that's what excites people. . . . You know, there's a goal. But if everyone's goals aren't aligned, that's not going to happen.*
> *(Senior Manager, Hospital, quoting a Project Manager)*

Starting with a goal

Project definition starts with a clear statement of goals or aims, answering the questions 'What do we want to achieve?' and 'What exactly will this project do to solve the problem, meet the need or take advantage of the opportunity?' Our experience in practice, teaching and research has taught us that one of the first challenges in developing a project can be defining the goal in a way that lends itself to implementation and achievement.

People often have a passion for their work, and the energy and commitment to innovate, but some also have the tendency to make the project goal sound grand and important. The place for that is in the project rationale, or the project impact statement that might be required by government or philanthropic funders. The project goal(s) are less elevated – they must express concretely what the project itself will achieve. If the goal(s) are stated in ways that are not '**deliverable**', the project is in trouble from the start – without clear concrete goals, it is almost impossible to design (and reach agreement on) effective strategies.

At this early stage, it is also important to remember that projects sit within the organisation, so the goal (and **objectives**) must fit the organisation's higher-level strategic intent if the project is to receive approval and effective support, and if its outcomes are to be sustainable. In our example, ABC Care Homes, having considered the importance of the problem, must decide what proactive steps to take to prevent falls and improve residents' mobility. ABC decided to fund a project focused on developing and trialling a comprehensive evidence-based falls prevention program. The system would use some established, validated elements (e.g. falls risk assessment) that are industry standards and don't need to be trialled. But the comprehensive approach including a trial exercise program is new for ABC Care Homes, and its impact needs to be evaluated prior to full implementation. Therefore, the project goal is as follows.

> ### Project goal
>
> To develop and trial a comprehensive evidence-based falls prevention program in ABC Care Homes.

In the early stages of a project, there are many reasons why it can be difficult to take the step of turning a worthy aspiration ('we want our residents to live as independently as possible') into an achievable project goal ('this project will develop and test a program for falls prevention in our setting'). Sometimes it is simply a lack of familiarity with the technical meaning of goals in project management, but it may also be due to conflicting priorities among staff designing the project or problems in matching the team's goals to the requirements of a funding agency. Whatever the reason, the process of getting to a focused goal almost always forces greater clarity about strategies, timelines and the meaning of success.

Now is the time to debate the need for the project, the evidence for effective responses, the project's relevance to the organisation or unit's strategic goals and the potential to gain allies and support. At this stage, debate about these issues can be enormously productive. Later on, when resources have been committed and movement towards the goal has begun, such debate can cripple a project's chances of success. Later in this chapter, we explain how to use evidence and analysis to establish the value and validity of the goals; depending on the level of debate, the evidence may need to be gathered early in the process.

One of the fundamentals of project management is the principle that you first decide *what* you want to achieve, then work out specifically *how* to do it. There is, of course, an interaction between the 'what' and the 'how' – people always tailor their goals according to their means as well as finding the means to achieve their goals. But the principle remains, and the staging of project development accordingly is important: proponents need to be clear about what problems are going to be solved (or what needs will be addressed) and what needs to be done; *then* agree on how and when it will be approached; and *then* get on with it.

Project objectives

Objectives, like goals, are statements of what you want to achieve, but at a lower level. If you are going to meet your goal(s), what are the main steps along the way – the parts that, taken together, will add up to achieving the goal? In other words, objectives are more specific, immediate actions or changes that must be achieved if the project goal is to be met. Objectives in turn form the basis for strategies, and hence the activities or tasks through which the project is implemented. The objectives for the ABC Care Homes project are as follows.

Project objectives

1. Review the evidence on what works in falls prevention and establish benchmarking with peer organisations.
2. Design and trial an exercise program for strength and balance tailored to our residents and our environment.
3. Implement a falls monitoring system.
4. Implement a regular falls risk assessment method to identify and monitor residents' risk levels.
5. Train and accredit staff in the use of falls prevention methods and tools.
6. Evaluate the impact of the trial.

As this example illustrates, objectives are part of a more detailed statement that specifies what needs to be achieved in order to realise the goal. They identify the approach to be taken to achieving the goal and can include targeted levels of coverage or completion. The SMART criteria (Doran, 1981) can be a helpful guide for shaping a statement of objectives. The acronym has different uses and definitions, but for our purposes, the following interpretation is offered:

- *Specific*: a clear concrete target or improvement
- *Measurable*: achievement can be assessed and measured
- *Achievable*: likely to be accepted in the setting as feasible or doable
- *Realistic*: can be achieved with the available resources
- *Timely*: can be achieved within the required timeframe.

For projects like the ABC Care Homes example that aim to trial health and social programs, there are many ways to work towards a clear statement of goals and objectives: they can be established collaboratively through 'brainstorming' exercises; evidence and other information can be gathered to assess alternatives; and past strategies within the organisation can be reviewed with the involvement of key staff, managers and other stakeholders (e.g. peer organisations or government departments). More formal techniques for gathering and assessing evidence might be helpful at this stage, and we explain some of them later in this chapter. For other types of projects, like the introduction of new **information and communications technology (ICT)**, or innovation to meet the National Emergency Access Targets, the goal may be effectively set by corporate headquarters or the health or human services department. The aforementioned methods can then be used to shape the objectives and other elements outlined herein to suit local circumstances.

Project scope and strategies

The next step is to briefly define the **scope** of the project and identify what approach will be taken to achieving the goal and objectives. Scope is a commonly used term for defining the reach of the project – what functions or systems are in or out, what target groups, what interventions and so on. If goals define the focus, scope defines the borders. At the initiation phase, scope is generally defined only at a high level (i.e. without details). As project planning progresses, scope sometimes needs to be narrowed as the practicalities of the project and the challenges it must resolve become clearer, but the reverse can be true – essential enabling or supporting aspects may need to be brought into scope. Scope is usually fully defined when questions of who, what, where, when and how have been answered, and the project can then be given limits. For the ABC Care Homes project, the scope is defined as follows.

Project scope

The falls prevention program will fully address all relevant National Aged Care Standards and (excluding the exercise program trial) will cover all facilities.

The next step is to design strategies. Collectively, strategies describe how you are going to achieve one or more objectives (and ultimately, the goal). Strategies constitute a course of action designed to achieve a specific objective and contribute to the broader goal (Eagar, 2001). But it is also true that a single strategy (like a method for engaging relevant stakeholders) can contribute to more than one objective.

For the project brief, only a general outline of the strategies is required. The aim is to give enough information to explain the approach that will be taken. Good strategies are:

1. based on evidence of 'what works'
2. feasible to implement, and affordable
3. acceptable to stakeholders while allowing them to address their concerns
4. consistent with organisational culture (style, values and skill sets)

5. consistent with relevant policies (organisational, industry, government)
6. aligned with relevant organisational and/or government strategies
7. designed so that, taken together, they address the challenges the project is likely to face.

The design of strategies is tailored to each project, and there are many influences that help to determine what combination is likely to work best. A lot of information and guidance is available, including a useful approach suggested by the Institute of Project Management. There are always many ways to get things done. With time and resource limitations in mind, as well as knowledge of the organisation's mission, culture and environment, strategies are selected because they are the optimal approach to achieving the project objectives with acceptable levels of risk. While the project brief may not include the detail of strategies for each objective, it is a good idea for the project proponents to be as clear as possible at this early stage. For the ABC Care Homes project, strategies to achieve objective 2 are as follows.

Project strategies for objective 2: Design and trial an exercise program for strength and balance tailored to our residents and our environment.

Strategies

1. Design a program in consultation with residents, families/carers and expert staff in one facility, and specify criteria and indicators of success.
2. Train a cohort of the resident activity team in the chosen program.
3. Determine the best pattern of program delivery (e.g. duration, group size, location) according to resident profiles.
4. Train resident activity team members to recruit participants and provide the exercise program.
5. Collect and analyse trial data.

Step 3: develop a project brief

Once the project goals, objectives, scope and strategies have been at least tentatively defined, much of the work has been done for an initial project design.

Many organisations have in-house templates or forms that assist staff to develop a project brief, often on one or two pages, and seek approval to proceed to further development. These tools are intended to ensure that the major questions are answered in a standard format. The value of such an approach is to limit the amount of work required before the project idea is tested, and to enable both top-down and bottom-up initiation (i.e. ideas that come from senior management or external stakeholders as well as ideas that come from staff). Project ideas can then be assessed early on for fit with the strategic directions of the organisation and other important criteria. See Template 4.1.

Each organisation will specify its own requirements for how projects are initiated, and there are many different terms for the templates or forms, including 'project proposal', 'concept brief', 'project brief', 'project scope' or 'project definition'. While these terms do imply some differences in approach, they serve the same purpose – and we use the generic term project brief.

Templates sometimes vary between different parts of an organisation, and to suit different kinds of projects. Well-designed templates can be a valuable way of guarding against sloppy thinking, as they assist proponents to identify whether their vision or good idea can really be translated into practical action. The template can also be used by senior management to get an overview of what projects are being initiated within the organisation, for the purposes of prioritising and also to monitor and manage the organisation's **project portfolio**. Like any tool, project templates can become bureaucratic impediments if they are poorly designed or inappropriately used.

Step 4: consult with stakeholders

Stakeholder consultation at the initiation phase both enables tailoring of the project brief and can increase the likelihood of critical stakeholders buying in to the project. The project team can identify stakeholders' needs, allowing better management of their expectations and early management of potential issues and concerns. Stakeholder consultation also provides valuable information that can improve project design and reduce project risks. In this early phase, stakeholder consultation is likely to be informal and limited in scope. The focus is on getting an early reading of the acceptability of the project idea, and of the concerns that need to be addressed in the project plan. See Chapter 5 for discussion of stakeholder engagement in the planning phase.

Step 5: finalise the project brief and seek approval to proceed

The last step of the project initiation phase is to bring together the ideas and knowledge developed in the first four steps to finalise a project brief. The project brief typically includes the following headings or elements:

Template 4.1 Project Brief

Project Title:	
Project Sponsor:	
Proposed by:	

1. **Background to the Project:** [Briefly explain the context and the problem or opportunity that gives rise to the project]

2. **Goal/s and objectives:** [What is the project aiming to achieve?]

3. **Rationale:** [Why should these goals be pursued through a project?]

4. **Scope:** [Briefly state the boundaries of the project i.e. what is included and what is excluded]

5. **Deliverables:** [What will this project produce?]

6. **Stakeholders:** [who has power and influence, who will be directly affected by the project? What are their concerns likely to be?]

7. **Timeframe and resourcing estimates:** [what is the likely duration of the project? Likely types and amounts of resources (labour and non labour) required? What are the likely sources of funding?]

8. **Risks, issues and key assumptions:** [Identify all known major risks and issues that the project faces, and outline the major assumptions that may affect the project's viability or success]

9. **Success criteria:** [The key success criteria against which the project will be measured]

Signatures:		Date:
Proposer:		
Sponsor:		

Template 4.1 Project Brief

- background and problem statement
- explanation of goal(s) and objectives
- strategies, timeline and scope
- expected benefits to the organisation and key stakeholders
- project resources estimate: budget and staff requirements.

Each organisation will also have its own requirements and processes for approval of project briefs, and this is the final hurdle of the initiation phase. Typically, the 'idea owner' and the project sponsor will take carriage of this last step, and take on board the discussions, conditions and decisions of the executive or board and begin preparing for the next phase.

Specialised methods for initiating large and complex projects
In the following sections, we explain some specialised methods for particular types of projects that are more likely to be undertaken in health and community services. We start with preparatory work often used in the initiation of large, complex or untested digital technologies or systems.

Implementation planning study (IPS)
An implementation planning study may be conducted prior to ICT or information system implementations (or contract signing), to identify and understand the solution to be implemented, the context and requirements of the implementing agency, and to confirm the implementation scope and approach. Most commonly conducted in partnership with the software or technology vendor, the IPS typically involves a series of workshops covering solution demonstrations and requirements, the system integration approach, infrastructure/technology, data migration, training, testing and change management. An IPS report is usually delivered by the system or software vendor, summarising the IPS activities, findings and decisions, which then informs both the decision to proceed and the resulting project plan.

Feasibility, proof of concept and pilot studies
Feasibility, **proof of concept** and pilot studies may be conducted to assess alternative strategies for many types of projects. Even in small projects, it is a good idea to check that the assumptions underlying the strategies are supported by the available data.

One or more of these methods can be used prior to project approval or in the first stage of a multistage project to assess the practicality of a proposed plan or method. This step is needed when there is significant uncertainty regarding the implementation solution or the project deliverable or an untried technology or model of care. A feasibility study is used to determine the viability of a method, approach or idea by assessing technical, legal, economic, operational and scheduling feasibility (Simplilearn, 2023). A proof of concept (POC), commonly used to assess software capability, is a small exercise to test the design idea or assumption. The main purpose of developing a POC is to demonstrate functionality and to verify that a certain concept or theory can be achieved in development (Singaram & Jain, 2018). A pilot study, pilot project or pilot experiment is a small-scale preliminary study conducted in order to evaluate feasibility, time, cost and adverse events, and to improve the study design prior to performance of a full-scale project (https://en.wikipedia.org/wiki/Pilot_experiment).

The project business case

Whatever's signed off in terms of the business case and the financial and the contingency is the starting point for the project manager.
(Senior Manager, Health Network)

In project management, a **business case** is essentially a project plan and financial analysis that quantifies and schedules the costs of a project as well as the benefits and direct cost savings or increased revenue arising from the project. A positive business case is one in which the benefits (which normally arise after the project is completed) outweigh the costs. The origin of the term lies in the small business field, where typically an owner of a small business needs to present a positive business case to their bank or potential investors in order to get the capital needed to open or extend the business – that is, it is essentially a plan that demonstrates that the business is capable of repaying the investor or financier. Preparing a business plan can be important for small business owners for other reasons, as it essentially forces the owner to answer the question: 'How can this business be profitable?'

The concept of a positive business case is a bit different for projects in health and community services. The question may instead be: 'Will this project enable us to do something differently or better without additional cost – can we make this pay for itself?' (the 'break even' argument). For private providers of services, the question may be: 'Can we make this pay for itself and generate at least an acceptable surplus?' And the business case is often really about the ongoing service or system, rather than the initial project that establishes its feasibility and effectiveness.

If there are potential returns from the ongoing service or system, but the costs of the project itself are significant and sources of funding are hard to find, a well-argued business case can give decision makers a compelling reason to find the money and make the investment. In some situations, a signed-off business case may be required to get a mandate for the project. In addition to showing how innovative and effective the proposed project could be, the business case needs to address how the proposed project can justify the resources required (or how implementation of its outcomes will be sustainable); how it will contribute to the achievement of the organisation's and/or funder's strategic goals; and, if possible, how it will complement or enhance other approved initiatives and thus maximise their benefits.

Writing a business case

The business case document will be used as a tool for raising interest among key stakeholders and potential funders. It should address the following questions:

- What strategic benefits will the project bring to the organisation?
- Why is the project good value for money, given that the organisation will make a considerable investment in the project?
- What are the consequences for the organisation if it were not to conduct this project?
- What is the evidence that supports the case (in a form that is useful for decision makers)?
- On what criteria will success of the project (and a decision to proceed with implementation of the result) be based?

Sometimes the business case needs to be approved first. The process of writing it will require some of the information needed for the detailed project plan. The business case should be as concise and clear as possible, while including all necessary practical details. There are plenty of business case templates available (e.g. www.projectmanagementdocs.com/template/Business-Case-Template.doc), and Table 4.1 provides a generic business case outline.

Table 4.1 Generic business case outline

Executive summary	A concise summary (ideally on two pages) of the content of the document, including all recommendations. It should read as a 'standalone' document and should not introduce any material not found in the body of the report.
Sign-off sheet	An endorsement clause for recording project sponsors' and proponents' signatures, either committing them to act on the business case, or recording their support.
Current situation	A statement of the background and current context with relevant facts and judgements backed up with evidence (expressed in numbers where possible).

(Continued)

Table 4.1 (Continued)

Future state	The intended, predicted or desired future situation or environment – the future role delineation, risk profile, service models etc. Any assumptions should be clearly set out and supported with relevant data or other evidence.
Policy issues	The broad policy, political, legislative and organisational constraints within which the business case must fit – for example, government goals and policies, social justice considerations, legislative or accreditation requirements.
Strategic alignment	How does the initiative align with the strategic goals of the organisation, sponsor or funder?
Gap/needs analysis	A statement of the problems, gaps or needs that the project seeks to address, supported with relevant data and analysis.
Options for action	All feasible options to address the problems or gaps within the policy constraints. Each option, including the 'base case' or 'do nothing' option, should be described in enough detail to establish workable alternative courses of action. Each option must be capable of standing alone.
Analysis of options	The analysis of options is both a qualitative and quantitative process. Components can include income and expenditure streams; sources of funds for capital and recurrent costs; economic analyses (e.g. cost utility, net present value) tables; risk analysis; volume of outputs or services; strategic considerations; and timing. The analysis of each option should conclude with a definitive result, since those results will be used for comparison between options, and selection of a preferred option.
Comparative evaluation and selection of preferred option	Based on the results of the preceding steps and a clear statement of the argument, criteria and process, the preferred option is identified (this explanation usually also appears in the executive summary).
Recommendations	Recommendations propose the preferred option in the form of a decision or action for decision makers to endorse or decline. Any needed information about decision-making processes and the management of differing perceptions or other issues in the approval process should be included.
Implementation plan	Specifies the team or individual responsible for implementation and outlines the main components of the project plan.
Appendices	Additional material used and referred to in the business case. For example, members of the project team, additional financial or service data and analysis, population profile or other demographic data, equipment lists and references.

What about projects with no positive business case?

For some projects, there is no way that the project results can be applied without additional costs – for example, the introduction of a new keyhole surgical technique will probably expand the number of patients who can be treated and therefore cost a public hospital or health authority more, even if the procedure itself is more efficient. A new diversion program for young people at risk of offending will probably bring no financial benefit or reduced costs or 'offsets' to the provider of the program; cost savings will be realised in other agencies, such as juvenile detention facilities. In this sort of case, the question may be: 'Can we justify this additional service to funders on the basis of health or welfare benefits, and thus savings to the broader service system?' This is essentially the argument that health or social harms will be prevented and money will be saved elsewhere in the human services system – even if there are extra costs for the organisation that provides the service. If this is the basis on which justification will rest, an economic analysis may be what is needed (see Chapter 6). The results of a **needs analysis** or other empirical evidence can also be useful, as illustrated in the following project.

Project Story: Positive health outcomes: negative business case

A primary health network (PHN) had identified that people with chronic diseases in their region were experiencing higher than average hospital admission rates. A check of compliance with clinical guidelines for chronic condition management in primary care by GPs and other local practitioners revealed that standards were being met and in some cases exceeded, so they needed to look elsewhere. There is evidence to suggest that patients and carers are particularly open to changing their practices at home immediately following a crisis that leads to admission, so the local hospital was a logical place to look.

The network approached the local hospital with proposals for improvements in the way the hospital assisted patients and carers to prepare for improved management of chronic conditions following discharge. The hospital quickly realised that engaging in the suggested changes in their practices would cost real money during the pre-discharge period (e.g. building in training and time for staff to provide direct coaching to patients and families), but that not enough of the cost benefits of improved effectiveness would flow to savings for the hospital. If the suggested measures worked, patients' wellbeing would benefit, and possibly their future disease course would change. However, the hospital did not have the capacity in its budget to fund the initiative, and there was simply no workable business case. They agreed with the PHN to work on a submission for research or philanthropic funding to test the effectiveness of the measures, and thus prove the health benefits and net cost savings over time to the local health system.

Projects and programs: what's the difference?

When projects are used to test or implement new health and care programs, there can be confusion between the purpose of the program and the goals and scope of the project. For example, a health service wishes to test a program that is already in use in another country that promises more effective early intervention and more active management of a chronic disease, such as diabetes. The program will need to be adapted for local use because of differences in health and care systems, and the changes involved for the health service are significant enough that the process of introducing the new program needs to be conducted as a project. And in this case, good evidence of the effectiveness of the new program in the local setting will need to be collected as part of the project, so the organisation can decide whether to embed the new program in their work.

The aim of the program is to reduce severity and progression of the disease among the participants. But the goal of the project is to conduct and evaluate a trial of the program in the local setting. If the *project* is successful, the organisation will have the evidence to make a decision about the *program*. For a project of this kind, it likely that the project brief will need to be supported with some additional information at the initiation stage. Now we describe some of the methods often used to gather and provide supporting evidence for this purpose.

Specialised methods for assessing potential programs in health and community care

Health and care programs aim to solve problems, address needs and improve people's lives. They must be informed by available evidence to quantify the problems, validate the needs and confirm their value in health and wellbeing improvement. Evidence is also needed to inform the selection of the best strategies in light of the relevant context and limitations. 'Evidence' to guide program development doesn't only mean findings from empirical research, it may also include:

1. case study reports or examples of best practices in similar organisations or fields
2. epidemiological, population and other demographic data which provide context and weight to the problem and related needs for a specific population group
3. established standards and norms that express technical knowledge and requirements (such as quality and safety standards and protocols)
4. learnings from other programs and projects and the lived experience of consumers

5. expert opinion from acknowledged leaders and those with special expertise
6. information about stakeholder or consumer preferences
7. policy and management reviews, and commissioned reports
8. organisational service performance data
9. research publications, in particular those that report experience and the results of evaluations of new strategies or methods and tools; and information about stakeholder or consumer preferences.

These types of evidence are also useful for other kinds of projects and not all will be required for any one purpose. And it is also true that the experience and expertise of the project team, stakeholders and other personnel within the organisation are important. Brainstorming sessions, advisory groups and community consultations generate different ideas and evidence.

Three important analysis and planning methods commonly used in programs (and sometimes projects) in the sector – needs analysis, **literature reviews** and **program logic** – are explained next. Not all programs or projects will warrant the use of these methods, which can be time-consuming and costly, and require some technical knowledge and skills.

Needs analysis

In health and community care (and other areas of public policy), needs are defined as socially determined requirements for services, experienced by individuals or families or population groups. The concept is useful for determining the focus of interventions, services and programs. Thus, services are seen to be worth funding because they can demonstrate that they are effective in meeting an established need (that is, they produce the intended outcomes).

The goal of needs analysis (or needs assessment) is to develop an understanding of the health or social problems experienced in communities by a particular group or population, and therefore the type and volume of services that are required. Needs analysis is undertaken to identify the sorts of interventions or strategies that can solve those problems and address those needs (Eagar, 2001; Royse et al., 2006; Royse et al., 2009).

Bradshaw's classic typology of needs (Bradshaw, 1972a, 1972b), summarised in Table 4.2, specifies different ways of thinking about and measuring needs. A good needs analysis can be a critical step for a program proposal, and it can also be a research project in itself, depending on scope and complexity. As always, it is important to be very clear about the purpose and

Table 4.2 Bradshaw's typology of needs (Bradshaw 1972a, 1972b)

Type of need	Explanation	Examples
Felt need	What people experience as need	Pregnant women may feel the need for more information on childbirth and potential complications.
Expressed need	Actual requests for services; a felt need expressed in the form of demand for services (people seeking the service) or through community action	The need for a place to exercise in a local community may be expressed as a demand for exercise classes or the use of a gym. Long waiting lists at the local GP clinics are a form of expressed need for more GPs to work in the area.
Normative need	Established standards based on research and/or professional opinion	The daily recommended allowances of nutrients in foods, or accepted standards that specify the amount of open space needed for a given population.
Comparative need	Level of need inferred by benchmarking against the volume of services in comparable settings	The availability of supportive care and education for patients with diabetes is compared with different geographic locations.
Latent or unmet need	A gap between known levels of need and actual take-up or availability of services or programs	The difference between the number of diagnosed diabetics in a region and the number who access care; or the gap between demand for emergency admissions and the capacity of local hospitals. Useful for predicting the level of demand for services when designing new facilities.

scope of the needs analysis; its intended users and what kind of evidence they will find convincing; as well as what will be acceptable and convincing for consumers, community and perhaps other stakeholders, like the local government authority.

Defining scope and focus of needs analysis

Well-designed needs analysis enables a systematic step-by-step approach to identifying and collecting relevant data and information. The first step is specifying the needs analysis questions. This may involve consideration of the following:

■   Does the problem affect a particular population, community or group, especially a group that is disadvantaged in other ways?
■   How prevalent is the problem – how many people experience it?
■   How severe is it – does it cause serious debilitation or minor inconvenience?
■   What is the service system capacity?
■   What barriers and obstacles to change exist?
■   Is this a study to argue for additional resources, or for the reallocation of existing resources to improve equity, or for reallocation of resources between different types of responses for the same need (e.g. prevention versus treatment), or between different types of needs?
■   Are there known effective interventions that should be included among the possible service responses? (Hawe et al., 1990; Smart, 2019).

Limiting the scope and focusing the questions is important not only for managing workload but also to minimise the risk of raising false hopes or identifying issues and problems that are well beyond the capacity of the organisation to address.

Gap analysis

As well as information about the number of people involved, information about gaps and potential capacity in the available service system – **gap analysis** – may also be needed. The knowledge that current capacity is not adequate for current demand or predicted increases can be used as the basis for deciding whether new services or service models are required, or simply the improvement of existing services. That is, could the (potential or actual) gap be solved through more efficient services, through different kinds of services or through bringing together the responses of different service providers?

For example, Indigenous people with cancer may be diagnosed later in the course of their disease than the general community, and the treating clinical staff might initiate discussions about the reasons for this and what could be done. Equally, community leaders may speak up and ask for changes in the way that members of the community are able to approach care providers or in the location and style of care. This kind of problem requires both genuine engagement of service providers and community representatives, and good use of data to understand the causes and potential solutions, and their costs and benefits. Community representatives will have the best insights into the reasons why patients seek care later or are less well served by local health care providers when they do seek care. There are four characteristics of current services that should be examined – awareness, availability, accessibility and acceptability (including cultural safety) – before decisions are made as to whether this is a case for a service improvement project or for new interventions or models of care. Measuring a gap in services to address the identified need and the capacity of existing services to address predicted increased need is as critical as measuring the need itself.

Data collection
Once the needs analysis questions have been finalised, methods for collecting data and information can be decided upon, with priority given to reliable sources that can provide meaningful and valid answers to the questions. Data can be from secondary sources (that is, already existing data collections, perhaps requiring new analysis) or from primary sources (data collected specifically for the needs analysis), and that usually means interaction with people. Some examples of common primary data collection methods include the following.

- focus group discussion
- community forum and consultation
- blood tests, weight measurement, fitness tests
- survey – email, web-based, telephone, paper
- personal interviews
- observational studies.

Organisations also conduct needs analysis for other purposes, such as analysing the need for a staff development program. The needs identified through such a process may lead to training and staff development activities, but they typically also identify other types of needs – for example, to overhaul the way work is done or the way jobs are structured or even the arrangements for staff car parking. Any of these identified needs might require the development and implementation of a project. And, if so, the detailed data gathered as part of the needs assessment will be a vital support for the project proposal.

Needs analysis report
The production of a needs analysis report is the final step in needs analysis. A needs analysis report is typically structured along the following lines:

- background and introduction, including purpose and focus of the needs analysis
- design and plan
- key findings (needs, problems, gaps, tested and possible interventions, feasibility and priority of tested interventions in the specific context)
- discussion of findings and recommendation of the best interventions or solutions for further action
- conclusion.

Needs analysis often results in a large amount of information, most of it very valuable. This can make it challenging to prepare a succinct report with a clear summary of the findings and conclusions and a limited number of recommendations. This is where a tightly defined and limited scope of analysis – specified at the beginning of the process – pays off.

Literature review
Literature review is a process of evaluating relevant information found in published research and other documents; it should describe, summarise, evaluate and clarify the evidence (Aveyard, 2010). That is, the quality of the evidence should be appraised based on methods of data collection and analysis, interpretation of data in the specific context, and relevance to practice or decision-making.

Literature reviews can be an effective way of defining a problem, finding the current thinking on a subject, or assembling the evidence of effectiveness for a new method or technology, intervention or service. Literature reviews can assist agencies to avert misguided or even harmful projects that fail because they either do not meet a need or suffer from serious technical flaws in the way they are carried out. In other words, literature reviews can provide the evidence for decision-making about whether and how a program and/or project should proceed.

The first stage in a literature review is defining the subject area and knowing what question is to be answered. The second step is finding the available evidence, which is likely to be a combination of peer-reviewed research articles and '**grey literature**' (e.g. policy documents, government reports, industry journals, press). For published research, electronic databases are generally used to find journal articles, which requires access to a reference library. See the end of the chapter for resources on searching electronic databases.

Journal articles and academic papers are valuable sources because they are subject to a peer review process intended to ensure their validity, and they can be more current than books. Sometimes, a search will find a recent published review of the literature (also called an evidence synthesis), which can save a lot of time. Research papers generally report on discrete research projects with clear aims and objectives, methods and analysis of results.

The difficulty with journal articles is that sometimes they, too, are reporting on material that is a few years old. They can also be very technical and difficult to read and understand. Readers sometimes find that the problems investigated and presented in the articles are not of great interest to practitioners, and that the articles create more questions than answers. Moreover, findings and suggestions may not be sensitive and applicable to the local context in which the projects operate (Liang & Howard, 2011; Liang et al., 2011).

Grey literature can be found using a search engine like Google or Bing, and by gathering policy documents in the workplace. Data and reports generated within the organisation can be particularly valuable, because they are current and local, and offer insights into both the needs of the relevant patient/client group, and the interventions or approaches currently in use. Being unpublished does not mean poor in quality. Much grey literature is of high quality and value and is often the best source of up-to-date information on certain topics that may not yet have been widely studied.

Using a search engine to find the websites of government departments, professional institutions and non-government organisations is the starting point for accessing the grey literature. However, search engines and other types of websites are increasingly driven by advertising and other commercial incentives. Specialised search engines like Google Scholar are more useful but, as always, the biases and integrity of sources need to be checked.

Finally, the thing to remember in evidence searching is the importance of organisation: taking notes, keeping records (not only of the source but also of details such as page numbers for easy reference later), highlighting important concepts and capturing interesting ideas and potentially useful quotes. There are several software programs (e.g. Endnote) designed to make it easier to record and cite references.

Making sense of what you find

The literature search will probably unearth many references and sources well beyond the scope of the project. Reading the title and abstract will identify those that can be set aside; others will have to be read through to assess whether they are relevant. Even if a paper is interesting, its quality and relevance still need to be assessed – that is, you need to critically appraise the evidence, and that requires some skill (Liang & Howard, 2011; Liang et al., 2011). The essence of the process is to read each relevant paper, summarise the method and findings in a paragraph or two, and then write a few sentences summing up the results. A standard step-by-step guide and forms to assist health professionals in searching and in assessing the quality of research is available at www.healthevidence.org (developed by the National Collaborating Centre for Methods and Tools at McMaster University in Canada).

After finding and assessing relevant evidence, the next stage is to tell the story of what the evidence means. This requires analysing the main findings from the sources, and writing the answer to the 'So what?' question – that is, taken together, what does this literature mean for the scope, focus, design or conduct of the program (and the benefits or use the organisation may make of its results)? Thus the literature review may help to set the parameters for the program as well as establish what is known about the topic.

Program logic

Program logic is a method for clarifying how a health or care program is intended to work, and how its **effectiveness** might be evaluated. A logic model, theory of change, or logframe starts from a goal statement, and then specifies and links inputs (the resources required), processes (what happens in the program), outputs (services or activities delivered), impact (the immediate results) and outcomes (the longer-term results). Based on systems theory, the logic model specifies how a program is designed to produce certain outcomes, and makes visible the relationships between, for example, the available resources (inputs) and the potential reach of the program (outputs). The model has been modified for many different settings, including in health and community care. The general structure is illustrated in Figure 4.1.

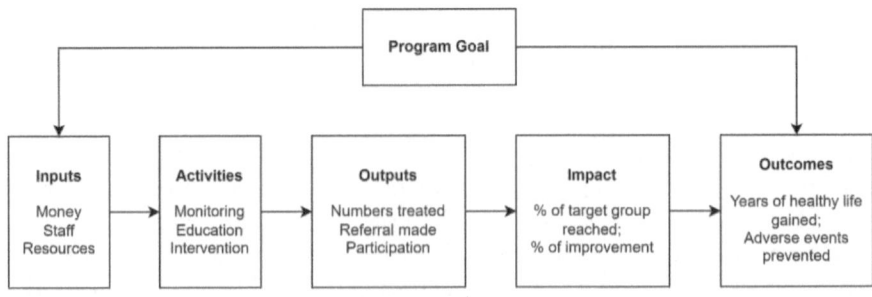

Figure 4.1 The logic model

A program logic model can be useful in the initiation phase of a project to assist with establishing the potential value of the program that the project will test. See the list of resources at the end of the chapter for more program logic resources.

In praise of opportunism

We have focused in this chapter on the need to test project ideas for feasibility and relevance to strategic directions and have advocated for both creative thinking and careful choices. However, there is also a place for opportunism, for several reasons. Sometimes an organisation needs to get runs on the board or build capacity and profile. Government responses to crises can also create opportunities. For example, during the pandemic, the imperative for governments to respond quickly provided significant opportunities for organisations to develop new projects and project management expertise. Organisations that can respond quickly to these opportunities, utilise the best evidence and develop feasible projects that align with government or corporate directions are well placed to both contribute to an effective national response and take advantage of the opportunity to remove impediments to modernising care.

Responding to grants and tenders

Potential external funding sources should be considered at the early stage of conceptualising project ideas. Seeking and securing funding is a significant task in itself. There are many potential sources of funding for projects in health and community service agencies, each with different criteria and requiring different approaches. Governments are important funders of projects, usually via a **tendering** or submission process. Potential project funds can also come from non-government sources such as trusts, foundations, charities and public donations.

When seeking external funds to support a project, the quality of the project proposal or funding application is critical. If resources allow, organisations sometimes contract consultants to assist with developing and writing funding applications.

A tender is an offer submitted by interested bidders (organisations that apply or 'bid' to win the contract) to the agency **commissioning** the project (sometimes called the 'purchaser'), usually in response to a 'request for tender' (RFT), also known as an 'expression of interest' (EOI) or 'call for tender' (CFT). Some governments use the competitive tendering process in order to obtain competitive pricing for the provision of services. So, there can be many opportunities for organisations to bid for and win contracts, often for ongoing service delivery, but also for projects. Government RFTs are sometimes advertised widely, both in the news media and on government websites, along with information about tendering policies and guidelines.

There are two distinct reasons for responding to a tender. First, it may offer an opportunity to obtain funding for a good idea that has been under consideration for a long time – or for a variation of it. The other scenario is a more opportunistic one: a tender appears for something that has not been previously considered or is perhaps not part of the agency's strategic directions but seems to bring other opportunities – and perhaps a bid is made.

The following questions and tips are designed to help with the process of deciding whether to respond to a tender:

- Consider who within the organisation will need to sign off on the application. Get their support as a first step.
- Consider who is commissioning this project and why. What are they looking for? Use networks and contacts to find out as much background as possible.
- If there is not an adequate match between the project and the funder's goals and scope, reconsider the value of applying.
- Consider whether the organisation has the necessary skills to carry out this project.
- Read the tender specifications and funding guidelines carefully, and always follow the instructions.
- Use relevant, up-to-date evidence to argue the importance of the project.
- Remember the application is to be read and assessed by the funder. Answer every question and respond honestly and in keeping with their expectations.
- Make sure the tender bid (or EOI) is realistic in terms of time and cost.

Government contracts can be very demanding about intellectual property (IP). Consider whether the project will generate new IP or use existing IP. If so, can the organisation's IP rights be protected?

Offering project tenders

For some organisations, projects usually mean engaging consultants, either through a tendering process or by directly engaging a particular company because of an existing working relationship or their successful track record. Deciding to tender out a project can be a tricky decision, given the challenges of preparing good specifications, and because of the tender process itself. Before putting out a project for tender, it may be useful to consider the following:

- Why is there a need to tender out this project? Is it because it is cheaper? Is there a lack of skilled staff? Or is it because the problem is best solved by an independent outsider with specific technical expertise?
- What kinds of people are needed to carry out this project? Can an external contractor feasibly achieve the required deliverables and outcomes?
- Does the organisation have the skills and resources to manage the tender process and contract?
- How long is it expected to take, and what will happen if it takes longer?
- How much should it cost?
- Are there any hidden costs to the organisation that have not been budgeted for?
- Is there an allowance for the costs of contract management, and of responding to the consultants' needs for information and access to staff?
- Are the required roles, responsibilities, accountability and monitoring methods clearly described?
- How will this project be evaluated?
- Have any IP issues been identified, and can they be resolved satisfactorily?

Essentially the tender process involves several steps, all necessary to ensure the best possible outcome and to fulfil the organisation's obligation to treat all bidders fairly. Key steps are:

- development of specifications for the project
- preparation of a request for tender (RFT) document
- call for expressions of interest and tenders
- establishment of a process for responding to queries from tenderers
- receipt and evaluation of tenderers' submissions
- notification of successful and unsuccessful bidders
- negotiation and signing of the contract.

Public sector organisations are usually required to advertise tenders for projects with costs over a specified dollar amount, and usually they are advertised on websites. The tender process must follow the principles of **probity** (the integrity of the tender process), which include fairness, impartiality, transparency, security, confidentiality and compliance with legislative obligations and government policy.

The discipline imposed by the tendering process can be helpful in forcing clear specification and adherence to the project plan. However, it can also cause problems when genuine contingencies arise and specifications or methods and timelines need to be changed.

Summary

- The initiation phase is when the ideas for a project are developed into a project brief suitable for consideration by decision makers in the organisation. There are five key steps in the initiation phase.

- Opportunities and ideas for projects originate from both within and outside the organisation, with many instigated by government policies or funding programs.

- Projects need clear goals, objectives and strategies. Attention to getting them right in the early stages will pay off when detailed plans are developed and implementation begins.

- Getting large complex projects to 'in-principle' approval may require the use of specialised methods to help ensure that the need for the project is established, that it is based on good evidence and that it represents good value for money.

- Projects are often made possible by funding bodies who offer grants or invite organisations to submit tenders. Applying for funding involves significant work, but success is more likely if submissions and tenders are closely matched to the funder's requirements and preferences.

- Organisations may decide to offer tenders for external consultants to conduct projects on their behalf. This is also a significant task in itself.

Readings and resources

On business case

Project business case template: www.projectmanagementdocs.com/templates/ business-case-template.html

On literature review and assessing quality of evidence

Cochrane Consumers and Communication. (2016). *How to GRADE the quality of the evidence.* https://cgf.cochrane.org/sites/cgf.cochrane.org/files/uploads/uploads/how_to_grade.pdf

Aveyard, H. (2010). *Doing literature review in health and social care: A practical guide.* Open University Press.

Fink, A. (201), *Conducting Research Literature Reviews: From the internet to paper.* (5 ed.) SAGE Publications.

Health Evidence at McMaster University: www.healthevidence.org

Health care safety and standards

Australian Commission on Safety and Quality in Health Care. (2017). *National safety and quality health service standards* (2 ed.). https://www.safetyandquality.gov.au/sites/default/files/migrated/National-Safety-and-Quality-Health-Service-Standards-second-edition.pdf

ACHS National Safety and Quality Health Service (NSQHS) standards: www.achs.org.au

Australian Commission on Safety and Quality in Health Care. (2017). *National safety and quality health service standards* (2 ed.). https://www.safetyandquality.gov.au/sites/default/files/migrated/National-Safety-and-Quality-Health-Service-Standards-second-edition.pdf

Institute of Project Management. (2013, March 05). *An implementation strategy for a project, The critical steps.* from https://projectmanagement.ie/blog/an-implementation-strategy-for-a-project-the-critical-steps/, accessed 5 December 2023.

On program logic

Australian Institute of Family Studies. (2016, November). *How to develop a program logic for planning and evaluation.* https://aifs.gov.au/resources/practice-guides/how-develop-program-logic-planning-and-evaluation

Australian Commission on Safety and Quality in Health Care (2017). *National safety and quality health service standards* (2 ed.). https://www.safetyandquality.gov.au/sites/default/files/migrated/National-Safety-and-Quality-Health-Service-Standards-second-edition.pdf

References

Australian Commission on Safety and Quality in Health Care. (2017). *National safety and quality health service standards* (2 ed.). www.safetyandquality.gov.au/sites/default/files/migrated/National-Safety-and-Quality-Health-Service-Standards-second-edition.pdf

Aveyard, H. (2010). *Doing literature review in health and social care: A practical guide.* Open University Press.

Bradshaw, J. R. (1972a). The concept of social needs. *New Society, 496,* 640–643.

Bradshaw, J. R. (1972b). The taxonomy of social need. In G. McLachlan (Ed.), *Problems and progress in medical care.* Oxford University.

Doran, G. T. (1981). There's a S.M.A.R.T. way to write management's goals and objectives. *Management Review, 70*(11), 35–36.

Eagar, K. (2001). *Health planning: Australian perspectives.* Routledge.

Hawe, P., Degeling, D., & Hall, J. (1990). *Evaluating health promotion: A health worker's guide.* MacLennan & Petty.

LeRouge, C. M., Tulu, B., & Wood, S. (2014). Project initiation for telemedicine services. *International Journal of Healthcare Information Systems and Informatics, 9*(2), 64–85. https://doi.org/10.4018/ijhisi.2014040104

Liang, Z., & Howard, P. (2011). Evidence-informed managerial decision-making: What evidence counts?: (Part two). *Asia Pacific Journal of Health Management, 6*(2), 12–21.

Liang, Z., Howard, P., & Rasa, J. (2011). Evidence-informed managerial decision-making: What evidence counts?: (Part one). *Asia Pacific Journal of Health Management, 6*(1), 23–29.

Royse, D., Staton-Tindall, M., Badger, K., & Webster, J. M. (2009). *Needs assessment.* Oxford University Press.

Royse, D., Thyer, B. A., Padgett, D. K., & Logan, T. K. (2006). *Program evaluation: An introduction* (4 ed.). Thomas Brooks/Cole.

Scott, B. K., Miller, G. T., Fonda, S. J., Yeaw, R. E., Gaudaen, J. C., Pavliscsak, H. H., Quinn, M. T., & Pamplin, J. C. (2020). Advanced digital health technologies for COVID-19 and future emergencies. *Telemedicine Journal and E-Health*, 26(10), 1226–1233. https://doi.org/10.1089/tmj.2020.0140

Simplilearn. (2023, October 19). *Feasibility study and its importance in project management*. Retrieved February 02, 2024 from www.simplilearn.com/feasibility-study-article

Singaram, M., & Jain, P. (2018, January 13). *What is the difference between proof of concept and prototype?* Retrieved February 02, 2024 from www.entrepreneur.com/en-in/technology/know-the-difference-between-proof-of-concept-and-prototype/307454

Smart, J. (2019, March 29). Needs assessment: Families and children expert panel practice resource. *Australian Institute of Family Studies*. https://apo.org.au/sites/default/files/resource-files/2019-03/apo-nid241741.pdf

CHAPTER 5

The planning phase

What will be done, and how?

DOI: 10.4324/9781003431701-6

Taking the time to properly plan a project can make the difference between project success and a troubled project that fails to deliver. In this chapter, we explain the need for planning and how it is done. Starting with the **project charter**, we then address project governance. Planning activities such as project scoping, defining **deliverables**, designing stakeholder engagement strategies, quality planning and other components of a comprehensive project plan, are explored in detail. Planning for evaluation is covered in Chapter 6.

Why plan at all?

> One who fails to plan is planning to fail.
>
> *(Attributed to Winston Churchill)*

Planning is the method by which the team works out how to make the project happen. A **project plan** addresses 'what, who, how, when and at what cost'. It makes a project team more effective in achieving its aims and more capable of acquiring and using the right resources and methods. Good planning means selecting achievable aims and **objectives**, designing feasible means, setting up a manageable work program, identifying risks and issues, making the best use of everyone's talents and establishing the basis for good decision-making.

Even though the use of project methods is now embedded in the practice of many organisations, and despite the obvious benefits of planning, there can be strong resistance to undertaking formal or detailed project planning. Often there is pressure to get a project done quickly, and it can be very tempting to get on with the actual work of the project as soon as possible, and either avoid planning or pay it lip service only.

There are many reasons for resistance to planning:

■ Planning can be difficult (it forces people to think – it requires negotiation, collaboration, consensus and decision-making); and some people lack the needed skills.

■ Taking the time to plan for a project that is on a tight schedule may be seen as wasting valuable time, especially because plans inevitably change during the course of a project.

- For most people, planning is not as satisfying as actually doing the work and starting to see progress.
- A project plan can be seen as too bureaucratic rather than as a working tool.

Failure to start with a clear plan almost guarantees that your project will not be successful, because there will not be sufficient definition of what you are going to do or how you are going to do it. Without an agreed project plan it is likely that there will be general confusion, a lack of common understanding and higher costs. Of course, the size and nature of the project will determine how elaborate the plan needs to be or can be. For example, process improvement projects often start from the basis that the right answer for how to improve the work is not known – plans then need to allow for decision points that will determine the rest of the project.

Executive and senior managers can be tempted to 'name the date' when the project will be delivered and then expect the project to be retrofitted to that timeline. Sometimes there are business drivers such as the opening of a building or commencement of a service. But often the date chosen is more arbitrary – for example, the end of the financial year or a media opportunity. Unrealistic timeframes that are not based on a good understanding of the scope, tasks and resources will jeopardise the project. Compromise, or finding the middle ground, can be the answer in these situations, where the **project manager** will need to understand the logic and assumptions of the decision makers, and may need to negotiate changes to aspects of the project (e.g. scope, resources or **procurement**) to meet the required timeline.

Sometimes circumstances mean that a project cannot 'start at the beginning' or that the rationale for the project has to be formulated after other decisions have already been made. Circumstances can also change during the life of the project, and this can mean that promises made by the project team cannot be kept, or important stakeholders might have another good idea that changes the project scope.

The value of planning can seem doubtful for **soft projects** (defined as complex undertakings aimed at intangible results). Most organisational change and service development projects have at least some of the characteristics of soft projects. However, experience in health and community services indicates that planning is especially valuable in conditions of uncertainty.

In reality, planning is often an iterative process and the project plan is a living document which may be extended, detailed and corrected regularly – what the PMI calls 'progressive elaboration' (Walenta, 2021). There can also be frequent movement between planning and implementation, particularly at the beginning of a project. For example, objectives might change when strategies are better developed in the early stages of implementation;

or detailed planning for testing, training and go-live for a new software platform may need to be done just before the activity commences. New possibilities might open up, or anticipated resources might shrink.

In spite of all these sources of uncertainty and variation, not having a plan is like negotiating the freeways of an unknown city without a map. You might be able to see the landmark you are headed for, but you are likely to end up somewhere completely different if you don't know the route. The key point is that hardly anything goes exactly according to plan, but having a plan helps you to deal with the challenges of real life, and real project work.

What's involved in planning?

Usually led by the project manager, project planning is a collaborative activity and how well it is conducted can set the tone for the life of the project. To get the best plan possible, it is important to reach out and engage with a range of stakeholders and experts in the organisation and in broader networks. Valuable input can be gathered from those who will be impacted by the project (including consumers), those who can assist in the planning and implementation effort, and perhaps vendors and third-party contractors. Skilful coordination of diverse stakeholder input is required. Project plans also rely on good use of information and data, and careful estimation of needed time and resources.

A good plan is comprehensive, enabling the team and the organisation to prepare for all aspects of the project. Even small projects may impact a wide range of stakeholders or require significant organisational change. Project plans are typically based on the **project brief** (see Chapter 4) which outlines rationale, goal, objectives, scope, strategies, timeline, budget and sometimes governance structure, and the plan is then developed in finer detail. It is also wise to plan for risks and issues, stakeholder engagement, quality, managing change (organisational and project), and communication. While not all the elements may be required for every project, additional components such as design, procurement, testing, training, and **contingency** plans may be required for some.

The time needed for developing a project plan can vary from days to weeks or months. It depends on factors like governance requirements or

Project management documents explained

Projects usually involve a lot of documentation, depending on the nature of the project, its size and complexity and the operating style of the organisation. To add to the potential confusion, there is limited consistency in what important project documents are called. However, there is a wealth of online templates and resources that can help, along with internal sources, and some templates in this book. Table 5.1 is a guide to the main documents.

Table 5.1 Project management documents

Name(s)	Purpose	Phase/chapter
Project Brief Concept Brief Project Proposal Project on a Page	To define a project idea, outlining goal, objectives, strategies, scope, budget and timing in a few pages. To seek in principle or final approval to start planning and preparatory work.	Initiation Ch 4
Project Charter Project Initiation Document (PID)	The authorising document for the project. A more detailed version of the project brief, developed during the approval process. Project governance is outlined, and updates added.	Planning Ch 5
Project Plan Project Management Plan	The guidebook for the team and stakeholders on the who, what, when, how and at what cost. Detailed strategies, work program, scope and boundaries, stakeholder engagement, communication, planning assumptions, approved budget and schedule. Includes Gantt charts etc.	Planning Ch 5
Budget	Detailed plan for how the available funding will be spent. Related documents include the business case.	Planning Ch 7
Quality Plan **Procurement Plan** Communication Plan etc.	Major elements of the plan, such as the quality requirements, may be documented in detail in stand-alone documents that are effectively attachments to the project plan. Others include evaluation plan (Ch 6), stakeholder engagement plan (Ch 5).	Planning Ch 5
Risk Register Risk Log	A risk management plan, supported with a risk log to track events and actions when risks eventuate.	Planning and Implementation Chs 5 and 8
Issues Register Issues Log	A chart of all 'issues' that arise during the project and can affect its proceeding as planned and action taken.	Planning and Implementation Chs 5 and 8
Change Request Register Change Log	A chart of all requests to add or amend aspects of the project and action taken.	Planning and Implementation Chs 5 and 8

Source: Adapted from Good (2023); Hoban (2023); Landau (2021); Mind Tools Content Team (2024).

standards, project complexity, and who will perform the work (less detail is required for fully outsourced work, more detail is required for in-house teams; Bondale, 2021).

There are no magic solutions for overcoming the difficulties of project planning and estimation. But some things can help:

- seeking advice from colleagues with relevant expertise
- consulting management and stakeholders early to ensure support and shared understandings of limitations and constraints
- identifying the most effective planning methods and approaches, with only the level of detail that is useful for each project
- reviewing the project plans of successful projects from within the organisation or elsewhere, and learning from the experience of other projects – many evaluation reports and case studies are available both online and inside organisations
- undertaking targeted training where needed
- seeking data that will assist in planning decisions especially from health information, decision support, quality and safety or business intelligence functions in the organisation
- contracting professional project planners or consultants to provide support and advice.

The project charter

The project charter (also known as the 'project definition' or **project initiation document** (PID) is based on the project brief. While the project brief is the document that decision makers approve, it is then updated with any necessary changes (e.g. modifications agreed with decision makers or clearer timelines) and becomes the project charter. The charter will also usually outline the approved governance arrangements and provides the mandate for the project. When projects or a subset of tasks are undertaken by external consultants, the project charter will also be a key part of the contract.

Getting the charter right is the vital first step after the project is approved, and this is where critical thinking is concentrated and the project design is fundamentally set. The project charter can be published to all who are associated with the project and then used as the basis for establishing the project and demonstrating management support for both the project and the project manager (Verzuh, 2020) as well as for preparing the full plan.

Project governance

Project governance is important to every project from the simplest to the most complex.

(Clayton, 2022)

Effective project governance is based on a structured system of rules and processes (Marker, 2021). Like corporate governance, project governance is about accountability, oversight and effective decision-making for the life of the project and enables alignment of direction and effort between the project team, executives and the rest of the organisation.

> *I can get things done quicker if, at the start of the project, we talk about governance, and everyone understands how decisions will be made.*
> *(Senior Manager, Hospital)*

While the right governance approach needs to be found for each project some of the key considerations are where the project needs to sit in the organisation, the weight of the decisions that it will make, the necessary reporting lines and the question of who carries ultimate responsibility for the outcomes of the project. The foundation roles to establish project governance include the **project sponsor**, the project steering committee (also known as the project board or project control group), the project manager and project stakeholders (Marker, 2021).

The steering committee

Steering committees, advisory committees and reference groups can help to make or break projects. The term 'steering committee' (also known as 'project board' in **PRINCE2** or sometimes called a 'project control group') implies some level of control and ownership over the project, indicating that the committee's decisions will steer the project in the direction the committee wishes it to go. Reference groups and advisory committees usually play a less hands-on role, providing advice and support, and helping the project to work well.

In the PRINCE2 approach, an empowered steering committee is chaired by the project sponsor (or executive in charge of the project). The committee takes responsibility for signing off the various stages of the project and its final outcome. It makes decisions that are needed at this level all along the way, and acts as a sounding board for the project manager and team.

The committee is made up of senior representatives of the major stakeholder groups – PRINCE2 describes the groups as those who will use or work with the results of the project (the 'users'), and those who are required to deliver services or capacity to support the project outcomes (the 'suppliers'). A deliberate role distinction is made: the suppliers are asked to monitor costs and feasibility, while the users are asked to focus on functionality and quality. One of our research participants highlighted this important distinction:

> *There is an opportunity to have the blend between skilled project methodologies and business interaction. . . . You know, the technical people should be able to ask the business 'If this doesn't work, what's*

the impact?', and the business should be able to say 'What are you doing that for? Is that really required?'

(Senior Manager, Health Network)

For large, complex projects consideration should be given to ensuring steering committees have adequate executive or even board oversight.

The duties of the steering committee or project board are to:

- be accountable for the project
- provide unified direction
- delegate effectively
- facilitate cross-functional integration
- commit resources
- ensure effective decision-making
- support the project manager
- ensure effective communication.

We suggest that the responsibilities of the committee are best outlined in the project charter, then refined and finalised in the early stages of implementation. Other groups that may be required depending upon the project, may be a board-level governance group, a project-specific **project management office** (PMO) and reference, working or advisory groups. It is desirable to limit the number of members on committees to about six or seven, a number that seems to balance the need for multiple perspectives with the need for each member to feel responsible for the committee's decisions. If the project is one in which it is impossible for all stakeholders to be represented by a manageable number of members, then the project may need a larger advisory group. This is not a project board, but more a forum for discussion and advice, and it is consulted on major issues (Clayton, 2022).

The role of the project sponsor

The sponsor or champion is somebody senior in the organisation who authorises the project (or receives authorisation from the CEO) and usually fulfils most or all of the following functions:

- providing leadership and a single point of accountability for the project as the project owner
- keeping the project aligned with the organisation's strategic objectives and the project business case
- chairing the project steering committee or working group
- acting as the supervisor of the project manager
- ensuring that the project team has good access to people and resources across the organisation, as needed

- keeping the executive informed of progress, and ensuring their continued support
- signing off (sometimes on behalf of the committee) on major decisions or variations as part of the project and receiving the final report.

To be effective, the role requires power (authority), a vested stakeholder interest, a vision and the ability to secure resources and to understand the human impact of the project (LeRouge et al., 2014). Our research participants report that project sponsorship is a growing part of management and executive roles, with an increasing amount of sponsor's time spent engaging with projects and project governance. The project manager typically leans heavily on the project sponsor when it comes to clarifying the decision-making framework and for escalation points above their control (Waldow, 2020).

If the project is contracted out, the equivalent role is generally played by the person who acts as 'the client' for the organisation and may be the person who signs the contract, and the functions are similar.

The project manager's role

It may seem obvious, but effective oversight of a project is not the sole domain of the project manager, but a shared responsibility with the sponsor, steering committee and other groups in the project governance structure. The distinction between project management and project governance is important, as many impediments to the project may be outside the remit of the project manager. In essence, the project manager's focus is on 'the application of knowledge, skills, tools, and techniques to project activities to meet the project requirements' (Marker, 2021). Project governance focuses on the mandate given by project charter, and ensuring the project stays on track by providing guidance, oversight and decision-making. The other key role of the project manager is to keep the sponsor and steering committee informed of the project status, **escalate** relevant issues, and provide information and options to enable them to make effective and informed decisions.

Project structures: functional and matrix

Planning for the location of the project within the organisational structure and specifying its reporting lines and access to decision makers can prevent (or minimise) unhelpful project politics later on. The project manager's role will likewise be made easier if their place in the structure and the decision-making systems is clear and appropriate to the task. The question of structure is more straightforward for external projects, where the team sits entirely (or mostly) outside the organisation. For internal projects, there are several structural options in common use, and no one right model.

Functional structures (where the project is 'owned' by the unit or department most involved, the usual employer of most of the project team) have several advantages. They tend to have maximum flexibility in the use of their staff; individual experts can be utilised for many different projects; and specialists can be grouped to share knowledge and experience.

However, a number of problems can also arise in this kind of structure. The project may suffer from a lack of focus and attention when it is competing with ongoing tasks, and the management of the unit may not be well placed to cope with project characteristics such as shorter timelines. The project may require the unit to work with other parts of the organisation or another service provider in a way that is at odds with its ongoing relationships.

When projects within a functional unit come unstuck, the typical outcome is that they slip down the priority list and are delayed, downgraded or allowed to fade away. The best predictors of success in this structure are that:

- The project is championed by the unit manager.
- The manager and team have authority to make decisions about the project.
- The project deals with an issue that matters to the staff in their daily work.

The main alternative structure is the matrix model, where project staff are drawn from functional units, thus cutting across the organisation structure for the life of the project. This structure may be best suited for organisation-wide projects and those that extend across organisation structures.

In the matrix model, the project manager reports to an executive or senior manager in the role of project sponsor, and the team members report to the project manager, at least for the purposes of the project. The advantages of a matrix structure are that projects and project teams can have a strong identity within the organisation, and resources can be allocated accordingly. The downsides can include conflicts between line managers and project staff, conflict for staff who work part-time on the project between their ongoing and project roles, and unclear roles and responsibilities.

The project plan

The project plan is the blueprint for the entire project and the guide for all project activities. With the project charter as the starting point, the remaining planning effort is directed at working out and documenting all the major resources and activities required to give life to the project. Some organisations have templates, software and defined processes for the development of the project plan and may stipulate what should be included in the document. Otherwise, there are a multitude of project plan templates available online that can be customised. Project management software can also be used to assist in the creation of elements of the plan including online Gantt charting, **milestones,** task dependencies and resource planning. The plan may be a single document or a series of formal documents that define what will happen in the implementation **phase** (see Chapter 8). Completed project plans can vary from about five pages to about 50 (or even more for large and complex projects).

The more carefully the plan is thought through, the more likely it is that the project will stay on track and the fewer surprises (or crises) there will be in the implementation and closing phases. Energy spent in developing the plan to a sufficient level of detail will result in greater understanding by all of what is expected of them as part of the project. In this way, much potential conflict can be avoided, or at least be identified and made more manageable.

For large complex projects, guiding documents that form part of the plan could include arrangements for **project assurance** and quality management, important assumptions, constraints and dependencies, organisational change management, testing, procurement and training, contract management, project logistics, transition to operations post-project, and approach to evaluation (see Chapter 6). Assumptions, constraints and dependencies are conditions that may need to be met before the project commences, or that may affect how and when it will progress. For example, it may be assumed that a government policy will be introduced by a certain date, or a project 'go-live' date may be dependent on a building redevelopment being on time.

If the project is a small one, some of these plan elements might not be needed, or need only a paragraph or two, but even small projects benefit from attention to each component.

In the next sections we work through the major components of the plan.

Strategies and work program: how the objectives will be achieved

The simplest way to think about the strategies for a project is to consider each objective and ask: How will it be achieved? What needs to be done? The strategies developed in the initiation phase and documented in the project brief or charter are the starting point.

The project plan should describe the strategies in enough detail for the project team, stakeholders and decision makers to understand how the project will achieve its goals and objectives, and if there were options, the rationale for the chosen strategy.

Goals, objectives and strategies: what's the difference?

Goals and objectives are just different levels in a helpful hierarchy for breaking down what needs to be achieved by the project. Strategies are statements of how objectives will be achieved, the method or approach that will be taken. If the goal is to establish a COVID testing clinic, an early objective might be to acquire a suitable site; and an important first strategy might be to engage a property manager to identify and evaluate site options within the desired area.

Whether you define something as an objective or a strategy depends partly on what your responsibilities are (or where you sit in the project). If you're the project manager, engaging a property manager is a strategy to achieve the objective of acquiring a suitable site. But if you're the property manager, preparing a list of suitable sites with costings might be your main objective. This is not confusing in practice because the plan is written from the point of view of the organisation.

Small projects may not always need all three levels of goals, objectives and strategies, but if so, it is the objectives that can occasionally be skipped, never the goals or strategies.

These are some questions that may be useful when identifying the need for particular strategies:

- If this is effectively an initial development and trial, how can the trial provide the best basis for broader implementation if it proves its value through the project?
- Is there a need for the approach to be piloted, the methods proven or the feasibility assessed?
- What technologies will be developed or deployed and what methods will be used?
- Will the project be staged and rolled out over time, or have a single implementation phase?
- For a staged implementation, which groups/areas would start first and what is the remaining order?
- Are there important standards, policies or guidelines that need to be taken into account in deciding on strategies?
- What approach will be used to engage stakeholders?
- What training and change management methods will be used?

Once strategies are fully developed in the plan, they provide the basis for the preparation of a work program, which may be captured in a Gantt chart for small projects and is often documented in a **work breakdown structure (WBS)**. A WBS focuses on the activities and tasks by which the strategies are implemented and sets out their sequencing and timing (see Chapter 7 for details and a worked example).

Defining and documenting project scope

The project scope is a statement of what is included in the goals and objectives of the project and potentially what is excluded. In other words, it is the limit or boundary of what the project will cover. For example, the scope for a project that will deliver training packages needs to define the number of packages, the curriculum for each, the delivery modes (e.g. online, face-to-face), the delivery platform, any assessment tool and the staff groups that the training will be delivered to. The **scope statement** should also state any **exclusions** such as training in software or staff groups who will not be included (and why). Defining project scope is fundamental to the planning process as it is the basis on which the resources for the project can be estimated, the team gathered and the project plan, budget and schedule determined.

Both failure to define the scope and '**scope creep**' (unmanaged changes to scope – usually expansion) can be major factors in projects failing to meet timelines and budgets. Many of the reasons for such failures are found in the way the project was designed and how the boundaries around it were drawn.

Clarifying scope by having a scope statement is the best way to safeguard the project from these risks. A scope statement should describe the major activities of the project and their limits in such a way that it will be absolutely clear if extra work is added later on (Verzuh, 2020). Often this is achieved by specifying what the project will *not* do (project exclusions), as these examples show:

- 'The system will be implemented in all Aurora Health campuses and locations but excludes the co-located services at Rolling Valley Community Health and Eastern Dialysis services.'
- 'Training will be developed and delivered to all ICU staff but will not include ongoing eLearning modules being delivered as part of the continuing professional development program.'
- 'The project scope includes the piloting and evaluation of the new medication protocol, but not its implementation.'

The scope statement can also define where the project sits in relation to a larger or related project.

Project scope management is the term for the process of controlling and tracking scope during the project and it may be beneficial for some projects to develop a scope management plan. The management plan would be based on the scope statement and would also detail the rules and change control procedures that will be used when changing the project scope is considered.

Defining deliverables

Project deliverables are the tangible outputs, services or results that the project must produce to achieve the project objectives. They are specific, measurable and time-bound, giving clear progress and completion indicators (Ostrowercha, 2023). Depending on the project they might include documentation, designs, hardware, **commissioning** of a new building, perhaps a piece of software, a process improvement, a new job design, a training package or any other product commissioned as part of the project. It is important that deliverables are documented, specified and measurable to enable the project team to produce them according to the quality plan, and to ensure that there are agreed acceptance criteria for handover to the deliverable owner.

Consulting and vendor contracts often include a detailed statement of the project's products or outputs that will be handed over to the client at the end of the contract. This concept can also be useful for internal projects, by forcing a clear delineation of the product or output in more concrete terms than the goals or objectives. A statement of concrete deliverables assists every team member to know what is expected of them and what they must deliver. It also helps stakeholders to understand what they can expect from the project.

Identifying and engaging stakeholders

> Stakeholders are essentially anyone who can be impacted by the project deliverables.
>
> *(Alie, 2015)*

Stakeholders are the individuals and organisations who are actively involved in the project, or whose interests may be affected as a result of the project, or who may exert influence over the project and its results (PMI, 2021). In order to successfully complete a project, a clear understanding of who the stakeholders are, what their expectations are and what motivates them is essential, and should be developed in the planning phase (Landau, 2023).

The project team needs to confirm and possibly expand the list of stakeholders identified in the project charter, plan for their engagement and identify their priorities, interests, expectations and allegiances, all of which can affect the project. This process is called **stakeholder analysis**.

While stakeholder identification is not always easy, most projects will have stakeholders who fall into the following categories:

- *senior leadership*: those who approve the finances and whose support for the project is essential
- *consumers, clients or users*: the people, groups or organisations that will use or consume the project's product or outcomes
- *partners and allies*: the organisations and individuals whose contributions or support is needed such as suppliers
- *performing organisation, division or department*: the organisation or department whose employees are most directly involved in doing the work.

Sometimes the project personnel themselves are also considered as stakeholders.

Once stakeholders have been identified, it is useful to consider the impact that a particular stakeholder group may have on the project, and how they will be managed. Stakeholders may have the power to veto or approve, delay, facilitate, derail or guide a project. Stakeholder analysis and engagement planning can be broken down into the steps outlined in Table 5.2. Only some steps may be applicable to a project depending on its size and complexity.

Stakeholder management in internal projects has its own challenges – for example, there is often no defined 'client' to accept or reject outcomes. Individuals may have roles in both supplying inputs to the project and using its outputs, and the interests of stakeholders are sometimes seen as a kind of zero-sum game – that is, one person's win is another's loss. In these circumstances, stakeholder paralysis is a real threat to projects that seek to change the way business is done.

A simple map of the stakeholders is a useful planning tool that can help with planning for active management of stakeholders' issues in the implementation phase, as represented in Table 5.3.

To complete the mapping exercise, stakeholders are identified and categorised as to whether they are supportive of or opposed to the project, and rated for their relative importance – that is, the amount of power or influence they can exert on the project. Strategies for managing the way individual stakeholders engage with the project can then be developed, with the aim of minimising opposition and maximising support.

Involving consumers

Consumers can be patients, clients, family members or carers and they need to be considered as a stakeholder group. Consumers can provide valuable information about how services should be designed and delivered to best meet the needs of people using those services. This can be important in the development of a new service, planning for a new hospital, the writing of information resources, the design and implementation of patient satisfaction surveys, the design of medicine packaging or the selection of staff (Health Consumers NSW, 2024).

Including consumer perspectives and learning from their experience is increasingly recognised as adding immense value to both organisations and projects as it can ensure measurable benefits and better health services. These are some of the circumstances in which consumer engagement is highly likely to be of benefit:

- The project will have a direct impact on care or services for patients/clients.
- The rights of consumers (e.g. to privacy, or self-determination) will be affected by the project.
- There are issues of equity of access and appropriateness of service for population groups with special needs (e.g. people with disabilities or

Table 5.2 Stakeholder analysis and engagement planning

Analysis or planning step	Description
1. Identify stakeholders	Develop a list of potential stakeholders using the project charter and other documents. Brainstorming, mind mapping or stakeholder mapping techniques can be used to generate and organise ideas. A simple example of a stakeholder mapping matrix is given in Table 5.3 below.
2. Analyse stakeholders	Determine stakeholders' potential level of influence, interest and impact. Existing project documents and active discussion will be useful for gathering information on stakeholders' needs, priorities and concerns. Use analytical tools to sort and prioritise stakeholders.
3. Plan stakeholder engagement	Define strategies to engage and communicate with stakeholders throughout the project. Methods such as workshops, meetings or feedback sessions can be planned and later used to involve stakeholders in decision-making and problem-solving. The plan should include specific levels of engagement and what is expected of each stakeholder (their roles and responsibilities) and the frequency and modes of communication.
4. Plan stakeholder management and monitoring	Make a plan for structuring and managing stakeholder engagement. Consider the methods for communicating progress and achievements of the project, as well as issues and changes; and how stakeholder feedback and concerns will be monitored and responded to.
5. Create a stakeholder register	A stakeholder register brings together information about stakeholder needs and is developed in the planning phase. The stakeholder register will be a helpful reference for managing stakeholder relationships throughout the project.

Source: Adapted from Project Documentation (n.d.).

Table 5.3 Stakeholder mapping

Likely response to project	Not important	Very important
Hinder	Problematic – need to be monitored	Antagonistic – need active strategies for management
Support	Low priority – keep on side	Champions – work ith them

mental illness, First Nations people, the homeless or those with cultur-ally diverse backgrounds).

■ There are established advocacy or interest groups who can offer exper-tise and who might affect (positively or negatively) the success of the project.

The next question is to determine how consumers can be involved. While rep-resentation (for example, on steering or advisory committees) is one method, it isn't necessarily the best way. Focus groups, surveys and consultative groups (focused on the consumer perspectives, experience and priorities) can make better use of consumers' limited time and energy. **Co-design** is a powerful method that is increasingly used in health and community care projects.

Project story: Co-designing with consumers

Co-design is a relatively new approach that our research indicates has rising importance. The concept is collaboration among equals, and it is used when agencies design services or products in partnership, and when community or consumer representatives work with agencies in planning and design. As one of the senior managers we interviewed noted:

> The co-design approach is very powerful to get that buy in and to ensure sustainability because when they have been involved in the design, whether . . . the outcome is good or bad, it's their outcome, rather than something someone is throwing at them.
>
> (Senior Manager, Health service)

One example comes from a large area health service in a capital city that had developed an innovative and effective approach to working with consumers at all levels of the organisation, in clinical units, community services, hospi-tal wards, management processes, board committees and of course in pro-jects. In a major hospital building project, a co-design process provided many opportunities for consumers to lead the decision-making. For example, selection of public furniture for the new building was led by a diverse group of consumers and community members with a focus on meeting their varying needs.

When the time came to specify the detailed design of patient rooms, the organisation was well placed to bring together a group of local community members and consumer representatives to test the planned layouts and furnishing. The group were well briefed, and then taken through prototype room models to test all the elements in the room and the interior design such as bed location, furniture, grabrails etc. In discussion they quickly identified several room features that wouldn't be suitable for some patients, and they proposed practical alternative arrangements.

While some of these alternatives resulted in changing specifications and some higher capital costs, this process ensured the finished space would be of a high quality to meet consumer needs and avoid the need for modifications after construction – a much more costly outcome. The recommended changes were incorporated, and it was described as a win-win by both staff and the community and consumer representatives.

Co-design is not always this smooth and it is easier in the context of effective ongoing consumer engagement. But when it works, it is powerful. Co-design requires effective foundations of consumer engagement, where relationships are prioritised and trust is built between members. This person-centred approach provides a safe environment where all members can listen without judgement, share experiences and ideas, and solve complex problems. It requires time, resources and support to build capability in all the co-design participants (including staff) to create effective outcomes. There is no single approach, and the co-design process needs to suit the consumer and the service.

Via co-design, solutions to jointly identified problems are grounded not only in actual problems considered in their context, but also deep understanding of the challenges that the end users face and the environment in which these challenges are embedded (Bird et al., 2021).

Many co-design toolkits are accessible on websites of both government and non-government agencies (see list at the end of this chapter).

Finding and integrating the consumer voice can be challenging. Groups often left out of consultation can be the most marginalised, vulnerable and hard to reach (Health Issues Centre n.d.). When the type of consumer input required has been identified, any existing consumer forums and channels within the organisation, such as a consumer advisory committee or a consumer liaison representative or team, can assist in matching the project with the right consumers. Another avenue might be to contact national or local health consumer advocacy groups. (Some Australian consumer organisations are listed at the end of the chapter).

Planning for human resource needs

> Projects can't succeed without people power.
>
> *(AIPM, 2022)*

Working out the human resource requirements and how to build the project team are critical tasks for many projects, and the process can often be started as soon as the project charter is released and while planning is underway. This can also be a good time to arrange for induction and training for new team members.

Often developing the detailed project plan is the first task of the newly appointed project manager, who may find that some of the key questions below have already been answered:

- What kind of skills and experience are needed to achieve this project?
- Are these skills available within the organisation or will they need to be sourced from outside?
- Which of those skills are needed by the manager and the team?
- What other people with particular skills are needed, how much of their time and how many of them?
- How will technical or specialist expertise not available among team members be brought in?
- What are the human resource policies and processes that will govern project team recruitment, and will any exceptions to normal processes need to be made?
- Who will the project manager report to?
- How much authority over team members will the manager have?

This is the time when organisations that have embedded project management practice, conducted succession planning and nurtured project capability and skills within the organisation (or have an established project management office) will see the benefits of their investment.

The organisational human resource (HR) function is a valuable support if the project team is large and team members are required to be drawn from across the organisation. The project may need a dedicated HR representative, an advisor on the team or a team member whose role encompasses HR liaison.

It may be best to commence recruitment for project team roles (and the project manager if not already identified) with an internal expression of interest. Our participants advise of many benefits of internal recruitment including providing a pathway forward for existing or previous (project) staff, making onboarding easier, rewarding good performance, showing that the organisation values current staff and enabling project work to become part of a professional or staff development plan.

Managers of staff who have expressed interest or applied for project positions will need to be consulted. It is important to ensure that adequate lead time is given for staff to move into the project and for backfill to be arranged. Backfilling some positions can be difficult, particularly for clinical, specialist or technical roles. For some, releasing the staff member part time onto the project may be an option.

Expectations about how long a member of staff may be seconded to the project need to be clarified, along with a process for extension of the secondment if the project is delayed. Consideration may need to be given to the future placement of project team members after the project is completed.

On the other hand, contracting for project management and team members may be a necessary or desirable strategy. Because of the uniqueness of each project, it is rare for an organisation to have all the necessary skills in-house for a major project. So, consultants and temporary specialist staff are often engaged either to work directly on a project or to backfill operational positions. The nature of the relationship between contracted staff and the project manager and/or sponsor needs to be well planned and communicated.

Consultants can add real value to a project by bringing high-order skills, up-to-date knowledge, the independence or objectivity of an outsider and a greater freedom to deliver uncomfortable messages or challenge the prevailing culture. On the negative side, working with consultants and contractors can be a knowledge drain for the organisation and may also require additional resources to manage the contract. However, contracts can include a requirement for the consultants to transfer knowledge and skills, and to hand over all the 'intelligence' gathered as part of the project (in the form of briefings and presentations as well as reports and other project records). This can help the organisation get value for money from the consultancy and will reduce the likelihood of future dependency on a particular consultant or firm.

Risk management

Risks are an inherent part of every project.

(Scavetta, 2021)

All projects encounter uncertainty, and there is always the risk that something will happen to jeopardise the budget, the quality, the timelines, the stakeholder support and, ultimately, the achievement of the project's aims and its sustainability.

Risk management is the means by which uncertainty is systematically managed to increase the likelihood of meeting project objectives (Verzuh, 2020). Risk management is essentially designed to answer three questions: What might go wrong? How will it be handled? What can we do to prevent it, or reduce its likelihood or consequences? The related task of managing problems, opportunities and errors that arise during the project is generally known as 'issue management' (see next section).

A risk management plan identifies and assesses potential risks to a project and outlines how risks are analysed and mitigated (Eby, 2023). The plan can borrow from the organisation's overall risk management approach, templates and tools, and should cover the what, how, when and who of managing project risk.

Contents of a risk management plan

- *methods*: the tools and approaches that are used to perform risk management activities including risk assessment, risk analysis and risk mitigation strategies
- *risk register*: a chart documenting all the risks identified for the project giving details such as date, description, category, severity, impact, probability, timing, trigger, mitigation, response plan, risk owner and notes
- *risk breakdown structure (RBS)*: like a WBS, an RBS is a hierarchical chart that identifies project risk categories and subcategories (e.g. technical, external, organisational or project management), then ranks each of the risks within the category (McAbee, 2022)
- *risk assessment matrix*: allows the team to analyse the severity, likelihood (probability) and impact of project risks so they can be prioritised
- *risk response plan*: explains the mitigation strategies that will be used to manage the response when risk events actually happen
- *roles and responsibilities*: the team members with responsibilities as risk owners (to monitor risks and coordinate responses) are specified
- *risk reporting*: details how the team will document and report risks during the project including how the risk register will be updated and how risk management will be periodically reported to governance groups and the executive.

Source: Scavetta (2021)

The first step is to analyse the project to identify the sources of risk. This is perhaps best achieved with consultation or a meeting with stakeholders to ask the critical questions, followed by analysis. What can happen to cause problems for this project? Will the new equipment be delivered on time? Will industrial activity impact on the timeline? Will the software pass testing? Are there enough skilled resources to complete a task? Will there be a change of government policy or corporate leadership?

After defining the possible risks, including their potential impact on the project (i.e. what is the result if the risk turns into reality?), each risk can be assigned a probability rating. Then a strategy (also called a contingency or treatment) can be developed to respond to the risks and reduce possible damage to the project and the organisation. The resulting plan then provides the basis for the project risk register during implementation. Table 5.4 illustrates one component of a risk management plan for a simple project of conducting a community survey.

Project risks are classified according to the likelihood of their occurring and the seriousness of the consequences or impact if they do. The likelihood may range from rare (e.g. the chances of an earthquake) to almost certain (e.g. the chances of short outages in computing or communication systems), whereas the consequences may range from insignificant to catastrophic (e.g. complete failure of the project or injury to patients). The risk level is assigned by plotting these two attributes of risk in the **risk matrix** (see Figure 5.1).

Once risks are understood, it is possible to identify contingencies – the 'what if' issues – and plan the response. Capital building and engineering projects usually include a contingency allowance – that is, money set aside for unforeseen circumstances, traditionally about 10 to 15 per cent of the total cost. Projects in health and community services are often budgeted with no capacity for a contingency allowance. But even if adding an actual contingency allowance is not possible, there is usually a way to slip in some flexibility or some discretionary resources. If something goes wrong, resources allocated to another component of the project could perhaps be shifted without impacting on the core objectives; or some potential slack in the project timelines could be taken up; or the scope could be squeezed by cutting back on less important elements. As part of contingency planning, it is important to plan for an escalation procedure. To 'escalate' means taking the issue higher in the organisation in order for it to be resolved or implementing the next level of action required to overcome an identified risk.

There are some types of project risks that are almost inevitable, no matter the industry or type of project.

Common project risks

■ *Technological risk*: There are high risks in projects involving technology and software development due to increased complexity of deliverables and considerations such as data security, compliance, information security, infrastructure and system integration. These projects can be challenging as they will often require changing workflows and work practices as well as training for staff and they have increased risk of impacting patient care.

■ *Communication risk*: Even with a comprehensive communication plan, maintaining effective communication of the right information to the right people at the right time can be challenging. Not keeping the team and stakeholders informed or not communicating changes, updates and decisions can impact project delivery.

- *Scope creep risk*: Changes to scope are likely to increase costs by creating the need for additional functions, expansion of eligibility for clients, or just extra features in the services or products the project will deliver. Sometimes scope creep has to be accepted, when added or changed elements are necessary or highly desirable for the project's success. It is important to have a method for identifying potential changes and making decisions about accepting or rejecting them.
- *Cost risk*: Project funds may turn out to be inadequate or misallocated between priorities if budgeting is inaccurate, costs increase more than anticipated or there is no allowance for contingencies.
- *Health and safety or quality risk*: Where project deliverables may impact adversely on patient care, staff or stakeholder health and safety.
- *Skills resource risk*: The risk of inability to recruit or acquire skilled staff to the project, as well as the potential for shortages in the organisation's workforce.
- *External hazards risk*: Some risks are outside the control of the project or the organisation, such as epidemics, extreme weather events, earthquakes and vandalism. These risks should be identified and contingency plans for the project should be made. The organisation's risk management plan can be a good place to start.

Source: Adapted from Indeed Editorial Team (2023)

Tips for effective risk management planning

- When identifying and assessing project risks as well as generating ideas for mitigation, it is important to involve governance groups, the project team and key stakeholders in the process and to ensure that those involved have a clear understanding of the project and its objectives.
- To decide which risk management tools and models will be used, gather risk management plans from the organisation and previous or similar projects as these will provide a guide to the risk assessment, categorisation, and severity criteria or models that are preferred. It is helpful to use formats that are familiar to governance and management groups.
- Use available project management software, templates or documents to avoid the need to develop the plan from scratch.
- Our experts advise that bringing together the risk, issue, assumption, decision and constraint logs within the risk management document or register (on separate tabs) may make cross referencing, monitoring and managing these factors more effective across the project (logs are explained later).
- Risks recorded in the risk register should be reviewed periodically during status review meetings (Sankararajan & Shrivastava, 2012).

Table 5.4 Risk management for community survey project

Element	Description	Example
Risk	Description of the risk	Not enough community members are willing to complete the questionnaire
Risk impact	What is the impact of the risk if it is realised?	Reliability of survey results is reduced
Likelihood	How likely is the risk to be realised (see risk matrix)?	Likely
Consequence	What is the severity of the consequence if the risk is realised (see risk matrix)?	Moderate
Level of risk	What is the level of realised risk considering likelihood and consequence (see risk matrix)	Moderate
Contingencies	What strategies can be used to respond to the risk and reduce the impact?	Extend the survey timeline. Use other means, e.g. focus groups or interviews.
Mitigation	How can the risk be minimised?	Promote participation through influential community leaders and staff
Risk owner	Person who has responsibility for managing the risk and contingencies	Project manager
Date logged	When was the risk identified?	22 April
Date of review	When was the risk last reviewed?	15 October

Consequence → Likelihood ↓	Insignificant	Minor	Moderate	Major	Catastrophic
Almost certain					
Likely					
Moderate					
Unlikely					
Rare					

Level of Risk			
Low	Moderate	High	Extreme

Figure 5.1 Risk matrix

Source: Adapted from PRINCE2 (Axelos, 2017, p. 130).

Issue management

Issues are any problems, situations, opportunities, questions and errors that come up in the course of the project and could impact the plan. The key difference between an issue and a risk is that an issue has already occurred and a risk is a potential issue that may or may not happen (Sankararajan & Shrivastava, 2012). Examples of issues include delay in the supply of a project resource, a policy conflict exposed by the project, technical failures, a key stakeholder either leaving or joining the project, procurement delays, or an unresolved disagreement within the project team.

Issues might be completely unforeseen in the project planning or may have been documented as risks that are then realised. They can be categorised as a major problem, opportunity, concern or situation. It is important to plan a method of responding quickly and effectively to any issues that arise (Bridges, 2022).

An issues plan can be developed using software or one of the many templates available online, but will usually have the following steps:

- *Create an issues log*: to capture all issues that arise, with a clear process for raising, escalating, responding and tracking progress in resolving them (who, what and how). Ideally this is an online collaborative document that is easily updated, can notify others and can support issue reporting.
- *Log issues*: enable nominated team members to log issues promptly, no matter how small. To promote rapid identification and logging, provide information to the team as to who can raise issues and how they can be raised, escalated and resolved.
- *Assign actions and develop an action plan if necessary*: ensure that one person is assigned responsibility for following each issue through to closing. If the issue is a realised risk, the risk should be moved to the issues log. Responsibility remains with the person who was assigned the risk or is reassigned if necessary.
- *Monitor progress*: regularly review, track and report (potentially weekly) on open issues to ensure they are appropriately followed up and actions taken. Tracking issue status via a project dashboard to assist transparency is a good method.
- *Assess impact*: define the escalation scale and make sure the actions taken are being measured.
- *Approve resolution*: create a process for ensuring that issues are only marked 'resolved' in the issues log when checks have confirmed that the actions align with the project objectives and that the issue is truly resolved.
- *Close the issue*: when resolved, close the issue on the log and move resolved issues off the active list.

An issues log enables issues to be documented when they arise and thus provides the basis for assigning responsibility and ensuring the issue is addressed.

It also establishes a record of how the issue was resolved or managed. The risk and issues logs can be kept in separate tabs in the one document to enable tracking of both. The contents of a simple issues log are illustrated in Table 5.5.

The quality plan

Every project aims to reach a standard of quality in its outcome, at the least in order to be fit for purpose, and perhaps to meet internal or external standards (for accreditation or other benchmarks). The project charter is again the source document for quality planning. What are the standards that each of the major deliverables or outcomes must meet? Are there process standards that apply (e.g. 'consultation with unions is conducted in accordance with the organisation's formal agreements')? Who needs to be satisfied with the quality achieved? The quality baseline may be expressed as **critical success factors** and key performance indicators (KPIs) which may also be documented as part of the project charter. Each project will have unique specifications, standards or criteria that need to be met. For example, a new information system for patient location search in a hospital might require an average response time of three seconds or less; a new strength and balance **program** for older people might have to achieve a high standard of safety. These requirements provide the elements for the project's quality plan. A simple quality plan for an emergency department project (introducing a new patient management system) is shown in Table 5.6.

Planning for project assurance

Project assurance is a discipline that seeks to provide independent and objective oversight of the likely future performance of major projects

Table 5.5 Issues log

Issue ID	Unique identifier, usually a number, assigned as each issue is identified.
Description	What is the issue, and what is the impact if it is not resolved?
Assigned to	The project team member (the project manager or sponsor) responsible for pursuing resolution.
Date identified	Date the issue was originally added to the log.
Current status/last action	The date of the last action, a description of the action, and the current status of the issue. Leave all the action/status lines in the log as a record of how the action was pursued and resolved. Keeping closed issues in a 'resolved' section of the log is one form of project history.

Table 5.6 Quality plan for emergency department patient management system

Quality of outcomes	Measurement	Who assesses
The flow of patients through the emergency department (ED) is efficient and safe	Meets specifications for timelines and continuity of care	Directors (medical and nursing) of ED
The information needs of clinicians are met	Meets specifications; no losses of information currently available	Senior medical and nursing staff representatives
Administrative staff can meet their workloads with current staffing levels	Workload of new systems is at worst equal to existing	Administration manager and staff
	Reports can be successfully run and data errors can be fixed	Administration/health information manager
Statutory or government reporting requirements are met	Statutory reports can be run	Health information manager
Patient care is not disrupted during implementation	No adverse impact on patients arising from the project is recorded	Directors of ED
Staff are consulted and engaged in changes affecting them	Meets organisational change agreement standards	ED Management Human resource consultant

for those responsible for approving, financing or insuring them (Project Assurance, 2021). Aimed at minimising the risk of project failure and enabling effective oversight of progress and outcomes, project assurance practices are increasingly common, and need to be specified during the planning phase.

To heed the lessons of past project failures, and in recognition of significant investment, many government-funded projects are subject to scrutiny via independent audit, gateway reviews and project assurance requirements. The **Gateway Review** is a project assurance methodology developed in the United Kingdom. It involves short, sharp and confidential reviews conducted by reviewers not associated with the project at six key stages of the **project life cycle**, also known as 'gates' (Australian National Audit Office, 2012). Gateway reviews and other forms of project assurance may also be stipulated in a third-party vendor contract.

The following is a list of common project assurance requirements that may need to be planned for:

- external/government representation on the project steering and governance bodies
- external/independent review of the business case
- independent audit of the project budget (and sometimes independent costings) and risk/mitigation plan
- regular performance reporting
- project assurance reviews
- gateway reviews – audit, reviews, actioning of review reports, reporting.

Source: Department of Treasury and Finance (n.d.)

Communication planning

Inevitably, almost all aspects of projects rely on effective communication, from policy decisions to meeting times. A breakdown in communication can be a project showstopper, and project communication management is one of the 10 key knowledge areas in the Project Management Book of Knowledge (PMI, 2021). Successful project managers use formal and informal communication methods across various channels to increase the chances that messages are received. They use simple language, stick to relevant topics, keep messages concise and, to the extent possible, include all information in one place (Wrike, n.d.).

A communication plan is the written strategy for getting the right information to the right people at the right time (Verzuh, 2020). A communication plan recognises that all the project stakeholders will need information on a more or less regular basis, so even a simple plan outlining who requires the information, what information they need and when they need it is useful.

A project communication plan addresses the following:

- communication with all project stakeholders, based on their roles, their information needs, and the channels and frequency they prefer
- how to communicate the status of the project at any given time
- the different types of communication and how they will be used, from formal written reports (plans, contracts, minutes, agendas, status reports), and email updates, newsletters, social media posts and instant messaging; to presentations and meetings (project, stakeholder, steering committee) and informal verbal communication, with groups and individuals

- the type of information that will be communicated, when, who is responsible and what technology or channel that will be used
- the path to escalate issues
- how the plan will be monitored and updated to ensure it continues to meet the needs of stakeholders.

Source: AIPM (2021)

Table 5.7 A simple communication plan

Target audience	Information	Frequency	Owner	Channel	Schedule
Project team members	Project updates or status	Fortnightly	Project manager	Face-to-face	Every two weeks on a Wednesday
Executive team	Project high level report	Weekly	Project manager and sponsor	Email	End of the week
Sponsor	Issue or risk escalation	As necessary	Project manager	Phone, email	As necessary

Source: Adapted from AIPM (2021).

A simple communication plan is outlined in Table 5.7.

As part of a communication plan, a standard format for reporting progress to stakeholders will help enable rapid and consistent communication. Template 5.1 shows a project **status report** (including communication plan reporting). It is also useful to think about how other reports and communication can be as timely as possible, whether through flyers, regular meetings (virtual or face-to-face), newsletters, email updates, intranet notice boards, message boards, the project dashboard, and/or instant message platforms or social media posts. It is important to get the right communication balance – too much and stakeholders can get overwhelmed or switch off, and too little can lead to misunderstandings and issues.

Managing project change

Projects never unfold exactly as planned, no matter how good the planning has been, and variations (or **variances**) are a normal part of project implementation. At the planning stage, it is important to anticipate the need for variations and design a process for identifying, documenting and managing project change. This is project change management, as distinct from organisational change management (addressed in the next section).

Template 5.1 Project Status Report

Project Status Report for period ending: [Date]

Project Summary

Project name:	
Sponsor:	
Approved budget:	
Actual Start Date:	
Forecast End Date:	
Project Manager:	
Current Phase:	[I.e. Initiation, planning, implementation, closure]
Current Status:	[Green, Amber or Red*]

* Indicator definitions: Green = as planned, Amber = signs of trouble, Red = in trouble.

Progress

Project Phases, milestones and activities	% Complete	Planned Start Date	Actual Start Date	Planned End date	Actual End Date

Key accomplishments last period:

Upcoming tasks for this period

Project Financials <Financial year>

Cost Item	Approved budget $	Actual $	Forecast overrun $	Comment

Key Project Issues

Issue No.	Issue	Management

Key Project Risks

Risk No.	Risk	Mitigation

Change Requests

Change Request	Change Description	Impact

Key Communications / Planned Events

Date	Description

Template 5.1 Project Status Report

There are a number of formal tools for managing project change, and they can be adapted to suit the needs of the project and the style of the organisation. PRINCE2 and other frameworks call for a register or log of changes and a process to formally request changes to aspects of the project such as scope, timelines and deliverables. This register can be stand alone or a part of project management software and records the following for each change: the problem/change title, originator, date notified, project manager approval date, sponsor/client/steering committee approval date, implementation notes and, if relevant, change to the project completion date. It is a good idea to have a change request form template developed and ready to go in the planning phase. See Template 5.2 for an example of a change request.

Organisational change management planning

An important challenge in the planning phase is to imagine what the organisational impact of the project will be, so that it can be effectively planned for and managed. It is likely that the project will entail some change in the organisation that impacts on business as usual (BAU) – what people do, how they do it and how that then affects patients or clients and their care. Projects can be a major method for introducing change, but other changes are likely to be happening at the same time – organisational change is now a normal part of doing business (Hicks, 2022).

Stemming from organisation theory and practice, there are a number of **best practice** change management models that could be considered to inform the organisational change management strategy including Lewin's change management model (Unfreeze, Change, Refreeze; www.managementstudyguide.com), the McKinsey 7-S model (www.managementstudyguide.com), Kotter's change management theory (Hicks, 2022, www.zendesk.com) and the Deming Cycle (Plan, Do, Study, Act; The Deming Institute, 2024). There are also many change management resources available on the internet, including models, frameworks, software and templates. Before commencing a plan or selecting a model, it would be sensible to understand what change management models are being used in the organisation, or any contractor requirements.

An effective change management plan is based on understanding what will change in BAU as a result of the project (Ramos, 2023). The impacts of those changes can then be predicted, and a management plan developed. It will vary for each project, but communication and engagement with stakeholders will inevitably be an important part, as will identifying likely sources of resistance. A change management plan is also likely to highlight the need for data and evaluation of the changes, so that the organisation can assess the necessary levels of response to any issues arising. The plan might also need to be changed as the project progresses and new implications or issues for BAU emerge.

Template 5.2 Change Request

1. Project Information

Project Name:		Ref/Number:	
Request Date:		Requested By:	
Project Manager:		Project Owner:	

2. Change Requested

Description of Change requested:	
Justification:	

3. Project Impacts

Scope	
Schedule/Time:	
Cost:	
Risk/Other:	
Priority:	

On approval by all parties, the required change/s will be subject to quotation /confirmation of cost

4. Project Status and Currency

Implementation Details:	
Current Phase:	
Implementation Completion Date:	

5. Approvals and Signatures

Project Manager:		Approved	Yes/No	Date
Project Sponsor:		Approved	Yes/No	Date

Template 5.2 Change Request

The change impact of a project may be significant for specific individuals, for a particular role and for the organisation as a whole. During the planning phase, the focus is on anticipating the impact of change, or how it is going to be identified later, so that it can be managed effectively. For projects that entail significant change in the way services are delivered, or the way business processes are conducted (e.g. introducing **an electronic medical record [EMR]**), it may be necessary to map the existing processes and the points of change during the planning phase in order to identify the change impact of the project.

'Process mapping' (or 'business process review') involves mapping workflows and information flows, sometimes using flow-charting software such as Lucidchart or Visio, to document current state and future processes. For example, when implementing a telemedicine service, a number of workflows (processes) for the clinical, allied health and administrative staff may be affected, including booking of the appointment, scheduling of clinicians' time, documenting the consultation, and billing. The patient perspective also needs to be considered.

It may not be necessary to conduct a full business process review in the planning phase, but simple high-level workflow mapping can assist in identifying aspects of the impact of change. These include who will be affected, and whether their role or responsibilities will change, as well as the location of their work and how they will carry out a process.

Workflow mapping will also indicate current versus future state – what is changing, what is staying the same and what will no longer be done – and the team can then quantify the magnitude of change, what decisions will need to be made, and what policies will need to be reviewed and updated. Depending on the magnitude of predicted change, the project steering committee may need a change impact statement (documenting prospective change effects) so they can make a decision to accept the identified changes and plan for their impacts.

The project plan should include strategies for identifying, quantifying and managing the early organisational impact of the project, including change impact statements, business process review, stakeholder assessment, change readiness assessment and policy review, as well as communication and training.

Other planning

Some large or complex projects will require further planning activities, and the following list describes some of them. Much of the content of some of these plans will be taken from the main planning documents. Some of them may be initiated during planning and be outlined in the project plan then be further developed during the implementation phase:

- *procurement management plan*: materials, products and services' minimum quality requirements, in-house or outsourced, contract requirements, expression of interest process, identifying suppliers, market analysis, vendor selection criteria, procurement resources and bid evaluation

- *contract management plan*: specifying deliverables and benefits, scope definition, budget including payments and terms, roles, responsibilities and key contacts, delivery schedule, communication plan, meeting schedule, performance monitoring and assessment, change management and process for amending the contract, managing issues and dispute management (AIPM, 2023)
- *training plan*: training needs analysis, development approach, curriculum, training materials, quality assurance process/validation, training delivery, resources and logistics, instructor recruitment and preparation, training evaluation and ongoing training requirements
- *test plan (for software)*: test goals, scope and approach, test strategy, test environments, test deliverables (cases, scripts, reports), testing activities, schedule, resources, logistics and approvals
- **go-live** *plan/checklist*: readiness and **go/no go** criteria, technical infrastructure, resourcing, communications including go-live meetings, support teams and help desk, go-live plan and schedule, testing completion, risk review
- *transition to operations*: defines cutover readiness, approach – cutover or parallel, product documentation (end-to-end solution), operational process, skill development and transition, handover process design, cutover plan, business continuity.

Planning project logistics

The project will need some systems for its own operation, and some physical resources. The project plan should address the establishment processes, and there are other questions to consider. The following checklist highlights key issues:

- Is the project visible and identifiable – does it have a name or logo?
- Should the project be officially launched?
- Is the project manager known and identified as being the project manager?
- Do people know the lines of communication and how to make contact with the project?
- Does the project have a home? Is there adequate space for project team meetings, and workspace for project staff?
- Are the necessary resources and equipment available, such as computers, mobile devices, workstations, system user logins, internet/intranet access, digital whiteboards, photocopiers and stationery?
- Have the software applications and platforms that will be used for work management, project management, virtual meetings, communications,

procurement, finance and budgeting, training, recruitment etc. been selected, procured and deployed?

The project information system

A vast array of information can be gathered, generated and stored during the life of a project. Project documentation and data include the project plan, training program, variation requests, progress and status reports, budget papers, scope documents, emails, meeting minutes and agendas, WBS, Gantt chart or schedules, contracts, policies, discussion papers, rosters, invoices and purchase orders, test plans and results, correspondence and workshop reports.

The system for managing project artefacts and data is called a project management information system (PMIS).

There are different types of PMIS software but most include tools for scheduling, task management, information collection and distribution etc. Some also have automated gathering and reporting on KPIs while others are simply a collection of files. A PMIS captures all project data and stores it in an organised way. It must make the information retrievable and searchable, and enable it to be sorted by category, shared and analysed (Keup, 2022).

Regardless of the size of the project, a system for dealing with the documents and data it generates is needed. For a small internal project this might entail setting up a shared file directory or wiki, a series of online templates and a simple online project dashboard that stakeholders and team members can access. For larger and more complex projects, utilising project management software may be required (see Chapter 3).

A project dashboard, using software or a template, shows essential data needed to prioritise tasks and help keep projects on schedule and within budget. It may also show task timelines, percentage of task and project completion, project status, task assignment and pending items such as decisions, actions and change requests. Dashboards are data visualisation tools that are useful for easily updating stakeholders and teams on task progress, project status, and completion percentages. Project dashboards need to be efficient, accessible and customisable, and should provide project metrics that inform priority areas of project monitoring and reporting (Eby, 2022).

We noted at the beginning of this chapter that reality hardly ever works out in the precise, rational way that planning methods seem designed to achieve. This is not an argument against making a logical, detailed plan, but it does point to the need for skilled management and flexibility. Expecting the unexpected is the only possible outlook for project managers.

Summary

- Project planning is critical for project success, and the project plan is the central pillar of project management.

- The rational planning approach involves the development of achievable aims, objectives and strategies in a logical order, even though reality hardly ever works quite that way.
- Planning methods depend on the type and nature of the project, and many specialised methods for particular types and sizes of projects are available.
- There are many resources available to support the development of the project charter and project plan including templates, guides, blogs and project management software.
- The foundation of the project plan is the project charter, which defines scope and strategies as well as aims and objectives and is the approved project mandate.
- The other elements of the project plan detail how the project charter will be implemented. They include the work program, human and other resources, planning for risk and quality, communication planning, change management (both project and organisational), project logistics and evaluation planning.
- Project governance determines decision-making processes, but can also be well designed for managing stakeholders and coordinating the advice and inputs the project needs.
- Risk and issue management planning involves identifying what might go wrong, what will happen to the project if it does, how likely it is to happen, what contingency allowances can be made, and what approach to take to deal with each major risk.
- The quality plan specifies the standards that the project's outcomes must meet, and how their achievement will be monitored.
- Additional planning elements may be required, for example procurement, contract management, training, testing, go-live and transition to operations.
- Project logistics include getting the project established (e.g. workspace, devices, name, logo), the information systems the project will need and the communication plan.
- Even after writing a great plan, project managers should expect the unexpected, and recognise that it may need to be updated.

Readings and resources

Planning tools, documents and templates

Malsam, W. (2023, May 1). *How to write a project charter: Examples and template included.* Project Manager. https://www.projectmanager.com/blog/project-charter

Project management tools: www.mindtools.com/pages/main/newMN_PPM.htm

Project communications template: www.projectmanagementdocs.com/
templates/communications-management-plan.html

Risk management planning: www.wikihow.com/Develop-a-Risk-Management-
Plan

20 common project risks: example risk register: https://www.stakeholder-
map.com/risk/register-common-project-risks.html

Project assurance plan template and gateway review process: https://www.
dtf.vic.gov.au/gateway-review-process/gateway-key-decision-points-
guidance-and-templates

On stakeholder analysis

How to make a RACI chart for a project (with example): https://www.
projectmanager.com/blog/how-to-make-a-raci-chart-for-a-project-
with-example

Consumer advocacy groups (Australia)

Consumers Health Forum Australia: https://chf.org.au/

Health Consumers NSW: https://www.hcnsw.org.au/

Health Issues Centre: https://hic.org.au/

On managing project change

Change management models: https://www.managementstudyguide.com/
kurt-lewins-change-management-model.htm

Change management plan template: https://www.iscm.com.au/pdf/change-
management-plan.pdf

On project management information systems

What is a project management information system? https://monday.com/
blog/project-management/project-management-information-system/

Benefits realisation management framework

Benefits realisation management framework: www.nsw.gov.au www.nsw.gov.
au/departments-and-agencies/customer-service/publications-and-reports/
benefits-realisation-management-framework

References

Alie, S. S. (2015, October 10). #1 *critical success factor* [Conference paper]. PMI
Global Congress 2015, Orlando, FL, United States. www.pmi.org/learning/
library/project-governance-critical-success-9945

Australian Institute of Project Management. (2021, March 18). *Your guide to project
management communication.* https://aipm.com.au/blog/project-management-
communication/

Australian Institute of Project Management. (2022). *The state of project management in Australia 2022: Leading projects through volatility.* https://info.aipm.com.au/hubfs/Reports%20and%20major%20content%20assets/The%20State%20of%20PM%202022%20Report%20FINAL.pdf

Australian Institute of Project Management. (2023, January 24). *How to create a contract management plan.* Retrieved March 13, 2024 from https://aipm.com.au/blog/how-to-create-a-contract-management-plan/

Australian National Audit Office. (2012). Administration of the gateway review process (Audit Report No.22 2011–12). *Department of Finance and Deregulation.* www.anao.gov.au/sites/default/files/201112%20Audit%20Report%20No%2022.pdf

Axelos. (2017). *Managing successful projects with PRINCE2* (7 ed.). The Stationery Office.

Bird, M., McGillion, M., Chambers, E. M., Dix, J., Fajardo, C. J., Gilmour, M., Levesque, K., Lim, A., Mierdel, S., Quellette, C., Polanski, A. N., Reaume, S. V., Whitmore, C., & Carter, N. (2021). A generative co-design framework for healthcare innovation: Development and application of an end-user engagement framework. *Research Involvement and Engagement, 7*(12). https://doi.org/10.1186/s40900-021-00252-7

Bondale, K. (2021, December 2). *How long does it take to put together a project plan.* Retrieved March 25, 2024 from www.projectmanagement.com/discussion-topic/177452/how-long-does-it-take-to-put-together-a-project-plan-#_=

Bridges, J. (2022, February 14). 8 Steps for better issue management. *Project Manager.* Retrieved March 13, 2024 from www.projectmanager.com/training/managing-project-issues

Clayton, M. (2022, April 29). *What does project governance really mean?* www.projectmanager.com/blog/what-does-project-governance-really-mean

The Deming Institute. (2024). *PDSA Cycle.* Retrieved March 15, 2024 from https://deming.org/explore/pdsa/

Department of Treasury and Finance of Victoria. (n.d.). *Gateway review process.* www.dtf.vic.gov.au/infrastructure-investment/gateway-review-process

Eby, K. (2022, April 27). Free project dashboard templates. *Smartsheet.* Retrieved March 13, 2024 from www.smartsheet.com/content/project-dashboard-templates

Eby, K. (2023, February 27). How to create a project risk management plan. *Smartsheet.* Retrieved March 15, 2024 from www.smartsheet.com/content/project-risk-management-plan

Good, L. (2023, November 20). *What is a project charter? Complete guide & examples.* Retrieved January 13, 2024 from https://project-management.com/what-is-a-project-charter/

Health Consumers NSW. (2024). *About us: Driving health consumer engagement and co-design in NSW.* Retrieved March 25, 2024 from https://hcnsw.org.au/about-us/

Health Issues Centre. (n.d.). *About us.* Retrieved March 25, 2024 from https://hic.org.au/about-us/

Hicks, K. (2022, May 2). Top 8 change management models: A comparison guide. *Zendesk Blog.* www.zendesk.com/au/blog/change-management-models/#georedirect

Hoban, S. M. (2023, October 13). What is a project initiation document & 7 easy steps to create one. *The Digital Project Manager*. Retrieved March 12, 2024 from https://thedigitalprojectmanager.com/projects/pm-methodology/how-make-project-initiation-document/

Indeed Editorial Team. (2023, October 14). 10 Common project risks (plus the steps to solve them). *Indeed*. Retrieved March 13, 2024 from www.indeed.com/career-advice/career-development/project-risks

Keup, M. (2022, April 14). A complete guide to PMIS. *Project Manager*. Retrieved March 13, 2024 from www.projectmanager.com/blog/a-complete-guide-to-pmis

Landau, P. (2021, April 08). *How to create a project brief(example included)*. Retrieved March 13, 2024 from www.projectmanager.com/blog/create-a-project-brief

Landau, P. (2023, September 1). Stakeholder analysis 101 (example & template included). *Project Manager*. Retrieved March 13, 2024 from www.project-manager.com/blog/stakeholder-analysis-101

LeRouge, C. M., Tulu, B., & Wood, S. (2014). Project initiation for telemedicine services. *International Journal of Healthcare Information Systems and Informatics*, 9(2), 64–85. https://doi.org/10.4018/ijhisi.2014040104

McAbee, J. (2022, June 21). *Understanding risk breakdown structure*. Retrieved January 23, 2024 from www.wrike.com/blog/understanding-risk-breakdown-structure/

Marker, A. (2021, October 12). Project governance: How little processes can have big impacts. *Smartsheet*. Retrieved March 13, 2024 from www.smartsheet.com/project-governance

Mind Tools Content Team. (2024). *Project initiation documents*. Retrieved March 29 from www.mindtools.com/a5ysls5/project-initiation-documents

Ostrowercha, K. (2023, May 08). The makings of project deliverables: A guide to defining objectives effectively. *Float*. Retrieved March 13, 2024 from www.float.com/resources/project-deliverables/

Project Assurance. (2021, November 17). In *Wikipedia*. https://en.wikipedia.org/wiki/Project_assurance

Project Documentation. (n.d.). What are the tools and techniques for conducting a stakeholder analysis? *Linkedin*. Retrieved August 25, 2023 from www.linkedin.com/advice/0/what-tools-techniques-conducting-stakeholder

Ramos, D. (2023, March 22). 8 Elements of an effective change management process. *Smartsheet*. Retrieved March 13, 2024 from www.smartsheet.com/8-elements-effective-change-management-process

Sankararajan, D., & Shrivastava, N. K. (2012). Risks vs issues. *PM Network*, 26(6), 28–29. www.pmi.org/learning/library/risks-vs-issues-project-failure-2328

Scavetta, A. (2021, September 15). *How to make a risk management plan(template included)*. www.projectmanager.com/blog/risk-management-plan

Verzuh, E. (2020). *The fast forward MBA in project management: The comprehensive, easy-to-read handbook for beginners and pros* (6 ed.). Wiley.

Waldow, D. J. (2020, October 27). *Your quick how-to guide to effective project governance*. Retrieved March 03, 2024 from https://monday.com/blog/project-management/project-governance-your-guide-to-the-decision-making-process/

Walenta, T. (2021, December). *How long does it take to put together a project plan.* Retrieved March 25, 2024 from www.projectmanagement.com/discussion-topic/177452/how-long-does-it-take-to-put-together-a-project-plan-#_=

Wrike. (n.d.). *What is project communication management?* Retrieved January 23, 2024 from www.wrike.com/project-management-guide/faq/what-is-project-communication-management/

CHAPTER 6

Planning for evaluation

Assessing project performance

This chapter explains project evaluation, why it needs to be included in **project plans** and evaluation methods suited to different projects and settings. It explains ways of incorporating evaluation design into the project to guide data collection throughout the **project life cycle,** to enable early identification of warning signs and to provide evidence of the project's success. It also explains the use of evaluation methods to capture and share learnings

DOI: 10.4324/9781003431701-7

from project experiences and enhance project expertise. Evaluation commences in the project planning **phase**, even for small projects, and is carried out in the implementation and closing phases.

What is evaluation, and why do it?

Evaluation is used to judge the value or worth of something by observing, measuring and comparing it against established criteria or standards (Hawe et al., 1990), including against project goals and **objectives.** In project evaluation, information is collected and analysed in order to understand the progress, success and benefits of a project. It focuses on understanding what happened and the reasons for success or failure. Project evaluation provides evidence to identify strengths and weaknesses, and to make decisions about the continuation or extension of a project; and it can also be used to demonstrate accountability to funders and communities (SACHRU, 2008). Evaluation can also assist organisations to learn from their project experience and apply that knowledge to the design and conduct of future projects.

In spite of these benefits, throughout our research for this book and its earlier editions, many participants have acknowledged that formal project evaluation is rarely undertaken (unless it is a stipulation of the contract or funding agreement), and funding is usually not available, a finding supported by other researchers (Gray & Wilkinson, 2016). Gray and Wilkinson (2016) also report a lack of expertise in project evaluation in some organisations, and a lack of easily accessible reports. Inadequate recognition of the benefits of evaluation among project staff, or a perception that it is 'too academic' and complicated, may also be a factor.

However, some participants in our research for this edition confirmed that evaluation is part of **project management** and can be conducted formally or informally:

> *What I personally like to do at the end of the project is put together a spreadsheet in a central location where all . . . who've been involved in the project, and stakeholders, can put their feedback to help inform the project closure report . . . it's basically a 'lessons learned' spreadsheet, where they can put their comments and feedback. . . . Rather than necessarily criticising the project, it's a nice sort of formal way of getting feedback about how a similar project could be done next time.*
> *(Project Director, Health Network)*

Our experts also noted that in projects where the goal is to test a new way of delivering care, and to establish its benefits, evaluation is fundamental to project design. And sometimes, funding for evaluation is built into the project budget (e.g. through funded **project assurance** activities).

We advocate for greater use of evaluation because of the potential benefits for project success rates and for the industry's **effectiveness** in implementing new ways of providing and supporting services. In a time when **evidence-based practice** in both service delivery and policy development are valued, and when mega-projects (with multimillion-dollar budgets) are funded with government or corporate involvement, there is likely to be intense scrutiny of both project outcomes and value for money – in this situation a good evaluation plan, executed well, can be essential.

Evaluation types and design

Because each project is different, the choice of method(s) is quite broad – the only constant is the need to plan your evaluation so that the right evaluation questions are asked at the right time, allowing the right information to be collected in the right way for each project. Project evaluation needs to be methodical and to produce valid conclusions based on reliable data and observations, but the **scope** and complexity will be tailored to the needs of the project and its stakeholders, and it usually doesn't need to meet the standards of traditional scientific research:

> *The reason why those evaluations have been more tangible and meaningful is because, while she's a researcher . . . she hasn't waited for it to be research-quality standard evaluation. She's more practical outcome-focussed. It has been solid data, but it's not academic grade.*
> *(Senior Manager, Home Care Service)*

It is helpful to think about different types of evaluation for answering different kinds of questions, and traditionally there are three main types described, with different purposes, as outlined in Table 6.1.

Table 6.1 Common project evaluation types and purposes

Types of evaluation	Key purpose
Process evaluation (e.g. survey of stakeholder groups, gateway review)	To assess the effectiveness of strategies and methods and how they are implemented, and to monitor progress. The focus is on measuring project outputs and deliverables, as well as analysing which processes or activities contributed.
Impact evaluation (e.g. statistical analysis of care indicators)	To measure the achievement of the project goal and objectives. The focus is on the immediate results at the end of the project.
Outcome evaluation (e.g. benefits realisation)	To measure the long-term results or benefits of the project. Impact and outcome evaluation both assess the effects of the completed project, but over different time periods.

There are many methods and data collection techniques that can be used and there are no rigid rules for making methods decisions. The art of evaluation involves creating a design and gathering information that is appropriate for a specific project, setting and policy context. But that doesn't mean starting from scratch each time – previous evaluation designs for similar projects as well as advice from experts can be useful.

Clinical and community care improvement projects will generally use some traditional quantitative data to measure the impact of changes on the effectiveness, timeliness or cost of care. But when projects are seeking to introduce new ways of approaching complex social problems (e.g. family violence), where the social, legal, economic and cultural context are important influences on what will work and how, methods such as 'realist evaluation' (Pawson & Tilley, 1997) and other interpretive approaches such as the theory of change approach are needed (Chen, 1990; Wadsworth, 2010). While these methods often include quantitative data, they generally emphasise qualitative methods including interviews, direct and indirect observation, focus groups and case studies.

Evaluation approaches can also be quite simple, as this case of a successful project in a community health service illustrates.

Project story: Evaluation in the community setting

A community health service had a request from a local general practitioner (GP) concerning the needs of an increasing number of Afghani women attending her surgery. She felt that their needs were largely social and emotional rather than medical, and asked, 'Could you do something for them?' The agency met with the women's unofficial interpreter, and after much discussion decided to establish an Afghani Women's Health Project with three project objectives:

1. Provide Afghani women with opportunities to voice their health needs.
2. Raise awareness among participants about local services and provide effective referral pathways.
3. Engage local service providers in providing care and support to Afghani women.

Discussion groups were held, resources were collected, and an Afghani Women's Health Forum was conducted, with invited speakers addressing important cultural and health issues. Other activities followed. Service providers in the area took part and were successfully engaged in broader responses to the needs of the group.

The project was evaluated in several ways. As the project leader said:

First, we asked the question 'Did we do what we set out to do – that is, did we successfully establish the project?' The answer to that question was clearly 'yes'. Second, we collected data on the numbers of women and service providers attending all the activities, and we collected demographic data about the range of women attending – age, education, family and work responsibilities etc. Third, we asked for feedback from all participants in our activities through both individual feedback sheets and group discussion. Finally, we involved the Afghani women in decision-making about future activities, thus reflecting on what we had done and identifying what worked and what didn't. In this way, we carried out both process and **impact evaluation** – we just did what seemed logical.

It was not possible in the timeframe of the project to do a formal **outcome evaluation**, that is, did the health of the women improve? – a complex question to measure in any setting. However, the project had both unforeseen and longer-term impacts. For example, the women identified a whole range of issues as important to their health, such as housing, immigration, work and education, which went well beyond the issues the agency had initially considered. The women also organised among themselves and became very involved in local housing issues. One woman went on to open her own restaurant, actively supported by the others.

There was also an impact on service providers, who were made aware of the group's needs and priorities. They realised that some of their normal practices should be changed if they were to meet the needs of this group. This realisation led to a series of cultural awareness projects in some of the local mainstream agencies.

But there was another way the staff knew that the project had been a success. 'When the group came to hold their meetings, they filled the place up with laughter, colour, food and good energy. That good energy lifted the spirits of everyone else in the place – hard to explain in evaluation terms but easy to see and feel in practice.'

Process evaluation

What the team should always look at is whether the project still makes sense, whether there is still logic in implementing that project, and whether there is going to be value. . . . Because [if not]. . . it's better to stop that project now rather than completely delivering it and not getting the value out of it and . . . wasting all of those resources.
(Senior Manager, Health Department)

Process evaluation focuses on how a project is done, whether project strategies have been implemented as intended and on the overall quality of the project activities and output – what is actually produced by the project. It addresses questions of what is done, when, by whom, to whom, and how well. Examples of questions that are often included in process evaluation are:

- Is the project operating as intended?
- Were project activities accomplished, and how well? If not, why not?
- What is the quality of each of the key project components?
- Are the interests of stakeholders being addressed?
- Is the project staying within budget?
- Are the planned outputs being delivered (during the project)?
- How satisfied are the participants/stakeholders?

Thus process evaluation can indicate the effectiveness of the chosen project strategies as well as communication, governance, **stakeholder** engagement etc. and the skill of their execution. It is undertaken while the project is in operation, and its results can be analysed and used during the project as well as at the end. Process evaluation can explain whether the project design is fit for purpose, where strategies are poorly implemented or whether issues and risks are effectively addressed.

Process evaluation doesn't have to be hard to do. A well-developed project plan includes **milestones**, standards and criteria for assessing how the project is going as it unfolds, and having this kind of real-time feedback on progress against the plan is already a normal part of project management. Information from process evaluation adds value for understanding the import of the results of normal project monitoring, the reasons for success and the **lessons learned** (Rowe & Sikes, 2006). Some of our participants recognised the importance of process evaluation and said it is commonly done in their projects – more so than the other types of evaluation.

When a project is trialling a new **program** or service, process evaluation can aid in understanding the relationship between specific program elements and outcomes (Saunders et al., 2005, p. 134). When a project is pilot testing a specific component of a large project before its implementation, process evaluation also tests the ease of implementation and whether project strategies and other key elements should be modified.

Process evaluation can be conducted on an ongoing basis and at specific points during the project. A general guide is:

- *Soon after a project has begun*: collect and document descriptive information on project characteristics that will not change, and baseline information.
- *During implementation*: collect data on progress against **deliverables**, timelines and objectives (e.g. recruitment, stakeholder engagement, conduct of planned activities and quality of resources used in the project).

■ *At the end of the project*: analyse and document achievement of activity targets (e.g. attendance at workshops or group fitness or uptake of a new method by staff) and quality of outputs.

Table 6.2 provides an example of the kind of data needed for process evaluation of a surgical admissions pathway project, using a combination of data already available from the project records, and some collected for the purpose of evaluation (*shown in italics*).

Impact evaluation

> *Impact evaluation serves both objectives of evaluation: lesson-learning and accountability.*
>
> *(OECD, n.d.)*

Impact evaluation measures the extent to which the project's objectives have been achieved. It focuses on the immediate results at the end of the project (whether good or bad, intended or not and direct or not). For example, in telehealth projects, one of the known unintended negative effects that may emerge during the project is the growing dependence of patients on technology and the increased isolation of clinicians due to reduced contact and interaction with colleagues (Alami et al., 2019).

Impact evaluation can be a simple process. At its most basic, the question is: 'Did we achieve the objectives of the project?' For example, if the

---

A word about impact and outcome

Readers may have encountered different usage of the terms impact and outcome. In Australia (but not in some other countries like the United States) 'impact' is used to denote the immediate results, and 'outcome' for the longer-term results. So, in public health interventions, the impact of an immunisation project would be measured in terms of the proportion of the target population who were immunised at the completion of the project, whereas the outcomes could not be measured until much later (i.e. fewer cases of vaccine-preventable diseases in the area). For a project that prepared an organisation for a change in funding arrangements, the impact would be measured by preparations being completed on time and a smooth introduction of the new system. Outcome could be assessed on the basis of successful management of services and budgeting under the new funding rules, but that would come well after the project was completed.

Table 6.2 Process evaluation of a surgical admissions pathway project

Goal: To introduce a surgical admissions pathway for urgent patients straight to the receiving ward, and to test both its capacity to reduce the overall length of stay for those patients and its impact on emergency department (ED) waiting times for all patients.

Process	Questions	Data source
Pathway development	Were staff representatives satisfied with the pathway development process?	Notes of consultations and workshops with staff representatives during the project; *notes of meeting held by an independent manager or clinical leader with staff representatives for this purpose, using questions prepared by the project team.*
Stakeholder management	Were staff representatives satisfied with the project overall? Was the change managed well? Were other departments (including ICT) satisfied with the project process?	Minutes of team and steering committee meetings; papers prepared by the team for the steering committee or other audiences; *notes of discussion at final steering committee meeting.* Minutes of meetings and other evidence of engagement; *notes of discussion with representatives of other departments.*
Communication	Were stakeholders well informed about the project, its progress and the nature of changes?	Summary of formal communication about the project with stakeholders; *notes of meetings held for evaluation purposes.*
Governance	Was leadership and decision-making for the project effective?	Minutes of steering committee meetings; summary of formal reports to the executive; *notes of discussion at steering committee and with executive held for this purpose; notes of other meetings held for the purpose of evaluation.*
Close and handover	Was the project closure adequate? Was handover effective?	Summary of closure activities; notes of all questions fielded by members of the project team or the surgical division executive in the first 30 days after handover; *responses to a survey of surgical wards, ED and other departments involved.*

objectives of the project were to install a new system or process and allow it to work, the question is: 'Is it installed and does it work?' For some projects, this may be all that is done, and all that the organisation needs. But the impact evaluation questions for larger or more complex projects require more thought, and the **project manager** may need to choose or design evaluation indicators to make the impact of complex changes measurable. For example, in assessing the impact of a new model of care that requires nurses to work differently, sick leave levels may be a good indicator of real acceptance of change, to complement data on the level of compliance with the new method.

Table 6.3 details some examples of impact indicators based on the five types of projects used in health and community care (see Chapter 1).

Planning process and impact evaluation together

While the distinction between the three types of evaluation is conceptually helpful, in practice many of the same methods are used. We suggest that process and impact evaluation be planned together. An essential part of project planning is to determine how and when activities and achievement of milestones need to be assessed (sometimes known as '**tracking**' in project jargon). The project plan will have defined and itemised the project goals and objectives, activities, quality standards and expected benefits (see Chapters 4 and 5), and these provide the foundation for evaluation of both process and impact. The evaluation plan should outline the questions of interest regarding the project's progress and outputs and specify the times at which they are to be considered, how and by whom. The plan should then outline the standards, targets or outcomes against which the impact of the project will be measured, along with how the measurement will be made and who will be involved.

Taken together in this way, process and impact evaluation assesses how the project went, what it produced and what difference it made (in the short term). Fundamentally, process and impact evaluation aim to answer the following five key questions:

1. How well did we do what we said we would do?
2. What worked and what didn't, and why?
3. What difference did it make that we did this?
4. What could we do differently?
5. What can be learned from the project to improve practice and inform other projects?

Table 6.4 provides examples of ways of breaking down and exploring answers to these key evaluation questions.

Table 6.3 Impact indicator examples

Type of project	Impact indicators
The development of new services, programs or technologies	An education program for teenagers in a local school district leads to a reduction in vaping uptake among participants
To improve existing care processes, work practices or service models	A new way of triaging emergency department patients results in shorter waits and improved patient satisfaction
The implementation of new organisational structures or systems, including those made possible by advances in digital health and care systems	Implementation of a new quality monitoring system leads to a reduction in adverse events
The construction, acquisition and commissioning of new equipment, systems and facilities	A new pharmacy ordering system has been implemented and is functioning at specified standards (e.g. timeliness, accuracy)
To design and conduct research projects, such as evidence reviews, needs studies and service planning	Published article in high-quality journal or policy change in the care system based on results

Table 6.4 Process and impact evaluation questions breakdown

Key evaluation questions	Breakdown of questions
1. How well did we do what we said we would do?	■ Have all planned project tasks and activities been completed? ■ How well has the project achieved its goal and objectives? ■ If the objectives changed during the project, how and why did they change? ■ Has the project developed resources suitable for future use? ■ Have the project team members developed skills as a result? ■ Did partnerships enhance capacity and capability?
2. What worked and what didn't and why?	■ What strategies worked well or not for involving the target population or staff? Why? ■ What strategies worked well or not for acquiring support from stakeholders? Why? ■ Have any of the activities and strategies been changed? Why?

(*Continued*)

Table 6.4 (Continued)

Key evaluation questions	Breakdown of questions
	■ Were any of the project goals/objectives not fully achieved?
	■ Did the project comprehensively address the problem?
	■ In what ways did the planning process work most effectively?
3. What difference did it make that we did this?	■ Did the project have any unexpected impacts?
	■ Were other initiatives started, alternative services proposed or new funding resources acquired as a result?
	■ Are the outcomes of the project sustainable, and will any new intervention or service continue beyond the initial funding?
	■ To what extent are the outcomes useful for uptake by other organisations, settings or communities?
4. What could we do differently?	■ What additional resources, skills or knowledge are needed to do projects like this one more effectively?
	■ Was additional support from stakeholders needed?
	■ How could we have improved stakeholder engagement?
	■ Did we develop realistic goals and objectives?
	■ Could the project results be made more widely available?
5. What can be learned from the project to improve practice and inform other projects?	■ What are the transferable learnings from this project?
	■ Will the evaluation results be available for new project planning?
	■ Are there project outcomes that should influence priorities for further projects, policy development or research?

The seven-step approach

Table 6.5 explains a structured approach to designing process and impact evaluation in seven steps. The first five steps are completed during the project planning phase so that both baseline data and process evaluation data can be collected from the beginning of the implementation phase.

Table 6.6 applies the seven-step approach to the evaluation of a project that implemented a new safety and quality system in a residential aged care organisation. The organisation had identified some problems with inconsistent quality of care for residents, and the system focused on both quality of care and resident satisfaction as well as job satisfaction for staff. The project was planned and implemented with the help of an expert group of researchers and was designed to engage both residents and staff as stakeholders. It included enhanced monitoring of adverse events and near misses along with training for all staff in the principles, methods and tools of the system.

Table 6.5 Evaluation in seven steps

Step	Focus	Details
1.	Definition of work	■ Review project strategies and activities and the expected immediate and longer-term outcomes to identify what aspects should be evaluated. ■ Check sponsor/funder/contract/stakeholder requirements on the types of evaluation they expect.
2.	Development of evaluation questions and success indicators	■ Develop questions, targets and key performance indicators (KPIs) that can be used to measure the completion and quality of the activities and the defined impacts.
3.	Selection of methods	■ Determine methods to be used to collect the required data for each target and KPI.
4.	Allocation of responsibility and tasks	■ Decide who will be responsible for the overall evaluation and who will undertake the tasks involved.
5.	Set timeline	■ Determine the timelines for collection of different types of data and for any data analysis and reporting that is needed during project implementation.
6.	Data collection, analysis and interpretation	■ Collect and analyse the data and interpret its meaning to answer each of the evaluation questions.
7.	Dissemination and application of results	■ Write an evaluation report that can be shared within the organisation and with stakeholders. ■ Consider presenting the results at conferences and publishing in journals, along with other ways that the results and learning can be available to future projects.

Outcome evaluation

Outcome evaluation measures the longer-term results or benefits of the project and is virtually always done after the project has been completed. This type of evaluation can provide strong evidence of value, but many projects simply don't have the resources to commit to outcome evaluation. While it can be difficult to look back, there are established frameworks and feasible techniques that have been well-tested in practice and some of them are described below.

Benefits realisation

Benefits realisation management (BRM) is used to identify, measure and track achievement of the desired benefits of a project (Vas et al., 2023) and

Table 6.6 Seven-step evaluation example: Implementing a modern approach to safety and quality in residential aged care

No.	Step	Details
1	Definition of work	To implement a modern approach to safety and quality in a residential aged care organisation, and to evaluate the process and impact of the new model on staff performance, staff job satisfaction, resident safety and resident satisfaction with care.
2	Development of evaluation questions and KPIs	Q1: Are managers and staff clear about the safety and quality model and their role in it? ■ % of staff who successfully complete a training course ■ % of staff who understand the model ■ % of staff who are able to use the new tools, reporting and monitoring procedures Q2: Has quality of care improved? ■ Improved resident satisfaction with care ■ Improved resident satisfaction with communication and support from care staff ■ Reduced number and severity of preventable adverse events
3	Selection of methods	Staff job satisfaction surveys Survey of staff who completed the refresher course Monitoring records of staff attendance and completion of training Monitoring records of adverse incidents Resident satisfaction surveys
4	Allocation of responsibility and tasks	Quality manager and project team manager will be responsible for designing survey instruments, collecting data and data analysis.
5	Set timeline	Baseline data on staff and resident satisfaction prior to project commencement Staff and resident satisfaction survey at the end of the project Resident care data monitored on a monthly basis.
6	Data analysis and interpretation	All data are quantitative and will be analysed using appropriate statistical techniques.
7	Dissemination and application of results	A report will be provided to senior management. A snapshot of the project and its outcomes will be shared across the organisation in newsletter format. Experience and learnings from implementing the model will be shared at national or international industry conferences.

is particularly (but not only) useful for **information and communications technology (ICT)** and digital projects. A benefit is defined as a net positive change in outcomes, including patient care and health or wellbeing outcomes. Benefits realisation methods have been widely used to demonstrate that the benefits of **electronic medical records (EMRs)**, if properly implemented, are far more substantial than the risks. They include higher patient and doctor satisfaction, real-time information tracking, fewer handwritten forms, fewer preventable errors, fewer dosage errors, and increased quality of care (Alanazi et al., 2020).

A benefits realisation plan (which defines expected benefits and sets targets and timelines) can be used to inform investment decisions. It is important that the plan specifies who will gather the information (PRINCE2 Wiki, n.d.). Its formal use is aimed at increasing the chances that the benefit will actually be delivered (NSW Government, 2024).

Like other evaluation planning, a benefits realisation plan is often developed early, at the same time as the **business case**, and updated in the planning phase. A benefits realisation plan typically contains the following information:

- the key outcomes (or benefits) to be achieved by the project
- the benefit type (bankable, productivity or health gain)
- baseline and target measures to be achieved, the data sources and expected delivery schedule for each benefit
- an overview of the monitoring capabilities (effort or cost, skills and people) required to measure each specified benefit, along with an outline of where those capabilities will be found
- an explanation of the risks that may threaten the achievement of each benefit, and how the threat will be handled.

The decision to implement clinical information systems and EMRs is often made on the basis of a proposal (or business case) that specifies anticipated benefits. For electronic ordering of pathology and radiology tests, one of the expected benefits would be a reduced number of inappropriate or duplicate tests ordered. For electronic prescribing, the expected benefits would include faster supply of medications and a reduction in medication errors. Benefits can be bankable (they can enable dollar savings, e.g. in consumables or space) or non-bankable – in the form of productivity gains (e.g. time savings) or improved patient satisfaction. It should be noted that benefits are often not realised until sometime after the project has been completed, and realisation plans often monitor benefit over a three- to five-year period.

Benefits realisation frameworks, management models and tools have evolved since the mid 1990s, and their use has matured with the implementation of clinical and electronic record systems (Askedal et al., 2017). For example, the **PRINCE2** benefit realisation framework has been used in major ICT projects by the National Health Service (NHS) in the United Kingdom (Axelos, 2017).

According to NHS England, one of the advantages of benefits realisation planning is that tracking of the achievement of intended benefits can be sustained after the end of the project; and the plan makes clear who is responsible (NHS England and NHS Improvement, 2021). The New South Wales government's Benefits Realisation Management Framework is a well-documented approach (available at https://www.nsw.gov.au/departments-and-agencies/customer-service/publications-and-reports/benefits-realisation-management-framework) and provides a clear guide to benefits management principles, processes, templates and guidelines, including implementation.

Economic evaluation

Economic evaluation assesses value by comparing the benefits and costs of a chosen option or initiative with an alternative option or the current situation (e.g. a different service or method of delivery compared to 'standard care'; Gray & Wilkinson, 2016) and provides evidence to compare and choose between alternatives (Drummond et al., 2015). It assesses the relative soundness and efficiency of interventions and at least in theory allows decision makers to be more rational in their decisions about which care options to fund or expand and which to cut (Carter & Harris, 1999). It is designed to help decision makers answer the question: 'Is this service/program/intervention worth doing compared with other things we could do with these same resources?'

Typically, answers to this question are most strongly influenced by estimates of the relative merit or value of the alternative course of action they pose. Because funding for health and community care is always limited, considerations of relative value become paramount. Are the benefits – for individuals or the population – worth the costs, as compared to other uses of that money?

The principle is that resource allocation decisions should maximise the efficient use of resources. In order to provide reliable guidance on this question for health or community care, decision makers also need information on the related questions of:

- *Efficacy*: Can it work in testing, and to what extent?
- *Effectiveness*: Will it work in practice in this environment and for this group of people?
- *Acceptability*: Will the people who are the intended recipients accept it?
- *Accessibility*: Will it reach those who need it?

There are three main methods for economic evaluation of interventions or services: **cost-benefit analysis** (CBA), **cost-effectiveness analysis** (CEA) and cost-utility analysis (CUA). The difference between them can be confusing. *Cost-benefit analysis* estimates (in dollars) the costs and benefits of a given intervention compared with another intervention. In recent years, cost-benefit analysis has been criticised precisely because it reduces complex values, such as quality of life, to dollar figures.

Cost-effectiveness analysis and *cost-utility analysis* express outcomes in non-monetary terms. Cost-effective analysis uses 'natural units' such as cure rate or reduction in the incidence of a disease (e.g. how much does it cost to prevent a single death through a cancer screening program). Cost-utility analysis attempts to express outcomes in quality-adjusted life years (QALYs) so that comparisons of benefit can be made between alternative conditions or service types (Drummond et al., 2015; Gray & Wilkinson, 2016). Health economists specialise in this sort of analysis, and use other techniques such as earned value management (PMI, 2021; Landau, 2022).

Economic evaluation is quite technical, and generally the services of an economist are needed. Recommended textbooks and online resources are included at the end of the chapter.

Post-implementation review

Post-implementation review (PIR) is conducted after a project is completed. It is a formal process of presenting and considering data to determine whether project objectives were met and how effectively the project was run, to learn lessons for the future, and to ensure that the organisation gets the greatest possible benefit from the project, including but not limited to its outcomes (Mind Tools, n.d.). It can also be used to guide funding and planning of future services or programs.

PIR is a flexible process that can be used to evaluate all aspects of a project. It is a good method to use when the organisation, project team and stakeholders would value capturing the learning from a project, both to make sure that the benefits continue to be optimised in business as usual (BAU) or because of its potential use to improve future projects. PIR can be also used to provide proof of delivery or compliance with standards, but it has a broader intention.

In planning for a PIR, consideration should be given to the method and questions that will be asked, as there are many ways to gather the necessary information to determine what worked and what didn't in the project. Westland (2018) offers some examples:

- *Gap analysis*: This method of assessing how a plan differed from the actual application is a powerful tool to see what benchmarks were met or not.

■ *Project goals*: Simply put, were the goals of the project achieved? Are the deliverables functioning as planned? What was the error rate of the project?

■ *Stakeholder satisfaction/benefit*: How satisfied were stakeholders? Were users' needs met?

■ *Cost*: How much did the project end up costing? What are the costs involved in operating the project's result?

■ *Benefits*: Did the project achieve the benefits projected; if not, why, and how can that be improved?

■ *Lessons*: What went well, and what can be learned from that experience?

■ *Report*: Documenting what was learned from the review.

A PIR may be conducted by an objective third party (either internal or external to the organisation); and it should include evaluation from the perspectives of all stakeholders and use information from evaluation activities conducted while the project was underway.

Consideration of the timing of a PIR is also important – long enough after project completion that the results have truly taken effect, but soon enough that those involved still have fresh memories and are still available.

Learning from the project experience

Every project brings a unique set of lessons to be learned, shaping how we approach future challenges.

(ActiveCollab, 2023)

Lessons learned are insights and experiences gained throughout the project life cycle (ActiveCollab, 2023) that, if captured and analysed, can inform the project team, guide future project endeavours and support positive organisational change. By analysing what went well and what didn't, project managers can identify areas for improvement, enhance project management and team skills, promote professional growth, avoid repeating mistakes (and reinventing the wheel), enable informed decisions for future projects or future phases of the current project, inform organisational **best practice** and share knowledge.

Project managers can plan for and implement a **lessons learned log** (see Template 6.1 and resources at the end of the chapter for examples). A log enables project members to add any insights or learnings during the project, which can then be discussed and assessed in the closing phase and key learnings or recommendations can be included in the project's final report. However, a lessons learned log alone will not capture all insights, teachable moments and potential project improvements in a meaningful way.

Template 6.1 Lessons Learned Log

Project Title:

Project Manager

Data Element	Definition/ Example
Number	Individual number of lesson being logged
Entered by	Name of person logging lesson
Subject	Lesson subject e.g. Requirements considered in design work
Situation	Lesson context or situation e.g. Requirements from key stakeholder (consumer representative) not included in design work
Recommendations & Comments	E.g. Ensure stakeholder analysis is not omitted or minimised in the planning phase due to time pressures
Actions taken	E.g. Stakeholder analysis template developed for future projects

Lessons Learned Log

Number	Entered by	Subject	Situation	Recommendations & Comments	Actions Taken

Template 6.1 Lessons Learned Log

A more detailed approach, as described by Eby (2021) and Rowe and Sikes (2006), is included in the Project Management Book of Knowledge (**PMBOK** Guide) which outlines a process in five steps, and defines the activities required to successfully capture and use lessons learned. This five-step process is summarised in Table 6.7.

Table 6.7 PMBOK lessons learned five-step process

Step description	Planning and implementation considerations
Step 1: Identify comments, recommendations, innovations, observations and areas for improvement for future projects or project phases	Plan to use logs, surveys and other sources of data or feedback Nominate someone (not the project manager) to facilitate lessons learned sessions Include what went well, what didn't go well and what needed improvement Define the timing and schedule when lessons will be identified in the project life cycle. Note that many of these activities might be undertaken in the closing phase Check for overlap with other evaluation methods being deployed (e.g. post-implementation review) so as to minimise duplication and streamline efforts
Step 2: Document and create a list of the lessons learned	Ensure input from all the project team and key stakeholders Use categories and key words to identify themes Create a report of findings
Step 3: Analyse the lessons learned findings	Analyse the list and findings report Share the findings and any recommendations for discussion and action if required The project management office could analyse the findings report against findings from other projects to identify organisational learnings
Step 4: Store reports in a shared database or repository	Arrange the software tools or platform for reports to enable access post-project by all interested parties Retain a copy of data or reports in the project archive Use keywords when storing your reports to make them easier to search for and retrieve
Step 5: Retrieve lessons learned reports	Consider retrieving lessons learned reports from previous or similar projects to compare insights.

Source: Adapted from Eby (2021); Rowe & Sikes (2006).

When planning for evaluation, the timing for lessons learned processes is important, and they don't have to wait until the end. Sessions might be helpful after any crisis or major change in the project, and in any case waiting until the end of a large project may mean that key lessons are missed. While a log is for use at any point, sessions or surveys can be conducted at key times such as at the end of each phase and in real time – when the lesson is being learned.

The post-incident review method is also commonly used in ICT and software fields and aims to bring people and teams together to discuss an incident: why it happened, what impact it had, what actions were taken to resolve it, and how the team can prevent it from happening again. One of the goals of completing a post-incident review is to respond to and learn from those incidents, turning them from frustrations to opportunities (Atlassian, n.d.).

Another approach used in some Australian emergency services, including police, fire service and ambulance jurisdictions is the Observation – Insight – Lessons Identified – Lessons Learned process (OILL) to synthesise observations, analyse them for insights and identify lessons (State Emergency Service, n.d.). The OILL process highlights that lessons are only identified by analysing observations and deciding on an action that improves things; and it is only when those actions are implemented that the lessons are really learned.

Collecting and using data

Some ways of collecting data are more intrusive for the people involved, and generally more costly to collect, than others. In addition to collecting data from primary sources (either by direct interaction with people or data from the project management information system [PMIS]), data from secondary sources (i.e. existing data collections) can also be used, perhaps requiring new analysis.

Depending on the complexity of the project and the type of evaluation questions, mixed methods and sources are often used. For example, for evaluating a training project, the number of training sessions and number of attendees will be available from training records. However, if we need to know the quality and benefits of the training session, then questionnaires or interviews on participant satisfaction and/or measures of improved competence in practice are needed, but harder to collect.

Both qualitative and quantitative data need to be relevant, accurately collected and recorded, and valid indicators of the things they are used to measure. For example, we can quantitatively measure participants' improved understanding of the topics that the training project focused on. We can also get some insight into participants' perception of the usefulness and effectiveness of the training by asking them open questions – a qualitative method.

If cause and effect relationships are to be attributed (e.g. if an improvement in the mental health of carers is to be claimed as a result of a project to increase access to respite services), then care must be taken to eliminate other possible reasons for the improvement (e.g. the carer's pension was increased at the same time). For more information on this and other methods questions, please see Readings and Resources at the end of this chapter.

External or internal evaluation

Project evaluation can be carried out by the project team themselves – 'insider evaluation' – and/or by contracted evaluation consultants – 'outsider evaluation'. Our interviews suggest that consultants are commonly engaged when projects are to be evaluated. The decision depends on whether the organisation has the required expertise and any requirements specified by funders.

> *Depending on the nature and the size and cost of the project, it may also have external project assurance. Having somebody else come in independently to do the health checks along with the progress of the project and that project completion.*
> *(Senior Manager, Health Network)*

For the people involved in internal evaluation, participation can assist in the process of finishing and moving on. Insider evaluation has the benefit of the participants' intimate knowledge and understanding of the project. It can encourage the development of critical reflection skills and assist in embedding these skills within the organisation. However, insider evaluation might be less rigorous because of the lack of evaluation expertise, or because of bias since participants are likely to dwell more on the positives. This can mean that the results of insider evaluation are viewed as being invalid or of less value than evaluation by outsiders.

External evaluation usually relies on a group of skilled specialists in a particular method or approach (e.g. economic evaluation), particularly for complex or large projects. But some of the benefits of fresh eyes and objectivity can also be acquired when expert staff from other parts of the organisation, who are not part of the project team, are engaged as evaluators.

Evaluation in practice: challenges and learning

Early preparation for evaluation, and building in data collection, reflection and review during the project, will enable the organisation to assess the project's impact, or at least its outputs, based on clear criteria and some solid evidence. It can also enable significant learning about how and why the project succeeded (or not), with potential benefit to the organisation's innovation capability. However, developing a good evaluation plan and fully implementing it can be challenging, and resistance to undertaking a formal project evaluation occurs for several reasons.

For example, an opportunity to evaluate a project that has made an unwelcome change in the role of a group of staff could become their chance to take revenge – resistance does not necessarily stop at the project's closing party. On the other hand, looking transparently at things that went wrong or need improvement, even with the best of intentions, is very confronting and tends to be avoided.

The project team can also have reasons to resist. If a **project charter** has been approved with very broad and unclear aims and objectives, it will be difficult to determine evaluation questions and establish evaluation measures/KPIs. In this situation, instead of moving forward with an evaluation design, the team could seek to amend the charter first. Towards the end of projects, the pressure to focus on the next goal or task also contributes to neglect of evaluation work.

Evaluation usually relies on a combination of data that is routinely collected by the organisation and data generated by the project staff. Good project design will minimise the workload required for correct and timely recording and collection of data – if it is too onerous, it is less likely to be done well.

Although evaluation frameworks are sometimes provided by governments or other funders to guide evaluation design, there is no one-size-fits-all approach. Even a well-designed evaluation strategy may bring difficult challenges for project staff, especially when there is inadequate training and preparation for completing evaluation tasks.

Some challenges are specific to the health and community service sectors, including the use of interventions intended to address complex social and health problems. Both understanding and demonstrating cause and effect between a service and the impact on patients or participants can be particularly difficult (Pawson & Tilley, 1997). Demonstrating the impact of illness prevention projects is sometimes even harder, and it may be necessary to use indirect or intermediate benefits as indicators. Sometimes, evaluation can only provide good-quality information rather than ready-made answers to inform decision-making (Larsen et al., 2005).

The engagement of many diverse stakeholders in health and community services projects can also bring challenges for project evaluation. Even if stakeholders demonstrated high levels of commitment to the project, they may become distracted by competing priorities, making it hard to secure their participation in evaluation activities.

There is no doubt that it is important to learn from project processes and outcomes, and evaluation provides a way to crystallise the learning and formulate desired changes in approach or method. Otherwise, the short-term nature of projects provides the perfect setting for reinventing the wheel (wasting energy and time) and repeating errors (reducing the chances of success). When the project has a direct impact on patient or client care, monitoring and review are essential to assess the impact and ensure there are no adverse effects on standards or access for the client population.

Summary

- Evaluation is a way of understanding whether a project has done what it planned to do, whether it produced the intended benefits, and why or why not.
- Evaluation is one of the tools to generate knowledge and evidence to guide the sector in better services, programs and project design.
- Process evaluation, impact evaluation and outcome evaluation are three conceptual categories for formal evaluations aimed at answering different questions and developing a better understanding of both the conduct and the achievements of the project.
- Evaluation planning is best approached in a logical, step-by-step way during the project planning phase. One way is the structured seven-step approach.
- Benefits realisation management, economic evaluation and post-implementation review are focused outcome evaluation methods used to quantify project benefits.
- Capturing lessons learned is a valuable approach to identifying insights and experiences gained throughout the project life cycle that can then inform the project team and future project endeavours.

Readings and resources
On benefits realisation

PRINCE@ wiki benefits realisation approach: https://prince2.wiki/management-products/benefits-management-approach/

Benefit realisation management framework: https://www.nsw.gov.au/departments-and-agencies/customer-service/publications-and-reports/benefits-realisation-management-framework

Online library of quality, service improvement and redesign tools: benefits realisation: https://www.england.nhs.uk/wp-content/uploads/2021/12/qsir-benefits-realisation.pdf.

On lessons learned

7 key steps in lessons learned in project management: https://activecollab.com/blog/project-management/lessons-learned, accessed 8 January 2024

Lessons learned log: https://projecttemplates.guru/templates/lessons-learned-log/

State Emergency Service, Tasmania, 2024, P5. The OILL Process and WebEOC: https://www.ses.tas.gov.au/emergency-management-2/tasemt/lessons-management/p5/

What is a lessons learned template? Guide with examples: https://monday.com/blog/project-management/lessons-learned-template/

On post-implementation review

What are post-incident reviews? https://support.atlassian.com/jira-service-management-cloud/docs/what-are-post-incident-reviews/

Mindtools.com, post-implementation reviews: https://www.mindtools.com/a192l7e/post-implementation-reviews

Post-implementation reviews making sure that what you delivered actually works: https://www.mindtools.com/a192l7e/post-implementation-reviews

What is post-implementation review in project management? https://www.projectmanager.com/blog/post-implementation-review

On economic evaluation

Mosadeghrad, A. M., Jaafaripooyan, E., & Zamandi, M. (2022). Economic evaluation of health interventions: A critical review. *Iranian Journal of Public Health*, *51*(10), 2159–2170. https://doi.org/10.18502/ijph.v51i10.10975

Turner, H. C., Archer, R. A., Downey, L. E., Isaranuwatchai, W., Chalkidou, K., Jit, M., & Teerawattananon, Y. (2021). An introduction to the main types of economic evaluations used for informing priority setting and resource allocation in healthcare: Key features, uses, and limitations. *Frontiers in Public Health*, *9*, 722927. https://doi.org/10.3389/fpubh.2021.722927

On earned value management

Reichel, C. W. (2006). *Earned value management systems (EVMS): "You too can do earned value management"* [Conference paper]. PMI Global Congress 2006, Seattle, USA. https://www.pmi.org/learning/library/earned-value-management-systems-analysis-8026

Earned value management: https://en.wikipedia.org/wiki/Earned_value_management

References

ActiveCollab. (2023, September 13). *7 Key steps in lessons learned in project management*. Retrieved January 08, 2024 from https://activecollab.com/blog/project-management/lessons-learned

Alami, H., Gagnon, M. P., & Fortin, J. P. (2019). Some multidimensional unintended consequences of telehealth utilization: A multi-project evaluation synthesis. *Internal Journal Health Policy Management*, *8*(6), 337–352. https://doi.org/10.15171/ijhpm.2019.12

Alanazi, S., Anbar, M., Ebad, S. A., Karuppayah, S., & Al-Ani, H. A. (2020). Theory-based model and prediction analysis of information security compliance behavior in the Saudi healthcare sector. *Symmetry*, *12*(9), 1544. https://doi.org/10.3390/sym12091544

Askedal, K., Flak, L. S., Solli-Sæther, H., & Straub, D. W. (2017, September 4–7). *Organizational learning to leverage benefits realization management; evidence from a municipal eHealth effort* [Conference paper]. 16th IFIP WG 8.5 International Conference on Electronic Government, St. Petersburg, Russia. https://doi.org/10.1007/978-3-319-64677-0_12

Atlassian. (n.d.). *What are post-incident reviews?* Retrieved January 08, 2024 from https://support.atlassian.com/jira-service-management-cloud/docs/what-are-post-incident-reviews/

Axelos. (2017). *Managing successful projects with PRINCE2* (7 ed.). The Stationery Office.

Carter, R., & Harris, A. (1999). Evaluation of health services. In G. Mooney & R. Scotton (Eds.), *Economics and Australian health policy* (pp. 154–171). Routledge.

Chen, H. T. (1990). *Theory-driven evaluations*. Sage.

Drummond, M. F., Sculpher, M. J., Claxton, K., Stoddart, G. L., & Torrance, G. W. (2015). *Methods for the economic evaluation of health care programmes* (4 ed.). Oxford University Press.

Eby, K. (2021, May 06). Guide to lessons learned in project management. *Smartsheet*. Retrieved January 08, 2024 from www.smartsheet.com/content/lessons-learned

Gray, A. M., & Wilkinson, T. (2016). Economic evaluation of healthcare interventions: Old and new directions. *Oxford Review of Economics Policy*, *32*(1), 102–121. https://doi.org/10.1093/oxrep/grv020

Hawe, P., Degeling, D., & Hall, J. (1990). *Evaluating health promotion: A health worker's guide*. MacLennan & Petty.

Landau, P. (2022, May 16). *Using earned value management to measure project performance*. Retrieved January 19, 2024 from www.projectmanager.com/blog/using-earned-value-management-to-measure-project-performance

Larsen, L., Cummins, J., Brown, H., Ajmal, T., Beers, H., & Lee, J. (2005). *Learning from evaluation: Summary of reports of evaluation of leadership initiatives*. Office of Public Management and the NHS Leadership Centre.

Mind Tools. (n.d.). *Post-implementation reviews*. www.mindtools.com/a192l7e/post-implementation-reviews

NHS England and NHS Improvement. (2021). *Online library of quality, service improvement and redesign tools: Benefits realisation*, 2021 p. 3. Retrieved March 25, 2024 from www.england.nhs.uk/wp-content/uploads/2021/12/qsir-benefits-realisation.pdf

NSW Government. (2024). *Benefit realisation management framework*. Retrieved March 25, 2024 from www.nsw.gov.au/departments-and-agencies/customer-service/publications-and-reports/benefits-realisation-management-framework

OECD. (n.d.). *Outline of principles of impact evaluation*. Retrieved March 25, 2024 from www.oecd.org/dac/evaluation/dcdndep/37671602.pdf

Pawson, R., & Tilley, N. (1997). *Realistic evaluation*. Sage.

PRINCE2 Wiki. (n.d.). *Benefits management approach*. Retrieved March 25, 2024 from https://prince2.wiki/management-products/benefits-management-approach/

Project Management Institute. (2021). *A guide to the Project Management Body of Knowledge (PMBOK guide) and the standard for project management* (7 ed.). Newton Square.

Rowe, S. F., & Sikes, S. (2006). *Lessons learned: Sharing the knowledge.* PMI® Global Congress 2006 – EMEA, Madrid, Spain. www.pmi.org/learning/library/lessons-learned-sharing-knowledge-8189

Saunders, R. P., Evans, M. H., & Joshi, P. (2005). Developing a process-evaluation plan for assessing health promotion program implementation: A how-to guide. *Health Promotion Practice, 6*(2), 134–147. https://doi.org/10.1177/1524839904273387

South Australian Community Health Research Unit (SACHRU). (2008). Planning and evaluation wizard. *Flinders University, Adelaide.* www.flinders.edu.au/content/dam/documents/research/southgate-institute/planning-evaluation-wizard/developing-case-key-questions.pdf

State Emergency Services. (n.d.). The OILL process and WebEOC. *Tasmania, Australia.* Retrieved January 08, 2024 from www.ses.tas.gov.au/emergency-management-2/tasemt/lessons-management/p5/

Vas, V., Gyambibi, L., Eftychiou, L., Al-Omari, H., Glass, J., Smith, M., & Matthew, D. (2023). Identifying value in healthcare transformation initiatives: An evaluation of an approach to benefits realisation. *BMJ Open Quality, 12*(4), e002349. https://doi.org/10.1136/bmjoq-2023-002349

Wadsworth, Y. (2010). *Building in research and evaluation: Human inquiry for living systems.* Routledge.

Westland, J. (2018, January 4). What is post-implementation review in project management? *Project Manager.* Retrieved March 01, 2024 from www.projectmanager.com/blog/post-implementation-review

Planning tools

Work program, scheduling and budgeting

In this chapter, we explain some key project planning tools for estimating the tasks, time, resource and budget requirements of the project – that is, for estimating the core of the work program. For small projects, this may be done relatively easily. However, for large or complex projects the use of

DOI: 10.4324/9781003431701-8

estimation tools, as well as consulting with experts and brainstorming with colleagues and/or project team members, may be essential.

The tools enable teams to break **deliverables** and strategies down into easily manageable tasks which can be implemented in sequence or in parallel, and to answer the 'when, who, how and how much?' questions that can seem too hard. The detailed understanding teams develop by using these tools also provides the basis for monitoring and measuring the progress and achievements of the project.

Work breakdown structure (WBS): tasks, sequencing and timing

> Running a project without a work breakdown structure is like going to a strange land without a road map.
>
> *(Joseph Phillips, 2022 cited in Keith K (n.d.))*

Project strategies cannot be implemented unless there is a clear action plan, with the necessary staff, resources and equipment at hand. First, the activities and tasks of a project need to be defined and broken down into manageable chunks. The simplest way to break down project activities/tasks into manageable chunks is to start with the goals, strategies and deliverables identified in the **project charter**. It is then possible to identify the activities/tasks that need to be done, break them down using subheadings and expand on them in a list format. This technique for breaking down and planning project tasks is called **work breakdown structure** (WBS). A WBS provides the basis for developing a project schedule as it defines all the work that needs to be completed (and in what order).

The WBS is a powerful tool for expressing the **scope** of a project in a simple graphical format. The visualisation of the project in this form can help with understanding the project scope, tasks and schedules as a whole, and their alignment with the project goals. It can also enable the **project manager** and the team to identify important but previously overlooked aspects of the work program. Documenting the full requirements of the project in this transparent form also enables the team and others to see the relationships and dependencies between the tasks, more accurately estimate the time required for the project and specify any deadlines (or critical points). The identification of **milestones** and **tracking** of progress against them is then easier.

Kloppenborg (2009) defines WBS as 'a tool that the project team uses progressively to divide the work of a project into smaller and smaller pieces' (p. 142). Similarly, the **Project Management Book of Knowledge** (PMBOK; PMI, 2021) defines the WBS as being oriented to deliverables and deconstructing the work in a hierarchical manner.

There are many techniques and rules of thumb for developing the WBS. Some tasks may take a long time to complete but are simple and straightforward; some require specialised knowledge and skills; some need to be managed independently; and others require teamwork. Identifying and detailing the activities and tasks can be difficult, and the ideas will probably flow faster if it is done by the team or a working group rather than an individual.

Types and components of WBS

A WBS is a hierarchical structure starting with one 'box' at the top level which represents the whole project and usually three more levels underneath. The project is then divided into increasingly small components in the lower levels of boxes in the WBS diagram. It apportions the entire project into logical chunks of work, which are then sub-divided and arranged in the right order (Hill, 2009). Please note that the terminology and software for WBS are variable, and the terms we use in the description that follows may not always be used.

The structure of the WBS is tailored to the project. Conceptually, there are two basic approaches: deliverable-based, where Level 2 of the chart has a box for each deliverable; and phase-based, where Level 2 has a box for each **phase** of the project (e.g. initiation, planning, implementation and **close**). But in practice, a combination is often most practical. For example, in a WBS mostly structured by deliverables, a Level 2 box covering the activities and tasks of detailed planning might also be included. In both approaches Levels 3 and 4 are used for the necessary activities and tasks.

Figures 7.1 and 7.2 illustrate the conceptual basis of the two approaches.

Regardless of the headings used in Level 2, the deliverables will be important in the WBS and need to be right. The statement of deliverables from the **project plan** or charter provides the basis but may need a little refinement for the purposes of the WBS as the project team gets closer to the question of what the project will really need to deliver. For some projects, a combination of the deliverables and the objectives from the project charter might be the best basis for completing Level 2 of the WBS.

Each Level 2 box will require a number of activities to be conducted, so activity is the next level down in the WBS. An activity is basically a manageable collection of related tasks that contribute to a single deliverable (Hill, 2009). Each activity in turn will require the completion of a set of tasks which form the fourth level.

The activities and related tasks that are required to complete a deliverable in a WBS are sometimes called a **work package**. A work package should be detailed enough to facilitate further planning, such as scheduling tasks and determining resources, and to assist the project manager to maintain **control** of time and resource use during implementation. However, these categories (tasks and activities) are highly variable depending on the scope and needs of the project (a small project's activity may be a larger project's

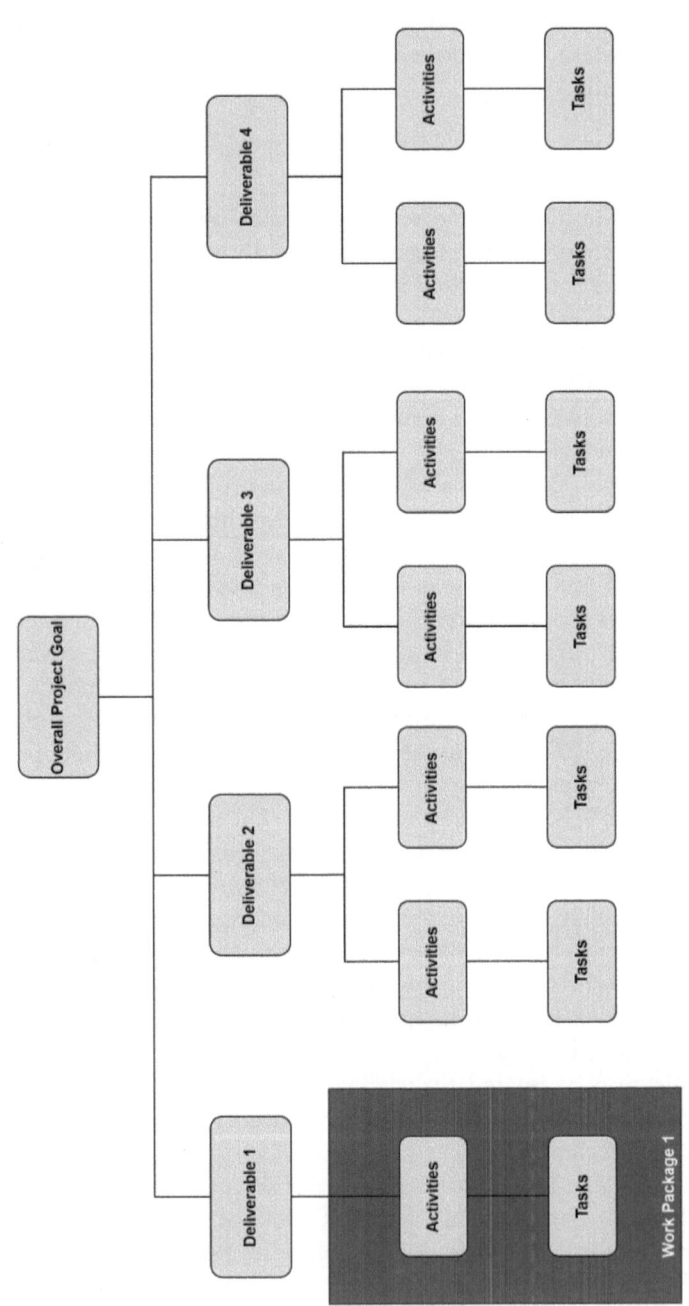

Figure 7.1 Deliverable-based WBS

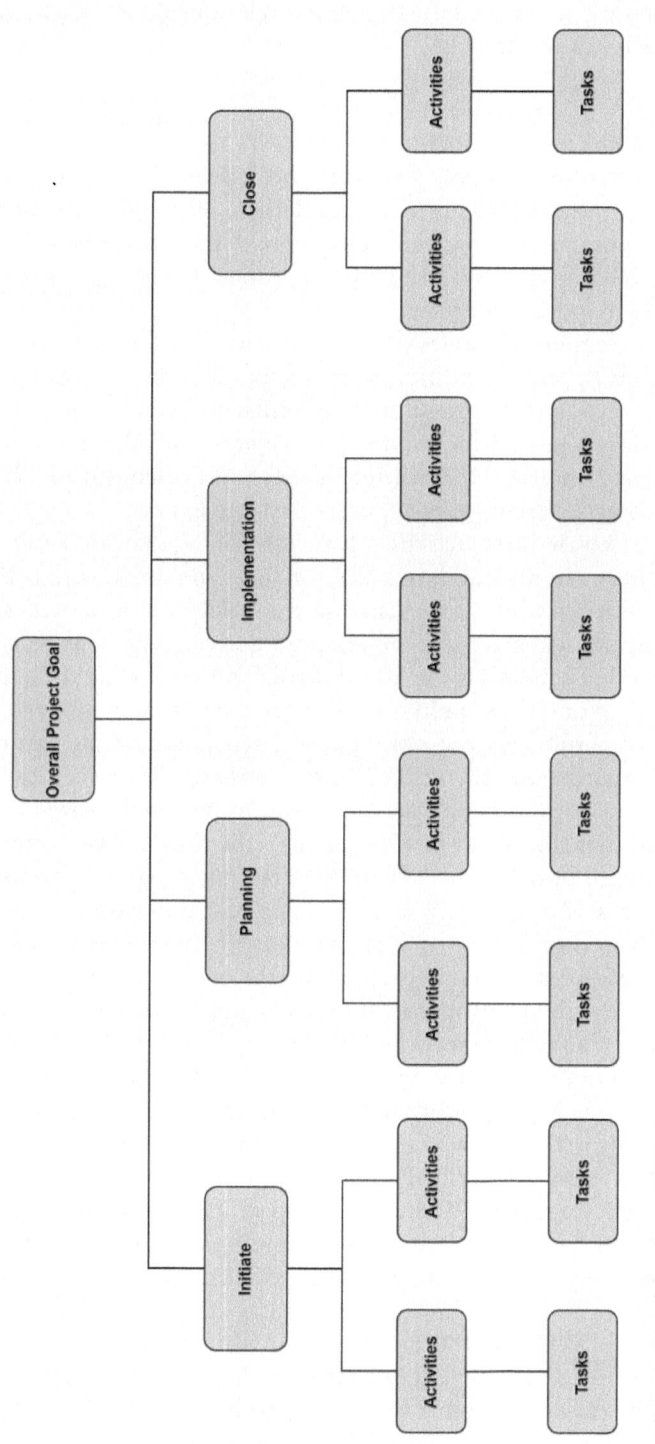

Figure 7.2 Phase-based WBS

task), and in some ways are defined by their relationship to one another and to the higher levels of the WBS.

Constructing a WBS

The common steps are logical: start with the deliverables (or phases), break each one into meaningful activities, and then into tasks, in descending order. It is important that each element in the WBS is described clearly, but briefly. The WBS is usually presented in a graphic format and is sometimes called a mind map for the project.

There are several other styles of WBS presentation. Level 2 can be structured according to responsibilities, bringing together the activities for which individuals or groups (often with specific skills) are likely to be responsible. Display by stages is used for multistage projects, and the deliverables for each **stage** are grouped. These different ways of presenting the WBS will suit the needs of different projects, users and audiences.

Normally, two or three activities for each deliverable are enough (Hill, 2009), but there are no standard rules for this. The guide is that the WBS enables the user to adequately visualise the sequence of activities. It can be hard to know when to stop dividing an activity into smaller elements (tasks). One rule of thumb is the 80-hour rule (Kliem et al., 1997): no single activity or group of tasks should require more than 80 hours (or two weeks) of work. But this rule may not always apply, depending on the nature of the project, its activities, and the skill and experience of the project team.

Another way of thinking about this question is to make sure that activities are set so that they don't last longer than the time between meetings of the project board or committee. This way, regular progress reports will be clear, tracking and monitoring will be easier, and the team will have some achievements to report. So, the best rule is the common sense rule – be as detailed as makes sense for the project and the team.

We have described above the top-down approach to constructing a WBS, but it can also be approached bottom-up – that is, by identifying all the work elements first and then grouping them to form the higher levels (Hill, 2009). In reality, the process often involves a mix of the two – that is, when specifying activities and tasks, any omissions or errors in the way the deliverables have been described come to light and can be corrected.

The construction of a WBS and the specification of individual work packages allows time, cost, schedule and even associated risks to be estimated individually, and also enables responsibilities to be allocated to project team members. Figure 7.3 outlines the activities and tasks of two work packages in the WBS for the project outlined in Chapter 4 that aims to reduce the incidence and severity of falls among elders at a high care nursing home. The residents' fitness and strength are one critical factor, so providing strength training was one of the deliverables of the project.

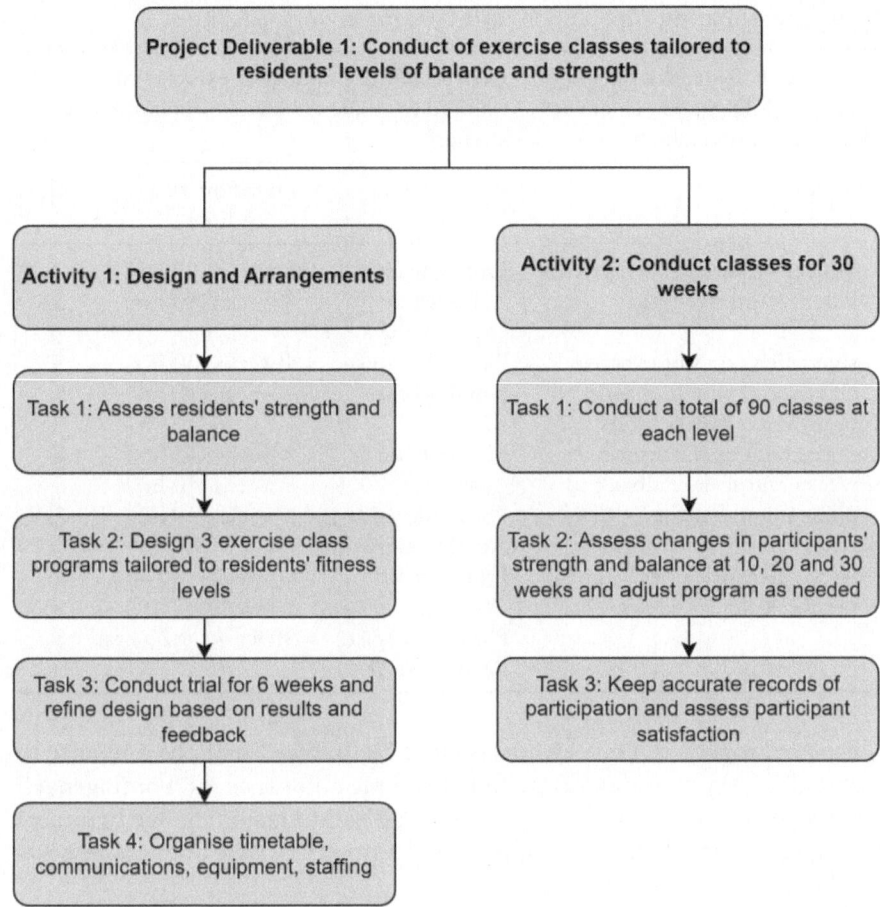

Figure 7.3 Work package example

Estimating time, and using scheduling tools

Managing time is important for projects, and estimating the time required for tasks and activities is a reliable way to establish a schedule and milestones against which progress can be assessed (PMI, 2021). The development of the WBS gives a starting point for performing the next difficult task of project planning: estimating the time required to complete each task and the whole project. This is best done bottom-up – that is, by first estimating the time required for each task and work package (Kloppenborg, 2009). In principle, the summation of the time required for the completion of all work packages gives the estimate of time required for the completion of the project. However, some work packages or tasks can be undertaken in parallel, so the whole may be less than the sum of the parts. It is also important to remember that the three factors – time, cost and quality – must be

Table 7.1 Estimating time and labour cost for a work package

Project goal: To reduce falls and severity of falls among elders at a high care nursing home	Deliverable 1: Conduct of exercise classes tailored to residents' levels of balance and strength		
Activities	*Resources*	*Duration and work time*	*Cost*
Conduct assessment on residents' balance and strength	Project team leader One nursing staff	8 weeks (60 hrs) 8 weeks (80 hrs)	$ $
Design three types of exercise classes and activities tailored to different fitness levels	Physiotherapist Nursing staff	4 weeks (30 hrs) 4 weeks (10 hrs)	$ $
Conduct trial of classes for six weeks and seek feedback to guide improvement	Project team leader Physiotherapist Nursing staff	8 weeks (15 hrs) 8 weeks (40 hrs) 4 weeks (40 hrs)	$ $ $
Provide exercise classes 3 times per week for 30 weeks	Project team leader Physiotherapist Nursing staff	30 weeks (80 hrs) 30 weeks (780 hrs) 30 weeks (820 hrs)	$ $ $

considered together. Time estimates can't be finalised without reference to cost and quality considerations, and also some allowance (or '**contingency**') for risks – obstacles that may cause delay or lead to major change in project strategies. Table 7.1 shows an approach to estimating time and labour costs for the work package outlined above.

The challenges in estimating time requirements relate to four factors. First, some tasks may require specialised skills and expertise, which makes it hard for non-experts to estimate the complexity and therefore the time and cost required. Second, good estimation requires a substantial investment of time and energy, which may be exactly what has not been allowed for in the project planning phase. Third, differing expectations of quality requirements between senior management and project staff can complicate this task, as can a lack of support or involvement by management and key **stakeholders** in the planning process. Finally, financial constraints can mean that balancing the time, resource requirements and quality of the project is challenging, and it is in detailed estimation that the financial squeeze becomes more visible.

One of the common mistakes made during estimation is overestimating the productivity of project staff (Usman et al., 2018). If non-productive time is not taken into consideration during estimation, the timescale (and/ or budget) for the project won't be realistic. There will also inevitably be tasks that are necessary but not directly related to the building blocks in the WBS such as stakeholder consultation and engagement (an important activity for project success but probably not a deliverable). On the other hand, overestimating the time needed for the completion of the project is equally undesirable, and it is worth examining the time allowed for individual tasks to find and remove unnecessary padding.

In the case of small projects, some form of brainstorming with colleagues may be a good approach. For large-scale and complex projects, estimates can be tested by seeking second opinions – from finance staff and by talking to people who are not involved in the project but have had experience in similar projects. Estimates from similar projects can also be used as a guide.

Gantt charting and other methods

The **Gantt chart** is one of the oldest **project management** tools, and one of the most commonly used methods of presenting schedule information (and of charting actual progress). A Gantt chart plots activities (in rows) against the timeline (in columns), thus showing the relationships between them. Gantt charts can also show the resources required for a particular task or activity, as well as the relationships between the tasks, milestones and baselines; and can be used to track planned and actual progress (Project Manager, n.d.; Shweta & Watts, 2024). Figure 7.4 presents a simple Gantt chart for a quality improvement project in an aged care organisation that aimed to improve overall service quality for residents. It used **co-design** principles to create a model for the 'Great Client Experience', which was then used as the basis for improvements in clinical governance and quality assurance.

For a simple project, a Gantt chart may be produced using a simple table format but for more complex projects, software is needed and many are available online. Gantt charts are useful in both the planning and implementation phases of the project, because they are simple, easily understood and very effective for showing the status of a task or a group of tasks against the schedule. Their limitations include the fact that they can be difficult to update if there are lots of changes and can be hard to manage in more complex projects. As a senior manager explained, Gantt charts can be very useful for getting input from team members or experts:

> *Invariably someone will say 'Have you thought about including . . .', 'Oh, you need to include these particular interface checks, or these checks of downstream systems' . . . a good project manager also leverages off expertise within the team and the organisation.*
> *(Senior Manager, Health Network)*

The many other project management charting and scheduling techniques include **network diagrams**, the **critical path method** (CPM) (see next section)

Project Title:

Implementing clinical governance to achieve consistently good care and a positive employee experience

2023

No	Tasks	Jan	Feb	Mar	Apr	May	Jun	Jul	Aug	Sept	Oct	Nov	Dec
1	**Staff readiness and engagement**												
1.1	Assess residential staff and leadership team change readiness, obstacles to change, and care-quality status												
1.2	Review Board Quality Committee meeting reports to understand current care quality and how these reports guide decision-making.												
1.3	To seek manager and staff's input on defining the Great Client Experience (GCE)												
2	**Engage consumers in defining quality care**												
2.1	Gather consumers input into the Great Client Experience via a formal process												
3	**GCE model co-design**												
3.1	Meeting with Residential Operations Manager to at five different residential sites to identify core clinical governance components required to support the achievement of the Great Client Experience												
3.2	Design key implementation steps at each Residential Aged Care sites												
3.3	Develop an implementation pathway incorporating input from above steps												
3.4	Review and develop a reporting system that effectively monitors implementation progress and outcomes												
4	**GCE model implementation**												
4.1	Residential Operations Managers develop local plans based on the implementation pathway, and commence implementation												
4.2	The Quality and CG Team assist with implementation, monitor implementation progress and identify and address barriers to implementation.												
5	**Completing process and immediate outcome evaluation and 'Guide' development**												

Figure 7.4 Simple Gantt chart

and the program evaluation and review technique (PERT) which is used to estimate uncertainty around project activities by applying a weighted average of optimistic and pessimistic estimates to evaluate the time needed to complete an activity (Program Evaluation and Technique, 2024). While CPM is used regularly, network and PERT methods are not as often used in health and community services, other than in some building and **information and communications technology (ICT)** projects, because there is often not the same focus on managing technical tasks and resources concurrently. Descriptions and tips on how to use them are included in many texts and available online.

Critical path method (CPM)

Developed in the 1950s, the **critical path method (CPM)** was designed to improve inefficient project scheduling that resulted in increased costs. Since then, CPM has become popular for planning projects and prioritising tasks, for some of the same reasons as WBS. But CPM is focused on generating a clear understanding of the minimum time to complete a whole project, starting with developing an understanding of the interdependencies of tasks (which ones can't start until another is finished; which can overlap?) along with estimating the time each needs.

The next step is to focus on the group of tasks that are interdependent and must happen in a certain sequence – that group is called the **critical path**, while the tasks inside it are called critical activities. A network diagram can then be created, as shown in Figure 7.5 – a chart depicting each task and the time it requires (in days in this case) with arrows to depict dependencies. Finally, the end-to-end duration of the critical activities can be calculated to determine the minimum time the whole project will require (Atin & Lubis, 2019, p. 1). Any delay affecting critical activities will result in extending the total project duration.

The aim is to develop a better understanding of the project's flexibility (or lack of it) and time efficiency, and it is often used in conjunction with WBS. CPM is useful because it helps project planners and managers to identify priority tasks that if delayed will impact the whole project; and to anticipate and avoid bottlenecks. It also enables timeline 'slack' (also known as float) to be identified. This is the number of days a task can be delayed before it affects the project's entire timeline (Asana, 2024; Ba'Its et al., 2020; Donato, 2023).

The calculation of a project's critical path can be done manually (with the use of a template or algorithm if needed) or more commonly by using project management or scheduling software.

Scheduling projects in stages

Larger and more complex projects are often better handled (and scheduled) in stages (e.g. building and ICT system implementation projects). This is helpful

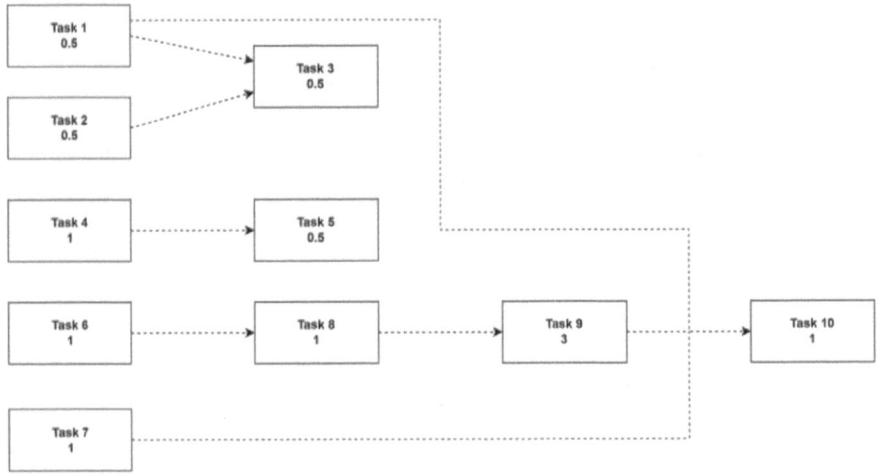

Figure 7.5 A simple network diagram

Source: Donato (2023).

when there are major unknowns which will only be clarified as the project progresses, or when there is major risk that needs to be mitigated. Projects that aim to design and test new models of care may be organised in stages because the testing process can't be determined until the design is known. Similarly, in research projects, the results of earlier stages of the study will often shape the later stages. Structuring projects in stages – where design/ redesign in the light of learnings from the previous stage is a planned strategy – can be an essential aid to maintaining quality, momentum and control.

Some of the breaks between stages may be designated 'go/no go' points, or gateways, where there is an opportunity to assess whether the project should continue or be substantially revised or abandoned. An example of a go/no go point might be the moment of **sign-off** following acceptance testing of software, or following a pilot go-live, to assess if further implementation can proceed. Staging of this kind can also assist in creating a more comfortable framework for the consideration of major changes.

The establishment of planned times and methods for deciding whether particular designs work, and whether the benefits and costs are in the right balance, can make it easier for decision makers to agree to proceed with projects, even though they have misgivings about some of the possibilities or find uncertainty difficult to manage. The inclusion of **process evaluation** in the project plan can be an essential aid in making 'go/no go' decisions or passing gateway points.

In order to design a project in stages, key decision points and decision makers need to be identified, along with specifying the criteria and information they will use. Important meetings need to be timed accordingly (while allowing for some slippage). In effect, each stage needs its own schedule. While this may sound daunting, it can actually make the task easier, because the planning is broken down into manageable pieces, and detailed planning for later stages can be deferred.

Budgeting

All projects require resources. At the project initiation stage, a rough estimate will have been included in the project concept brief, or a full **business case** may have been developed (see Chapter 4) but in the planning phase, a detailed comprehensive budget is needed. A budget is a financial document that projects income and expenses. It is a written forecast or plan of what managers expect to happen in the future, quantified in terms of dollar inflows (revenue) and dollar outflows (expenses). Organisations use budgets as planning tools to allocate resources and to enable financial control of their overall operations. For a project, the budget specifies all costs involved in completing the project and the funding or revenue required to cover the costs (when revenue and costs are equal, this is a 'balanced budget').

A well-planned budget provides the basis for project cost control and helps the project manager to effectively monitor actual costs against the approved budget and predict any potential savings or shortfalls. It provides important information to guide overall project monitoring and control and indicates where action is required (to reduce overall expenses or change practice and systems to reduce supply costs).

It is important to get the budget right – too small and there will be cost overruns that could derail the project; too large and approval is less likely. For externally funded projects, the granting body is unlikely to be convinced by a budget that seems either too large or too small – understanding how their money is to be used is part of their core business, so they usually have a reasonable idea of what things cost. A good budget is built on good estimation of tasks, time and costs, and on consideration of uncertainties and risks; and it makes adequate funds available for achievement of the project goals.

It is also important to check the project budget with finance staff in the organisation and, where relevant, others with expert knowledge. Finance staff will be familiar not only with what things cost but also with general and organisational policies that determine what costs are allowable and how they should be allocated.

Budget development

The ease of developing a budget depends on having a clear project plan backed up with a WBS or equivalent. A thorough analysis of the scope of work and activities, tasks and timelines along with labour and other needed resources is the first step for budget development. The literature on project budget development and control (Hill, 2009; Kloppenborg, 2009; PMI, 2021; Roberts, 2011) generally recommends that the next steps should be:

- assigning realistic monetary values to the required resources, based on estimates for each item – thus forming a preliminary budget
- identifying risk factors and allowing for their potential impact on the budget – the risk management plan provides a good basis for calculating a contingency allowance for risk.
- presenting and discussing the preliminary budget with senior management (and perhaps financial sponsors if relevant) to test that the thinking and calculations are in line with expectations, and to explore the reasons for any differences and then resolve them.

During this step, reviewing the planned and actual expenditure of previous projects can also provide information to guide more accurate estimation. Comparison of budget and actuals will highlight underestimation and may indicate costs that were overlooked.

After estimating the requirements of each major activity in the project plan, it is a good idea to stand back and consider whether any cost items have been overlooked before finalising a total budget estimate. For example, have the time and costs of any **gateway reviews** between activities been included? Does this estimated budget seem comparable with those of other projects of similar size and complexity?

In the implementation phase, the budget becomes the primary document for monitoring and controlling costs. The budget format depends largely on the project itself and on organisational systems and financial management practice, but a single spreadsheet can be used to list all project revenue and expenditure items. Expenditure items can be grouped according to type, for example labour (staff) or non-labour (equipment/materials) items and fixed versus variable expenses. Budgets are normally 'cashflowed' (that is, costs are allocated over the weeks or months of the project) so that expenditure can be monitored against time and linked to progress.

Identifying and estimating costs

Cost estimation is an unavoidable part of developing a budget. Some actual costs of required resources can be hard to confirm, but project managers may be able to get valuable help from the organisation's finance staff. Those who assist with estimating will need good instructions about what to include, and the expected size or volume of the resource (e.g. programming time to capture the data from a new care process; duration of a group health education program; number of participants for a community activity; or how many test kits are needed for a new approach to monitoring a chronic disease). However, budgeting is an exercise in uncertainty:

> *The challenges of trying to get precise quotes from vendors, and the lead time into these projects, they're going to want to re-quote by the time you go live anyway. . . . So, you know, sometimes indicative figures should be enough. And you've got to have the right culture to accept that.*
>
> *(Senior Manager, Health Network)*

For projects in health and community services, the following key types of resources are generally required, and their costs need to be estimated:

- All personnel (labour) required by the project including those who are directly involved in project implementation, who are managing and/ or advising the project. The personnel may be internal to the organisation, such as project team and technical support staff (whose labour costs should be included, even if only as an 'in-kind contribution'); and those external to the organisation whose services/expertise may be purchased e.g. legal advisers, consultants, statisticians, agency staff and so on. The organisation's financial policies will clarify the need to include labour on-costs (typically up to 25 per cent on top of base-rate salaries, to cover the costs of superannuation, workers compensation insurance, leave entitlements and any penalty rates).
- Equipment, services and materials that are needed for conducting the project including for setting up the project office, and all consumables.
- Specialised resources or products that need to be purchased as part of the deliverables (e.g. hardware and software needed to implement a new patient management system, or access to a gym to trial a physical activity program for people with a chronic condition).
- Overhead costs – while many resources that will be used by the project will not need to be met from the budget (e.g. office space, furniture and utilities), some easily forgotten overhead costs may need to be met. For example, a facility may need to be kept open outside normal business hours for the activities of a project, and security costs may need to be budgeted for.

Costs should not be 'guesstimates' but should be estimated as accurately as possible. Estimates are made based on data from the organisation's finance and payroll systems for the cost of personnel, together with prices from suppliers and quotations for any externally provided services or equipment.

If the project will last for more than one year, costs should be indexed for inflation or salary increases (finance staff can advise on formulae for doing this).

Detailed estimating is often one of the first tasks challenging a newly appointed project manager. Because it is sometimes difficult for one person to come up with a comprehensive list, team brainstorming and fact-checking can be the fastest way to develop one. If a working group was formed at the project initiation phase, this group can contribute. For capital projects, independent cost consultants are usually required.

Project managers in health and community services often report difficulty with estimating staffing requirements, timelines and other costs correctly. Sometimes the budgeting requirement is paid lip-service only for small internal projects, and those responsible simply incorporate the project costs in their ongoing operational budgets. When this works, it is simple and perhaps more comfortable, but when it doesn't – for example, by causing unexpected cost overruns – the consequences can be troublesome for the budget holders. It is a good idea to be clear about those costs that will be absorbed in operational budgets (with the agreement of the budget holder) and those that need to be included in the project budget.

Direct and indirect costs

Expenses or costs can be categorised as direct or indirect. **Direct costs** are incurred by and for the project – that is, they would not be incurred by the organisation otherwise. They may include the following:

- salaries, wages and other benefits (e.g. superannuation) for those working directly on the project, including the project leader, project officers and other personnel who contribute (perhaps on a part-time or sessional basis) to getting the project done
- communication costs, such as project-specific telephone charges, printing and postage (e.g. for a community mailout or phone survey)
- transport and travel costs incurred by project staff specifically for project activities (e.g. taxis, flights or special courier services used by the project)
- equipment and computer software or hardware used solely for the project (e.g. tablet devices hired for participant voting in community meetings)
- project staff training and professional development
- consumables used in project activities (e.g. refreshments supplied to focus groups)
- materials to be produced by the project such as training materials, promotional flyers, procedural manuals etc.

Indirect costs or overheads are incurred for a common or joint purpose and therefore cannot be readily attributed to a particular project. These costs may be necessary for the project but are shared with other activities within the organisation. Project indirect costs may include:

■ salaries, wages etc. for staff who don't work on the project, but who administer or otherwise support the project as part of their ongoing job, such as department manager, reception or ICT staff
■ general-purpose equipment, computers and software such as word processing programs
■ office space, meeting room and utility costs
■ general-purpose office supplies, internal courier services and general postage
■ routine printing, reproduction and photocopying, basic telephone charges
■ subscriptions, organisational memberships, practice books, and journal and magazine subscriptions used by the organisation
■ insurance, such as for public liability
■ financial management
■ supervision of project leader.

When developing a budget, all direct and indirect costs need to be included. In some circumstances expenses normally charged as indirect costs may be charged to the project as direct costs. For example, large complex projects that involve extensive data accumulation or surveying may need to employ an administration officer to support this work rather than using existing administrative staff – this would be a direct cost. Similarly, some overhead costs are routinely allocated to their end use, and if the project is included in this procedure (e.g. a large project may require a cost centre in its own right), these costs will be allocated as if they were direct.

Getting the budget right: not too little, not too much

Budgeting can be hard for many reasons, including that it may be a new role for project leaders/teams. The art of budgeting is to set the costs correctly, without either padding the budget through unrealistic assumptions (like zero delays in recruitment or allocation of staff) or, on the other hand, overlooking or underestimating significant cost items. Health and community service agencies face constant pressure to reduce costs without compromising service delivery, and project budgets are usually not immune from this pressure, so the principle of cost containment needs to be applied throughout the project planning process, particularly in relation to salary costs, which are often the biggest single item.

The golden rule of budgeting

The 'golden rule' for developing a good budget is to ensure that all cost items in the budget are allocable, allowable, reasonable and necessary, and are being treated consistently (Dobie, 2007; Martin, 2002).

- A cost is *allocable* to a particular project when it can be directly attributed to it – that is, the cost really belongs to the project. For example, a project leader purchases equipment to be used for work on a funded project. The equipment is allocable to the project as a direct cost. The project leader also purchases toner for her office printer, which is used for all of her unit's activities. This item is not directly attributable to any one project, is therefore not allocable and may not be charged as a direct cost to the project. Instead, costs of using the printer for project work can be allocated to the project on the basis of either an actual usage charge (e.g. using a project pass code for the printer) or a formula or rule of thumb (e.g. 20 per cent of the printing cost is allocated to the project).

- Only costs *allowable* by the organisation's policy or the rules of a grant, or accepted as common practice, can be included. For example, a project leader has a project officer working on the project. This is an *allowable* direct cost of the project. However, the project leader may consider discussing the project with the project officer over dinner. If meal expenses are not allowed by the organisation's policy, this is not an allowable cost and may not be built into the project budget.

- A cost must be *reasonable* and *necessary* for the performance of the project. For example, a project leader purchases lab supplies to be used for the project. The supplies are reasonable and necessary for the project and may be charged to the project as direct costs. At the same time, the project leader considers purchasing a car, as a lot of local travelling will be required during the project. This is not reasonable or necessary in this case, as it is more appropriate to hire a car or reimburse staff for use of their own vehicles or use public transport.

- Costs incurred for the same purpose in like circumstances within the organisation must be *treated consistently* as either direct or indirect costs. That is, if the organisation generally treats a particular type of cost as direct (and therefore allocable), the same cost can't be treated as indirect anywhere within the organisation. The reason for this rule is to avoid incorrect or double charging. Similarly, current practice should be used as the guide when deciding how to name and categorise each budget item, for consistency in accounting treatment. That is, if lab supplies (for example) are to be used in the project, they should be categorised in the same way as they would be in normal use.

Sources of funding and other resources

In health and community services, the resources needed for the project may be acquired from four major sources:

1. External funding (from government or non-government funders).
2. Internal allocation of funds from operating budgets or other revenue sources including donations and sponsorships.
3. 'In-kind' funding (resources but not cash). This can be either internal (e.g. staff time, office space or administrative support) or external (e.g. access to meeting rooms in the local hospital for a medication management workshop being run by the community health service).
4. Partnering with other organisations in collaborative projects. As the need to work across health and care programs grows, collaborative projects are also more common and important. Funding bodies and policy initiatives often reward collaboration and partnership arrangements, in all fields, including research and teaching. Collaboration routinely involves both cash and in-kind contributions.

Each funding source brings obligations and expectations, from formal contract obligations to expectations for acknowledgement and appreciation (e.g. if the organisation's volunteer or fundraising group funds the project).

There may be resources that are readily accessible to the project without cost or obligation. For example, in the case of a project aimed at improving medication management skills for people with high blood pressure, brochures may be freely available to the project from the local health department. These contributions should be included in the detailed budget, even when the dollar value is zero, in the 'in-kind' category. This practice ensures that the real resource requirements of the project are reflected in the budget, and also makes it clear to funders, stakeholders and sponsors that the project has attracted more resources than the ones they are being asked to fund or support.

Constructing a detailed budget

A budget usually includes five categories in the expense section as detailed in Table 7.2. However, the grouping of budget items can be different between organisations depending on their accounting practice.

Finance staff can be very helpful with getting the categories and grouping right. They are also more likely to support the project manager with budget problems during the project if they understand the budgeting decisions and if the budget has been correctly structured and documented. If a WBS has been prepared, the details of work packages provide the basis for writing a detailed budget. The activities and tasks are already specified, and it is then more straightforward to identify the resources required and estimate their costs.

For calculating the staffing budget, it is a matter of deciding the payment level and the amount of time for each role that is required. For example,

Table 7.2 Budget categories and items

Budget categories	Items
Labour costs (staffing)	■ Salaries ■ Consultancies ■ Agency costs ■ Oncosts: superannuation, recreation leave, sick leave, possibly workers compensation insurance, allowances etc.
Administrative costs	■ Staff supervision ■ Financial management ■ Administrative support
Operational costs	■ Stationery and postage ■ Meeting costs (venue hire, catering etc.) ■ Office space/rental ■ Travelling expenses ■ Telephone/fax/mobile/internet ■ Advertising and marketing costs ■ Printing and promotional materials ■ Staff training and development ■ Contractor costs (e.g. design of evaluation survey or evaluation contract)
Capital costs (major asset purchase)	■ Equipment and office furnishing ■ Purchase of ICT hardware and software
Other items	■ Necessary items specific to the project and not included above

if a nurse with expertise in high blood pressure education is needed for patient education in medication management, the first step is to find out what classification or salary level should be offered for this nurse specialist (based on education and experience requirements). The next steps will be to calculate how many days or hours of time are needed for all required tasks (e.g. preparation of workshop materials and data recording), and for how long (how many weeks or workshops).

Once all required resources for each work package have been listed, they can be entered into the budget template. A good budget template can also be a reminder of what may have been left out. Most organisations have their own budget templates and tools, and many funding bodies have a prescribed budget template as part of the application requirements. There are also many online budget templates that can provide a good starting point.

For a project where a WBS may not be justified, or may not yet have been completed, a good estimation of project costs can be prepared by listing all the essential tasks in the project Gantt chart, entering the resources required to complete them, and then calculating their costs. Table 7.3 is an example of a budget for a one-year falls prevention project in an aged care facility.

Table 7.3 Project budget example

Resource (itemised)	Funds sought from Dept. of Health (DoH)	In-kind donation from Aged Care
Staffing		
Project team leader 0.4 FTE (Health Service Manager Award Level 2 Year1)	$49,658	
Physiotherapist 0.5 FTE (Health Professionals and Support Services Award Level 3/PO3)	$41,500	
Nursing staff 0.5 FTE (Registered nurse – level 1 paypoint 3)	$46,002	
Administration support 2 hrs/w (SACS Vic Award Class II Year 2)	$2,980	
Total staff on-cost (23.5%)	$32,933	
Staff training and skills development		
Three days' training for project team leader	$1,500	
Half-day team-building training for project manager	$380	
Administrative costs		
Project team supervision from Director of Aged Care Facility (5 hrs/month, $89/hr including on-cost 23.5%)		$5,355
*Insurance and financial management (5% of total program costs)		$11,374
Operational costs		
Office rental ($85/w)		$4,420
Telephone/fax/mobile cost (2 mobile $60/m + $60/m landline)		$2,471
Stationery and other printing ($165/m)		$2,059
Recruitment costs (e.g. project staff and facilitators)	$2,904	
Capital costs		
Laptop computer with software	$2,530	
Two telephone sets	$605	
Evaluation costs		
**Internal evaluation cost (2% of total project cost)		$7,961
External evaluation consultant ($250/hr × 46 hrs)	$11,500	
Total cost	$192,492	$33,640
Total cost including 10% GST	$211,742	$37,004
Total funds being sought from DoH		$211,742
Total donation in-kind		$37,004
Total budget		$249,432

* Calculation of 5% insurance and financial management: 5% of total cost of annual expenses, including funding being sought and donation in-kind (excluding evaluation cost).
** Calculation of 2% internal evaluation cost: 2% of total cost of all expenses for the whole project (both years), including funding being sought and donation in-kind.

Budgeting for contingencies

When the budget is taking shape, it is helpful for the project manager and working group to make time to reflect on the uncertainties in the project itself that could affect the budget – these are called contingencies. The risk management plan (see Chapter 5), along with the budget document, provide the starting point. The source of funding for the project or organisational policies may also determine the level or percentage of contingency that can be built into the budget or business case.

To identify the need for a contingency budget, the following questions might be relevant:

- Does the budget include any identified contingency funds, or estimates that already allow for potential contingencies?
- Are there any special expectations by senior management or the funder that have cost implications?
- Is there any professional expertise that is critical to the project and may be hard to find? If so, what are the implications?
- Are there any expected difficulties in recruiting staff? Can any existing staff be allocated to the project?
- Have evaluation costs (based on the evaluation plan and funder requirements) been included?

Answers to the above questions may have different but significant effects on the project budget. For example, if difficulties in staff recruitment are expected or internal recruitment of staff is impossible, staff recruitment costs need to be included in the project budget. The impact of delay in staff recruitment on the project costs, and perhaps on its timing, should be factored in. Sometimes a potential project is just too complex to estimate with confidence – and perhaps too complex for the organisation to conduct. Scaling it down, or restricting the project to just a first stage, might be necessary.

In the next chapters we move to project management in action and discuss how project teams manage what happens when the plan meets reality.

Summary
- The work breakdown structure (WBS) is useful for estimating the time and resources required for the project. It enables sequencing of project tasks, and estimation of their duration.
- Estimation of time and costs is important to good project planning. However, estimation is never perfect for something that has never been done before or something that is large in scope and complex.
- Gantt charting and critical path method are commonly used to visualise the work of the project in relation to sequencing and time required. They assist to improve the quality of estimation.

- A budget is used to plan expenses and income for the project and provides project managers with the ability to measure actual results against plans and expectations.
- Budgets should be based on experience, a good understanding of the project and its tasks, and team effort. Budget development should be guided by the important features of costs – budget items should be allocable, allowable, reasonable and necessary, and be treated consistently.

Readings and resources
On WBS
22 work breakdown structure examples to download now: https://www.stakeholdermap.com/plan-project/example-work-breakdown-structures.html

What is a work breakdown structure? https://www.workbreakdownstructure.com/

On Gantt charts
What is a Gantt chart? https://www.projectmanager.com/guides/gantt-chart

What is a Gantt chart: The ultimate guide: https://www.forbes.com/advisor/business/software/what-is-a-gantt-chart/

On PERT
Program evaluation and technique: https://en.wikipedia.org/wiki/Program_evaluation_and_review_technique

On CPM and network diagram
Critical path method: How to use CPM for project management: https://asana.com/resources/critical-path-method

20 free critical path templates: https://templatelab.com/critical-path/

Critical path method: https://digital.ahrq.gov/health-it-tools-and-resources/evaluation-resources/workflow-assessment-health-it-toolkit/all-workflow-tools/critical-path-method

How to make a project network diagram (free tools and examples included): https://www.projectmanager.com/blog/network-diagrams-free-tools

References
Asana. (2024, February 28). *Critical path method: How to use CPM for project management*. Retrieved March 23, 2024 from https://asana.com/resources/critical-path-method

Atin, S., & Lubis, R. (2019). Implementation of critical path method in project planning and scheduling [Conference paper]. *IOP Conference Series: Materials Science and Engineering, 662*(2), 1–6. https://doi.org/10.1088/1757-899X/662/2/022031

Ba'Its, H. A., Puspita, I. A., & Bay, A. F. (2020). Combination of program evaluation and review technique (PERT) and critical path method (CPM) for project schedule development. *International Journal of Integrated Engineering, 12*(3), 68–75. https://doi.org/10.30880/ijie.2020.12.03.009

Dobie, C. (2007). *Handbook of project management: A complete guide for beginners to professionals.* Routledge.

Donato, H. (2023, January 08). *What is critical path in project management?* Retrieved January 13, 2024 from https://project-management.com/what-is-critical-path/

Hill, G. M. (2009). *The complete project management methodology and toolkit.* CRC Press.

Keith, K. (n.d.). 10 project manager quotes that ring true. *Cornerstone Dynamics.* Retrieved August 12, 2024 from https://www.cornerstonedynamics.com/10-project-manager-quotes-that-ring-true/

Kliem, R., Ludin, I., & Robertson, K. (1997). *Project management methodology: A practical guide for the next millenium.* CRC Press.

Kloppenborg, T. J. (2009). *Contemporary project management: Organize, plan, perform.* South-Western Cengage Learning.

Martin, V. (2002). *Managing projects in health and social care.* Routledge.

Phillips, J. (2022). *PMP project management professional all-in-one exam guide* (1 ed.). McGraw Hill. https://www.accessengineeringlibrary.com/content/book/9781260467475

Program Evaluation and Technique. (2024, March 20). In *Wikipedia.* https://en.wikipedia.org/wiki/Program_evaluation_and_review_technique

Project Management Institute. (2021). *A guide to the Project Management Body of Knowledge (Pilot study guide) and the standard for project management* (7 ed.). Newton Square.

Project Manager. (n.d.). *What is a gantt chart? (Examples & templates).* Retrieved January 13, 2024 from www.projectmanager.com/guides/gantt-chart

Roberts, P. (2011). *Effective project management.* Kogan Page.

Shweta, Bottorff, C., & Watts, R. (2024, February 02). *What is a gantt chart? The ultimate guide.* Retrieved March 13, 2024 from www.forbes.com/advisor/business/software/what-is-a-gantt-chart/

Usman, M., Britto, R., Damm, L.-O., & Börstler, J. (2018). Effort estimation in large-scale software development: An industrial case study. *Information and Software Technology, 99*(C), 21–40. https://doi.org/10.1016/j.infsof.2018.02.009

The implementation phase

Making it happen

DOI: 10.4324/9781003431701-9

The implementation **phase** is when plans come to life and strategies are implemented. Also called the execution or launch phase, it is when the project team actually do the work to produce the **deliverables**; and the **project manager** coordinates and directs project resources to meet the project goals (Watt et al., 2014). Implementation also involves monitoring progress and measuring performance to ensure the project remains within its expected timeline, **scope** and budget; and handling any problems or issues in a way that keeps the project running smoothly (Indeed, 2023).

Depending on the project's implementation strategy (see Chapter 4), the implementation phase is usually the longest and most intense phase, and it is where the project manager may experience both highs and lows. No matter how careful the planning, there is no such thing as a perfect **project plan** because circumstances change and unexpected things happen. The project manager's role, especially during implementation, can feel like being a juggler – having to manage the tasks, the team, the deliverables and the communication on a daily basis but also keep an eye on what's coming next and fix whatever goes wrong.

In this chapter we discuss getting started and executing the plan – establishing and managing the project team, leadership, problem-solving, effective **stakeholder** communication and change management – and the important tasks of **control** and monitoring (controlling scope, schedule and budget, managing risk and getting back in control when problems happen).

Getting started: assess the plan

Transition from the planning phase to the implementation phase may be subject to formal or informal **gateway review**, approvals or signoffs which may mean a lag between the end of planning and the beginning of implementation. In some cases, the **project charter** and plan are approved pending funding or budget approval. The project manager may be newly appointed to the project or the organisation and may not have been involved in the initiation or planning **phases**.

In any case, at the start of the implementation phase, it is a good idea to review the project plan, the **business case** and any associated documentation both for familiarisation and to check and update if needed.

> **Questions for project managers: assessing the plan**
>
> - Is the plan realistic?
> - Was the planning detailed enough? Are there any glaring omissions?
> - Have project activities commenced already?
> - Have the appropriate approvals been received to start the implementation phase?
> - Are there any aspects of the plan that are no longer feasible?
> - Do the assumptions, dependencies and constraints remain correct?
> - Has the business case changed and is it up to date?
> - Has the project governance been established?
> - Has the clock started on the project timeline?

If there are problems with the plan at the commencement of implementation, now is the time to address them – the sooner the better. For the project manager new to the project and/or the organisation or unit in which the project sits, the first step is to understand the project's history and context. Finding out the background to the project, how it developed and who was involved can assist later on if the project seems to hit brick walls, is being 'white-anted', or when something is happening that you just cannot put your finger on.

As the project is getting started, it's often a good idea to think about potential risks and sticking points that are likely to arise and how they could be resolved. This requires careful listening, honest thinking and informed logical analysis. It can be helpful to stand back from daily concerns and really analyse what's going on around the project and where the problems are likely to come from. One method is to imagine the story of how this project succeeds: what are the key mysteries that are solved and the turning points that will make the difference? This technique can be used to identify the negatives as well: if this project were to fail, what would the causes be and who would be the villains of the story? These techniques are a kind of rehearsal for managing and leading the project and can be used in preparation for important presentations or meetings as well.

Executing the plan: leadership, motivation and teamwork

Projects depend on relationships.

(Berkun, 2008)

Implementation of a project is about leading and motivating people, together with coordinating human and other resources to carry out the plan. Leadership, particularly for motivation and good teamwork (working together to a common purpose or shared goal), is essential for successful project outcomes.

Tips on project leadership

- Do not lose sight of the goal of the project – however strategies and work plans are implemented, they must be focused on achieving this goal.
- Timelines are important but circumstances can require some flexibility (not too much or you lose control of the project).
- Problems and potential problems must be identified and dealt with – they are unlikely to just go away and might get bigger and come back to bite you at the most inconvenient time.
- Attention to detail is essential – it can help you identify problems and keep your eye on emerging issues, so keep good notes and records.
- Keep your eye on the ball – work the project; it will not happen by itself.
- Walk your talk – make sure that you do what you say you will do and model good **project management** practice.
- Hone your communication skills – be a good listener and approachable; provide clear, easy-to-read written reports that are short and to the point.
- Use your facilitation skills, especially in meetings – make all meetings productive, or people will stop attending.
- Recognise the skills and work of others – give credit where credit is due, but also deal with non-performance.
- Take responsibility – beware of blaming others for problems.
- Encourage good working relationships – through good humour, a positive attitude and a 'we can do this' approach.
- Aim to be someone who creates and gives out good energy – rather than a black hole that sucks the energy out of others.

Establishing the project team

Recruiting a project team can be a challenging and fraught process, sometimes undertaken in a rush to commence the implementation phase, or sometimes decisions about who will be part of the team have been made during the initiation and planning phases. The recruitment process can be formal or informal and will depend partly on whether recruitment is internal, external or a mixture of both. If external, the formal recruitment process will include internal approvals, advertising, shortlisting, interviews, letters of offer and contract; or engaging with a contractor to provide specified services. The process may be more informal when organisational rules allow and leaders prefer.

Internal recruitment involves the secondment (or release) of staff to the project team. This may be a formal process of advertising project positions internally, then interviewing, followed by selection and appointment. Alternatively, people may be identified and approached by the **project sponsor** or manager – and some negotiation with their usual line manager will be needed. Internal recruitment can be a sensitive and emotionally charged process, with line managers sometimes perceiving that they are losing quality staff to the project with negative effects on their department. The availability of funding to support backfill, so that the staff member's normal work can continue, might also be a critical consideration. It is important to be flexible, communicate well and negotiate with managers regarding the terms of the secondment, lead times, commencement dates and duration, availability of backfill funding, dual reporting and how the process of transition at both ends of the project will work.

Tips for effective project team recruitment

- Clarify expectations about the recruitment processes required for the project from an organisational, human resources and industrial relations perspective.
- Clarify the requirements and attributes of the roles, including qualifications, skills, award classification, salary range and conditions.
- Develop position descriptions for each project team role and ensure that the sponsor or steering committee approves them.
- Use an open recruitment process (including advertising the project team positions and conducting interviews) if possible, both for getting the best people and for satisfying general staff expectations of fairness and opportunity. But circumstances or organisational culture might not support this.
- Involve the key stakeholders and clarify your authority in the decision-making regarding project team appointments.
- Communicate effectively and often with all the stakeholders, in particular the managers to whom the staff report.
- Be familiar with the policies and processes for effectively transitioning staff onto the project team, including employee contracts, credentialling, variation of employment forms, timesheets, rostering systems, budgeting and cost-centre management.

Managing project staff

Building a project team that works well together is a key part of project success. All the normal requirements of good people management and effective teamwork apply. Good management of a project team also requires effective responses to three important issues outlined below.

The problem of two bosses

Some team members may report only to the project manager (especially if they are full time on the project) or they may continue to be supervised by their normal line manager throughout. Openness between the two managers involved can help avoid a situation where the team member feels pulled in two directions. A clear delineation of the split in reporting relationships is essential. For example: Who approves leave? Who does performance appraisal? Who can make demands on the person's time and for what? How will the managers keep each other informed in a way that is fair to the staff member?

The challenge of rapid skills development

In many cases, team members may have only some of the skills the project needs. Although the project cannot wait for long-term skill development, all team members need to be confident in the specific methods and tools that will be used in this project. It is therefore usually a good idea to hold training workshops for the team to explain and finalise the project's chosen methods, systems, applications, tools, templates and reports, and to train team members in their use. Topics such as running effective meetings, process mapping techniques and interviewing skills could also be covered. Competence can improve rapidly when some training (and opportunity to ask questions) is provided; when data bases, tools and templates are used consistently across the team; and when team members are able to use the project manager and other leaders as models. Staff should be given the opportunity to identify their areas of interest and strength as well as those areas where they lack skills or confidence. Then either their roles can be structured accordingly, or skills training can be adapted.

The question of retention of a temporary team until their work is really done

Finally, towards the end of the project, there can be a tendency for team members (and maybe the manager) to focus on returning to their units or seeking other opportunities, rather than on finishing the project. It is a good idea to raise this issue at the beginning and work out strategies for meeting both the needs of the team members and the needs of the project, including identifying any opportunities for team members in ongoing support or business-as-usual roles arising from the project.

At the least, the manager and maybe one or two others could be contracted until well after the expected completion date to allow for slippage and for project closing and bedding-down activities. This will give them a period after the project is practically completed when they can focus on their next moves while completing project closure. Team members and the project manager could also negotiate agreements with the operational manager to cover problems with timing or any other aspect of return to the operational area and agree in advance on a process to be followed if these contingencies arise.

Early attention to these important issues, and establishing an environment of safety and clear expectations among the project team, will pay off in enhanced capacity to deliver results and weather storms as the project progresses.

Problem-solving

During the course of the project, it might become obvious that the project team has gaps in its skills and knowledge, or conflicts might emerge between team members or other groups and individuals. While problems like skill deficits can be serious, conflict can be one of the most challenging things that a manager has to deal with, inside or outside a project. Discussion with the project sponsor or human resource advisers can give useful insights and also ensure that the project manager has senior management support to actively address the problem.

It is important to keep an open mind in order to recognise problems as they begin to emerge in the project team. While there are many techniques and methods for dealing with conflict, basic problem-solving skills are particularly relevant.

Tips for problem-solving: use the process

- Accept that a problem exists and resolve to take action.
- Dispassionately gather the facts.
- Define the problem.
- Understand what is causing the problem.
- Engage the team in contributing to both understanding the problem and finding solutions.
- Agree to the solution.
- Plan the response and implement it.

Effective communication

Good communication makes a project successful.

(Carroll, 2023)

During implementation, the communication plan developed in the planning phase is put into action. If the plan was developed some time ago, it is a good idea to review it with any new stakeholders to ensure it meets their needs and then update the document with any needed changes to communication types, channels and frequency. The communication approach may need to be updated from time to time throughout this phase.

Communication within a team, across multiple teams, and with vendors and clients is a complex activity that requires constant attention. Poor communication can have a detrimental impact on the project, leading to misunderstanding of the project goals and objectives, conflicts among stakeholders and the project team, missed deadlines and lack of buy-in and commitment to the project. Carroll (2023) suggests the following tips for success in ongoing project communication.

Tips for effective communication

- When the topic is a priority, follow up on emails, documents, and messages with a phone call or in-person meeting.
- Use a variety of ways to communicate: one-on-ones, group discussions, texts, phone calls and online video meetings.
- Talk with individuals when there is an issue, don't wait for status meetings.
- Try to find the 'just right' amount of communication, and don't go into detail with people who don't need that. People won't listen as well if you overdo it. Listen to feedback and corridor chats, as well as giving information.
- When the project is underway, keep up regular project meetings to keep things moving. Set a meeting schedule that makes sense and stick to it.
- Take advantage of online meeting platforms and collaboration methods, not just with remote team members.
- Keep your focus on the goal and objectives. Help people not to get distracted with exciting or troubling developments.
- Be concise, transparent and clear always.
- Remember that communication is about building relationships. Get to know your team, stakeholders and important suppliers – with their different communication styles and priorities.
- Keep trying when people are unresponsive, especially with wary or hostile stakeholders. Follow them up, keep it professional and friendly, and make sure regular reporting gets to them.

Source: Adapted from Carroll (2023)

Communication is at the heart of stakeholder management. To get feedback from stakeholders, Abudi (2013) suggests checking in with them from time to time on whether communication about the project meets their needs by sending a brief email or survey that asks:

- What is working in how we communicate with you about the project?
- What is not working or not effective in our communications?
- Where can we improve our communications with you?

Other stakeholder monitoring tools such as **stakeholder analysis** updates or **lessons learned** reports can be used to collect and analyse data on stakeholder perceptions, opinions and attitudes as the project progresses.

Conducting effective meetings

Project meetings fulfil many important functions in most projects. They will be more effective if they are properly scheduled, have a well-structured agenda, and if brief minutes that specify required action and reporting are recorded. There will be different types of meetings with different participants – project team huddles, **steering committee** meetings, executive briefings, vendor meetings, stakeholder consultations – which will probably require different approaches to decision-making, structuring the agenda, facilitating discussion and reporting progress and outcomes. Meetings vary widely in their purpose (co-ordination or programming of work information updates, decisions, review), formality, format (virtual, phone conference, face-to-face) and setting (board room, office, corridor, walking, online) and all but the most informal of catch-ups can benefit from agreed objectives, a clear agenda and minutes.

Good meeting and facilitation skills can help to save time, diffuse conflict and make things happen. There are two underlying principles in facilitation. The first is the need to be efficient: people are busy and don't want to waste valuable time in unproductive meetings. Being clear about the purpose of each agenda item, and what the meeting needs to achieve to progress it, will help everyone kee`p on topic. The second is participation: people need to have their voices heard and feel that they are contributing if they are to have some ownership of the project and maintain their commitment.

Tips for effective meetings

- Always have an agenda, no matter how small and informal the meeting.
- Regularly review the meeting membership to ensure that the right people are there.
- Know the meeting timelines and stick to them: start on time (habitual latecomers will probably get the message), put time limits against agenda items and stick to them unless there is a very good reason not to.
- The chair or facilitator does not have to know the answer to every question – put difficult points back to the meeting or agree how they will be 'parked' and dealt with later.

- Keep things moving along; do not let participants ramble.
- Encourage some people to speak.
- Be prepared to shut others up – nicely!
- Keep on track; don't be taken off into irrelevant issues.
- Look for answers to difficult problems.
- Make sure every issue has an action, even if it is just 'defer to next meeting'.
- Make sure each action has an owner who is responsible for making it happen.
- Keep notes or minutes in whatever form works for the group, share them with all members and make sure they are properly retained and accessible.
- Revisit the minutes before the next meeting and deal with any matters arising.
- Keep a record of attendance.

Achieving sustainable change

Often the major implementation challenge the project team faces is achieving change through the project. Usually the whole purpose of a project is to bring in something new or to do something differently – that is, to innovate. Innovation is defined as the process of bringing into practice new ideas, methods, products, services, or solutions that have a significant positive impact and value. It involves transforming creative concepts into tangible outcomes that improve efficiency and **effectiveness** or address unmet needs (Jain, 2023). In health and community services, as in other spheres, innovation happens when a new process, technology or system is introduced, even if the agency is not the first in the world to undertake that particular change.

During the implementation phase, the change management strategies outlined in the project plan for identifying, quantifying and managing the organisational impact of the project will be enacted. These activities may include change impact statements, change readiness assessment, business process review, protocol development and policy review, as well as communication and training. As noted in Chapter 5, change is an ongoing process, and the project's change strategies will require monitoring and review throughout the implementation phase – are the strategies working? It may be that despite enacting all the planned change strategies a key stakeholder or group remains resistant, or an assessment of change readiness shows that the organisation is really not ready for the change to proceed.

Change fatigue is also commonly reported by staff in the sector due to constant, concurrent and often competing changes, and the magnitude of broader policy and social developments. Organisational change fatigue is a general sense of apathy or passive resignation towards organisational changes by individuals or teams (Change fatigue, 2024). It can threaten the success of change management efforts and the project itself. New strategies to counteract or avoid change fatigue may need to be considered by both the project and the organisation, such as prioritising one project (or change initiative) over others, providing backfill for staff to attend training, providing additional support during the **go-live** period, or quarantining staff to enable them to focus on only one change initiative at a time.

In the following section, we focus on projects that need to achieve sustainable change in some aspect of the existing work system, power structure, working relationships, roles or responsibilities of people and teams – that is, where the change will affect people and their work. A lot has been written about achieving change in organisations, and much of it applies to projects. We briefly review some of the major theories and approaches to change that are relevant to project management and the politics of change, and then address the ways people respond to change, particularly when there is resistance.

Participative approaches to implementing change

The organisational change theorists tell us that while directive processes can achieve change quickly, it is the more participative approaches to change that create a sense of ownership and involvement among the major players (Management Study Guide, n.d.). The main criticisms of participative change processes such as organisational development are the slow pace of change (which is usually achieved in small, incremental steps), failure to deal with the difficulties of participation, and lack of acknowledgement of issues of power.

Projects offer a middle path to achieving change, combining clear authorisation and support by management with well-structured participative approaches. That is, leaders make strategic decisions and set the parameters, and use project methods to engage affected staff in designing and implementing operational change accordingly. The project approach enables the setting of clear goals and scope, and ensures they are authorised before the project begins. That is, management accepts its responsibility to resolve the question of 'should we seriously try this?' up front, before the work commences. The project can then work with staff and other stakeholders so that the question of 'how can we really do this?' is settled using the insights of those who know how the work is actually done. While there are no guarantees, this method helps project teams and sponsors to get the best answers while also pre-empting or handling resistance from those who are affected, as well as to hold stakeholders to the project mandate.

Managing participation

While participatory approaches to change are useful, it is important to avoid 'death by process' – endless meetings, surveys, workshops and interim reports that waste time, cause the project to lose momentum and reduce good will. The challenge is to balance openness, transparency and consultation with maintaining momentum and sticking to the project's goals and scope.

There are two main levels to managing participation. One is the project's leadership structure, including the engagement of stakeholder representatives in committees etc. The second is broader participation by staff generally and by members of stakeholder groups. The key to success with these methods is structured participation, with well-designed processes that ask the right questions at the right stage and recognise that people want to have their say but are also busy. The givens – what is not negotiable, such as decisions already made by the executive or board, or the implications of government policy – should be explicit in order to set the boundaries within which there are areas of discretion.

Depending upon the project, stakeholder and context, different approaches to participation might be needed. For some difficult topics, the use of confidential one-to-one or small group discussions with project staff or trusted members of a stakeholder group has a place. Where it is useful to know the views of larger groups of affected staff (i.e. where their views will influence a decision), straw polls using computer-based 'voting' or its low-technology equivalents such as sticky notes or dots on wall posters can accurately capture the majority view efficiently, and avoid a discussion dominated by the loudest voices. Sometimes, engagement by the project sponsor or an independent expert can promote acceptance by a conflicted group.

The general principle is to use appropriate methods to gather meaningful results with a clear approach to analysing and using the outcomes. Most importantly, there needs to be a method of closing off the participation exercise and moving on.

The politics of change: managing the shadow side
Good change management helps, but those opposed to change also have strategies, and often some power or authority. Organisations too are constantly managing tensions – between providing a service and balancing a budget, between their espoused policy and their actual practice, between professions and managers, and between innovation and the comfort of traditional ways.

While some elements of the power structure (such as formal hierarchies, controls and resource allocation) are overt, much of the politics of the organisation, and of some projects, happens in what Egan (1994) originally called the 'shadow side'. According to Egan (1994, p. 41) the shadow side is:

> all the important activities and arrangements that do not get identified, discussed, and managed in decision-making forums that can make a difference. The shadow side deals with the covert, the undiscussed, the undiscussable and the unmentionable. It includes arrangements

not found in organizational manuals and company documents or on organizational charts.

The shadow side is outside ordinary managerial intervention and can affect productivity and the quality of working life, both positively and negatively. Negative elements can include:

- a culture that accepts poor performance or bad behaviour by favoured individuals
- decision-making processes that are covert and not documented
- manipulation of meeting agendas and minutes (matters not discussed at all, actions not completed, or decisions not minuted accurately).

The shadow side can also be positive, for example when informal networks are used to support positive changes, or when skilled staff work around dysfunctional procedures in the interests of efficiency. There will always be a shadow side, and organisations will always have politics. The question is not whether, but to what extent and in what directions (helpful or harmful) organisational politics operate.

Good leadership, a focus on important common goals, tolerance of difference and debate, and open communication will tend to minimise the space that the shadow side has to work in. In other words, bringing important issues into the open and dealing with them in a careful way will reduce the need for shadow-side activity. Projects can be an opportunity to shine the spotlight on forgotten cupboards and remote attics in the organisation, and to deal constructively with shadow-side issues (but judgement is needed to decide which doors to open when).

Project managers by and large do not have a strong or stable power base and learn to cultivate influence instead. The need for influence is made stronger by the fact that projects often exist outside ongoing structures, and so resources must be negotiated and bargained for. Lack of authority – for example, to manage performance of project team members – also limits power, and project managers may even be managing their peers or their superiors. They have less managerial control in this situation, and so interpersonal and influencing skills become very important.

This has many implications for project politics. The first is that project managers must understand and acknowledge the political nature of most organisations, especially the influence of key stakeholders. The second is that project managers must learn to cultivate appropriate political tactics.

One such tactic is to use the 'what's in it for me?' principle. For example, departmental or unit loyalties and interests are usually more immediate and more powerful for most people than commitment to organisation-wide concerns, especially in large organisations. It can therefore be helpful to analyse proposals and issues that arise in the project from the point of view of each of the departments or groups whose contribution, or acquiescence, is needed. When people respond to a proposal by asking 'what's in it for me?', they are offering the project manager an opportunity to explain why they should support the project (and perhaps also to explain how any potential negative impacts will be attended to).

Alternatively, power can be enhanced through tactics that level the playing field. In health and community services, knowledge and expertise are highly valued, and project leaders who hold or develop a superior knowledge base, and use it to add value for stakeholders, can enhance their power or influence and thus be more effective in negotiations (Pinto, 2000). External thought leaders can also help to challenge outdated assumptions and inspire interest in doing things differently.

In real life, the champions of change juggle opportunities, problems, the shadow side of the organisation and their upward management issues – and a combination of good luck, good ideas and good management gets them through.

Understanding and managing resistance

Whatever model or strategy for change management is used, the 'pointy end' of change management in projects is dealing with the response typically labelled resistance. When changes are proposed, the people who will be affected begin calculating gains and losses in relation to two basic questions: 'What's in it for me?' and 'Will it really happen?' There are some good reasons for the tendency to resist change. Those who are comfortable with the way things are will often see, perhaps correctly, that they have something to lose, including some of the power or influence they currently hold. And they will often have some power that they can use in order to resist.

On the other hand, those who stand to gain from a proposed change, either personally or because they support the goals of the change, are in a position of uncertainty. Their active support generally depends not only on whether they can see that there is something in it for them, but also on whether they believe it will really happen. Being engaged from the start is also important:

> *I still see examples where people or project teams go ahead and deliver whatever they want to deliver, and then when the time comes and the stakeholders who have to implement it say 'you know what this doesn't work for us'. It's like building a bridge from two sides and then they don't meet in the middle.*
>
> *(Senior Manager, Health Department)*

Resistance can occur anywhere. Individuals and groups with and without official power find ways to resist change, and senior managers whose areas are affected by the project might also use tactics of resistance. Prosci (n.d.) asked participants in his research to identify the primary reasons employees resisted change, and they identified several root causes:

- lack of awareness of why the change was being made
- impact on current job role
- fear rooted in uncertainty due to past failed changes
- lack of visible support from and trust in management or leadership
- lack of inclusion in the change.

For project managers who lack hierarchical authority, there can be times when the relatively greater influence and power of the sponsor is needed – this is part of their role. But regardless of formal power, there are two basic ways to shift resisters: buy them off (build in something that will benefit them) or change their hearts and minds, or both. It may be possible, for example, to convince them that change is needed through well-presented data and analysis. For some people, being brought into the tent (i.e. included on committees or in formal and informal meetings) will be enough to move them from mild resistance to open-minded monitoring or even a position of support.

There is usually great value in meeting with stakeholders who are resisting change or opposing the project. It is much easier in face-to-face meetings to understand the stakeholder perspective (and assumptions) and genuinely work towards resolving identified issues.

When project changes are made in response to feedback from stakeholders, the situation should be presented openly and with appreciation. It is the project manager's responsibility to follow through with any needed adjustments to the project plan, including its timetable or strategies.

Project story: Working on resistance to change

An **electronic medical record (EMR)** implementation project at Goodhope Hospital was running to schedule with the planning phase completed and implementation underway. The project manager was attuned to the need for close engagement with key stakeholder groups including the pharmacy department whose contribution was pivotal for the successful design, configuration, testing and implementation of many EMR modules including orders and medications management.

The pharmacy manager and several senior pharmacists had fully participated in planning activities including protocol, policy and workflow reviews and workshops. However, the pharmacy manager had not attended the previous two steering committee meetings and recruitment of pharmacy staff to the project team was delayed waiting for approval for secondments. Several future state workflows were not agreed, and pharmacy staff were raising significant concerns about the impact of the system on patient safety.

The project manager had a good relationship with pharmacy staff and was very aware that there had recently been a shakeup of the pharmacy leadership team. Several senior pharmacists were on parental leave, resulting in a depleted and less experienced pharmacy workforce. There had also recently been an increase in complaints from patients and ward staff about long waiting times for medications.

The situation got serious for the project when the pharmacy manager emailed the project manager to advise that, due to the pharmacy workforce issues, the needed pharmacy staff could not be released to the project for a further three months. He also advised that pharmacy could not support or endorse the proposed EMR work practices until patient safety concerns were properly addressed.

The project manager immediately set up a one-on-one meeting with the pharmacy manager. Her priority was to understand the changed circumstances in the pharmacy department and their concerns about the system, and to find a way forward. The meeting was intense but good-natured with both people gaining an understanding of each other's issues and priorities. The project manager clarified that funding for backfill of seconded staff would match the actual costs, and that workflow designs were not final and would be tested before final decisions were made. She also confirmed that patient safety was a key principle of system design and explained the safeguards that would be part of the system. She reassured the pharmacy manager that the workforce impacts of the system implementation would be assessed, managed and funded if necessary.

To move forward, it was agreed that secondment of staff to the project would be progressive to enable implementation activities to proceed and for the pharmacy department to recruit backfill staff. The project manager also agreed to attend a meeting with pharmacy staff to discuss any contentious workflows and to agree on decision-making processes for workflow design. It was also agreed that the pharmacy manager could join the steering committee remotely if required.

Keeping the momentum of the project going was a critical consideration for the project manager, and the project plan had in fact anticipated some of the issues the pharmacists raised. But the planning could not anticipate that there would be major disruptions for the pharmacy department at the same time. The agreed solutions had an impact on both the project timeline and the budget, but it was manageable.

In one of the foundational theories on managing change in organisations, Lewin (1958) analysed the change process as a struggle between the driving forces for change and the restraining forces for maintaining the status quo. He suggests that the change agent should first of all identify and analyse the strength of the forces for and against the change, and then decide what strategies are needed to support the positives and weaken the negatives.

Tips for managing resistance to change

- Try to get the management of changes right from the beginning. A structured change management approach at the start of the project can minimise or even prevent some resistance.
- Project teams should assume there will be resistance and work to address and reduce it. Understand the likely sources of resistance, and the root causes that will drive objections, then act on this knowledge before the resistance impacts the project.
- Address resistance openly and formally, to help ensure that it is understood and dealt with throughout the project. Create a change management strategy based on analysis and using special tactics for addressing the problems and sources. Prepare resistance response activities in case of persistent, pervasive resistance.
- Acknowledge the symptoms of resistance (passive like not coming to meetings, or active like not complying with a mandated change in practice) but identify and address the root causes, including through conversation with relevant individuals.
- Engage senior leaders as sponsors of the change but also as resistance managers. This is where the project sponsor and other leaders of people can really help, by demonstrating their support for the change, and influencing stakeholders.

Source: Adapted from Kempton (2024)

Two paradoxes: projects that change and hierarchy versus project mandates

We have argued throughout this book that project management is all about change. But there are two paradoxes that should be noted. The first is that this reality applies to the project itself as well. The emerging iterative nature of some projects in health and community services means that the nature of the change can't always be specified and mandated at the beginning of the project (unlike when, for example, the project goal is 'build a bridge'). For example, the real solutions to problems in models of care or support systems are often not known at the beginning of a project, which may be exactly why a project approach to the problem has been chosen. In this case, the project team and the stakeholders need to be flexible in their expectations of what will emerge at the other end, how and when. While the project plan is vital, the need to plan for variation is also strong. Project managers must avoid falling in love with their plans and tools.

The second paradox is the fact that senior managers may, in effect, be asked to disempower themselves and at the same time impose more discipline on themselves (Partington, 1996). While the organisational change literature argues that support from top management is essential if change is to be realised, in practice there is often tension between project-based authority (held by the project sponsor and manager) and the functional authority of line managers. As Partington notes, 'it is natural for managers at every level to struggle against the abandonment of hierarchies' (1996, p. 18).

Projects may also effectively ask managers to exercise their authority differently, and with more discipline. By locking managers as well as staff into specified goals, strategies, deliverables and budgets, projects can be seen as a temporary and partial stay on the ability of senior managers to change their minds and to manage discrete parts of their operations separately and incrementally.

The solution to this second problem is a long-term one that must be tackled by the organisation as a whole. However, the project manager who is aware of these issues can at least understand some of the sources of resistance from above and can then design ways of working through or around them.

Control and monitoring in the implementation phase

Controlling a project is about monitoring, measuring and reporting progress regularly to identify **variances** from the plan – and taking corrective action when it is needed (PMI, 2021, p. 237), using the methods and tools selected in the planning phase. (See the project templates in individual chapters for some examples). Project control happens throughout the implementation phase, with the aim of keeping the project on track to meet its goals and objectives.

The information for a good control system should be accurate, reliable, valid, readily visible to participants, timely and both diagnostic (what is happening?) and prognostic (what impact will it have?). Regardless of the nature of the project, it is likely that data on expenditure (compared to budget), task/activity completion (compared to the schedule) and performance (compared to the specifications) will be monitored. Meredith et al. (2021) suggest that while it is easy to focus on monitoring data that are easily gathered, monitoring should concentrate primarily on measuring important indicators of progress and output (e.g. the extent to which system design has been completed), rather than on intensity of activity (e.g. the number of meetings that have been held).

In the rest of this chapter, we briefly address controlling the scope and schedule, the budget and resources, project quality, and risk and contingencies before turning to the challenge of managing projects when they get into trouble.

Keeping to the plan

The completeness and quality of project planning will quickly become evident in the implementation phase. Any deficiency may not be the project manager's doing, as they do not always have the benefit of being involved in the project from the beginning – but the project manager is the one who must ensure that the project progresses as smoothly as possible and who must deal with the consequences of any planning deficiencies.

The tasks of planning, monitoring and controlling are cyclical during implementation. That is, the cycle of planning, checking on progress, comparing progress to the plan and taking corrective action if progress does not match the plan is followed by another round of planning to incorporate any necessary changes (Meredith et al., 2021).

The general methods for monitoring adherence to plans are status collection and assessment against the baseline provided by the plan. Information to measure the progress of both the entire project and the activities within it can be collected in many ways, from financial reports showing actual costs versus budget, to routinely collected data on e.g. timeliness of care, to project-specific progress indicators or corridor chat about emerging issues. When the data generated are meaningful and reasonably accurate, the information can be a powerful impetus towards goal attainment – achieving **milestones** and outcomes – for teams and stakeholders.

Controlling project scope: change control

During the implementation phase, changes to the plan ('variances' or 'variations') are normal and to be expected. The scope that was agreed, planned for and documented may be challenged or require modification for legitimate reasons. There could be a change to the deliverables, the target implementation group, a contract, the budget or the schedule. For example, during an information system implementation, there may be a need to include additional functionality in order for the system to work; or the timing for a go-live might need to be extended to ensure that all defects and issues are fixed.

In this phase, '**scope creep**' (unmanaged expansion of the project's scope) is a common and serious threat, leading to cost blowouts, missed deadlines and unmet expectations. If there are significant variances (and they jeopardise the project objectives), the plan can be adjusted by repeating the relevant planning process – for example, re-estimating the staffing levels.

It is almost inevitable that as soon as the project plan and scope have been written and signed off, changes will occur. The important issue for control is to ensure that variances are identified, assessed and documented, the plan is adjusted accordingly, and the variance is formally accepted by the authorised group or individual.

The tools to manage and control project scope include:

- a change request process, most commonly using a change request form (see Template 5.2)
- a process for assessing the impact of the change request on the project, such as impact on the budget or schedule
- formal review and approval (or rejection) of change requests by the project governing body, which then gives authority to the project manager to revise the project accordingly.

When the project is being conducted by external consultants, the contract will usually include a provision for variations. This protects the consultant from escalating costs due either to fickle decision-making by the client or to genuine contingencies, things not reasonably foreseen. The contract will also usually contain clauses that enable the client to extract additional work if the variation is of the consultant's making (e.g. poor modelling) or to reduce or withhold payments if the quality standards are not met.

Controlling the project schedule

Project timing tends to blow out most often during implementation, as project teams find that the actual time needed for the scheduled work is longer than the amount of time planned (Watt et al., 2014), or that time for decision-making about changes causes delays.

A chart or graphical display in the form of a dashboard is the most common and simplest way to represent data in order to monitor and control the timing of a project. A bar or line graph can easily show progress in each aspect of a project compared with the plan. Virtually any aspect of a project can be measured, and the priority is to chart the critical factors for project success. Items that are often charted in this way include:

- project task progress (percentage completion of project tasks as a whole by week)
- staff utilisation (e.g. percentage usage by week)
- performance (e.g. number and magnitude of variations)
- individual task hours and percentage complete
- customer satisfaction measures or milestones.

For projects that are structured in several distinct stages, the finishing of one stage, **sign-off** and commencement of the next (sometimes called a gateway) is another opportunity for controlling the scope and schedule. At the commencement of the new stage, progress and the results of the previous stage can be assessed for any implications, and the potential for variations.

For more complex or multifaceted projects, it will be important to monitor critical activities and the project's **critical path** in order to manage the project schedule (see Chapter 7). The total duration of the critical path is the minimum time you'll need to complete a whole project. Any delay for critical activities will result in extending the total project duration (Donato, 2023).

If the project is running behind schedule, Watt et al. (2014) suggest two schedule compression tools to get back on track – 'crashing' or 'fast tracking'.

- Crashing: When you absolutely have to meet the date, you can sometimes find ways to do activities more quickly by adding more resources to critical path tasks. Crashing the schedule means adding resources or moving them around to bring the project back into line with the schedule. Crashing always costs more and doesn't always work. There's no way to crash a schedule without raising the overall cost of the project. So, if the budget is fixed and you don't have any extra money to spend, you can't use this technique.
- Fast tracking: Sometimes there are two or more activities planned to occur in sequence that could actually be done at the same time. This is called fast tracking the project. Completing tasks in parallel rather than sequentially is risky (e.g. completing user acceptance testing and functional testing at the same time). There's a good chance you might need to redo some of the work done concurrently.

The alternative is to change the schedule, and this can be the best course of action. It is important that the schedule is kept up to date with all approved changes (and version controlled) to ensure that any monitoring correlates to the correct plan.

Controlling the budget and resources

Costs are usually highest in the implementation phase. The estimation and budgeting of project costs (see Chapter 7) is difficult and often poorly done, which can mean in turn that it is difficult to control the costs of a project and keep within budget. And if the budget is not altered when the scope or schedule of a project changes, there is little chance that the costs will match it.

Monitoring of actual and forecast expenditure against budget is probably one of the most familiar control methods in the management toolkit.

Good information is an important aid to the control of costs, but in the end hard decisions may be required. There are several kinds of possible **contingency** responses – finding other sources of funding, reducing the scope, taking up the slack in one part of the project to support another part's shortfall, or moving team members around to meet priority needs.

Managing quality

In the implementation phase, the pressure to cut corners in order to maintain progress may be significant. If key performance criteria (KPIs) have been defined in the planning phase, the focus during implementation is first to ensure that they are understood and accepted by stakeholders. This is one of the reasons why it is a good idea to set up quality assurance mechanisms that are transparent and require reporting to the sponsor or project steering committee on a regular basis.

The second focus of quality monitoring is to ensure that any variation from the quality plan is logged, documented and resolved at a high level. A procedure for acceptance of variations to the quality plan (change requests) should be formalised (usually through the project steering committee or the sponsor).

Some project teams appoint a 'quality partner': a friendly expert adviser/ auditor who takes a watching brief, not waiting for the documentation of problems, but working confidentially with the team to prevent them. An experienced project manager or a person with expertise in quality in the relevant area could play this role.

Managing risks and issues

During the implementation phase, the risk (and issue) plan and the risk register (see Chapter 5) should be regularly reviewed and updated, with existing risks reviewed and reassessed, and newly identified risks added. High and major risks should be reported to the sponsor or project steering committee via the agreed reporting processes (see the project status report, Template 5.1). If risk events occur, they should be reported immediately and the planned response initiated. For major risks, this will almost certainly require 'escalating' the problem to the required level of organisational authority.

Managing evaluation

The project plan should address how the project will be evaluated, specifying the criteria for judging success, on what data or evidence that assessment will be made, and how it will be collected and analysed (see Chapter 6.) Data to enable evaluation will need to be collected and monitored during implementation. The collection of **process evaluation** data need not be intrusive (or worse, destabilising). Minutes of meetings, as well as qualitative assessment by the team, sponsor and perhaps quality partner, can be used to garner information – as can indicators such as levels of attendance at meetings and capacity of the committee to make decisions in a timely way.

The work of implementing the evaluation plan should be built in as much as possible to the project's routine record-keeping and processes, so that the needed information and evidence on which a summative assessment can be made is available when the project is at completion.

Status reporting

The purpose of a **status report** is to advise the steering committee, project sponsor and other stakeholders whether the project is on track to deliver the planned outcomes, and to highlight where their decision-making or direct help is needed. Regular status reporting helps to ensure that the team and the project committee have a clear view of the true state of the project, and that management stays properly informed about progress. Frequent communication of project status and issues is a vital part of effective project risk management. A status report can be a formal document that is presented at meetings, or it can be a regular email or verbal update to key stakeholders.

Status reporting can commence as early in the project as required – for example, in the concept or planning phase – and early reporting can assist in both managing risk and keeping the project on the radar of important stakeholders including senior management. The right frequency of status reporting will depend on the size of the project and the requirements of the steering committee or project sponsor. Too much detail can overwhelm busy project stakeholders – with the effect that they do not read the report or know what to action. The use of high-level indicators, such as RAG reporting (using red, amber and green 'traffic lights') can enable stakeholders to quickly understand where things are off-track and to focus their attention.

There are many status report templates available on the internet (e.g. at www.projectmanager.com), and many organisations already have one in use. It is also a good idea to check with the project sponsor and the steering committee on their preferences for status reporting. Template 5.1 outlines the information that is commonly documented in a project status report.

Being mindful of the concept of 'managing up' may be useful when reporting on project status and progress. Managing up is 'consciously working for the mutual benefit of yourself and your boss' (Greene, 2023) and understanding 'how to effectively communicate with your superiors' (Herrity, 2022). Applying managing up principles to effective communication with the project sponsor and steering committee would mean communicating proactively and concisely, understanding their management style, providing the right information where they are required to make decisions, understanding the bigger picture and owning up to problems or mistakes.

Some projects also require the development of a **benefits realisation** plan (see Chapter 6) that will need to be updated and finalised during the implementation phase.

When things go wrong

If there is going to be trouble in a project, it tends to rise to the surface during the implementation phase. Sometimes the problems relate directly back to the project design and plan. Perhaps the stakeholder issues are not resolvable, or the decision to proceed in the first place was not a wise one, or the political environment in the organisation has changed or is not supportive. Often, the ability of the project team to handle unexpected crises and deviations from the plan is the determining factor in whether a project is successful or succumbs to these problems.

The earlier that signs of trouble are detected, the more effectively they can be dealt with. As noted above, one effective way of avoiding nasty surprises is to have regular status reporting both from and to the project team, the steering committee or other stakeholder groups, and the customer or sponsor.

Warning signs when a project is in trouble

If problems are emerging, there will be warning signs in interactions with the project team, the sponsor and stakeholders. The project manager needs to assess and respond actively to them. Examples of warning signs that may jeopardise a project include:

- essential support systems are not working or are significantly behind schedule
- senior management is not delivering on promised interventions (e.g. mandating requirements for staff to participate in training in new systems or procedures)
- the project itself is falling behind schedule to a point where agreed timing for project deliverables will not be met
- essential resources (such as provision of ICT services) are not forthcoming
- stakeholders fail to turn up to important meetings, or the sponsor or steering committee members are habitually unavailable
- a key quality indicator is not met (e.g. software failing testing)

- the need for the project outcome is fading because of external changes, or it is losing internal priority
- the project team is dysfunctional
- a key person is lost to the project
- the project objectives are looking unachievable – the outcome will not be sustainable (or profitable), or the service or product will not work well enough.

Escalating issues

If signs like those above are emerging, decisive action is probably required. Carroll (2023) advises that there are three main types of issues that require **escalation** during the course of a project: scope issues and delays in work; major decisions or change that needs to be made; and resource bottlenecks or changes to the team.

Escalating the issue – taking it higher in the organisation – should not be avoided or seen as a failure. An escalation process and criteria may be defined in the project plan and can be as informal as calling the project sponsor to brief them and request advice; or it could involve more formal discussion at a steering committee or executive meeting.

Escalating project risks and issues effectively and at the right time is almost an art form that can challenge even senior project managers.

Tips for successfully escalating a project issue

- Before escalating a matter, ensure that the necessary analysis and data gathering is done.
- Avoid frequent and unnecessary escalation, as it could backfire when you really need it.
- Understand and be respectful of any contractual or service-level agreement processes and give an appropriate amount of time for the other party to respond.
- Escalate only to the right stakeholders, and do not involve everyone in the issue.
- Arrange a separate meeting, call, or explicit email to escalate a matter, and keep it focused on the specific issue.
- Don't make it personal.
- Suggest solutions.
- Involve two levels up in escalation depending on severity.
- Document everything.

Source: Adapted from Good (2023)

The best outcome for a troubled project may be to terminate it before further investment is made and additional costs are incurred (e.g. through industrial action, which damages good relations between management and staff).

Finally, we note that most of the successful project leaders and managers we have interviewed in recent years have war stories about projects that succeeded only after great adversity. Sometimes adversity is a necessary struggle to resolve an unknown factor or an error in the project design, and in the end it improves the project outcomes.

Summary
- The implementation phase is where the planned project actions are taken and strategies implemented.
- Project management is a set of methods, but it is also an art that requires flexibility and persistence.
- Leadership, motivation and teamwork are essential in creating successful project outcomes, and project managers need team-building skills and the ability to run effective meetings, as well as problem-solving skills.
- Projects are powerful enablers of change, and organisational change theorists suggest that participative approaches to change are likely to be more effective and sustainable than top-down approaches. Senior management needs to set the parameters and explain the 'givens'.
- Managing change is a political process. While some elements of the power structure are overt, many are embedded in the shadow side of the organisation and outside ordinary managerial intervention. Projects can provide an opportunity to bring important issues into the open and deal constructively with the shadow side.
- Change management strategies identified in the project plan are enacted in the implementation phase and require monitoring to assess their effectiveness, and to identify resistance or signs of change fatigue.
- Project managers must listen to and understand the dynamics of resistance to change, paying particular heed to the forces for and against change, and stakeholder groups.
- Control and monitoring of the budget, quality, schedule, risks, issues and stakeholder engagement are key activities in the implementation phase.
- There are many reasons why projects get into trouble and require issues to be effectively escalated and managed. Sometimes projects only succeed after great adversity.

Readings and resources
On implementation
Agile project management: Project Management Institute. (2021). *A guide to the Project Management Body of Knowledge (PMBOK guide) and the standard for project management* (7 ed.). Newton Square.
Project implementation overview: https://opentextbc.ca/projectmanagement/chapter/chapter-17-project-implementation-overview-project-management/
The 6 steps of project implementation (with tips): https://www.indeed.com/career-advice/career-development/project-implementation
Project plan execution: www.mastering-project-management.com/project-plan-execution.html
Action learning: https://en.wikipedia.org/wiki/Action_learning

On problem-solving
Seven steps for effective problem solving in the workplace: www.mediate.com/articles/thicks.cfm

On effective communication
Managing communications effectively and efficiently: https://www.pmi.org/learning/library/managing-communications-effectively-efficiently-5916
Effective project management communication strategies: https://project-management.com/effective-project-management-communication-strategies/
Your guide to project management communication: https://aipm.com.au/blog/project-management-communication/

On managing up
The dos and don'ts of managing up: https://www.idealist.org/en/careers/managing-up
14 tips to manage up at work (and why it's important): https://www.indeed.com/career-advice/career-development/how-to-manage-up.

On innovation
What is innovation? Definition, types, examples and process: https://ideascale.com/blog/what-is-innovation/

On change management and overcoming resistance
Prosci methodology: https://www.prosci.com/methodology-overview
5 tips for managing resistance to change: https://www.prosci.com/resources/articles/tips-for-managing-resistance-to-change

Contingency model of change management: Dunphy and Stace's model of Change: https://www.managementstudyguide.com/contingency-model-of-change-management.htm

Embracing the shadow side of organisational life, HRzone: https://hrzone.com/embracing-the-shadow-side-of-organisational-life/

On project manager influence

Lead with influence: https://projectmanagementacademy.net/resources/blog/leading-with-influence/

Up & down the organization: putting influence management to work on projects: https://www.pmi.org/learning/library/techniques-to-influence-others-to-meet-project-goals-9102

On monitoring and control

Project implementation: the end-all guide: https://monday.com/blog/project-management/the-end-all-guide-to-project-implementation/

5 phases of project management [PMBOK Version]: https://guides.visual-paradigm.com/5-phases-of-project-management-pmbok-version/

What is critical path in project management? https://project-management.com/what-is-critical-path/

On keeping to the schedule

Project implementation overview: https://opentextbc.ca/projectmanagement/chapter/chapter-17-project-implementation-overview-project-management/

On project escalation

A guide to escalation in project management: https://project-management.com/a-guide-to-escalation-in-project-management/

References

Abudi, G. (2013, October 29). *Managing communications effectively and efficiently* [Conference paper]. PMI Global Congress 2013, New Orleans, USA. www.pmi.org/learning/library/managing-communications-effectively-efficiently-5916

Berkun, S. (2008). *Making things happen: Mastering project management.* O'Reilly Media.

Carroll, A. M. (2023, May 25). *Effective project management communication strategies.* Retrieved February 02, 2024 from https://project-management.com/effective-project-management-communication-strategies/

Change Fatigue. (2024, February 19). In *Wikipedia.* https://en.wikipedia.org/wiki/Change_fatigue

Donato, H. (2023, January 08). *What is critical path in project management?* Retrieved January 13, 2024 from https://project-management.com/what-is-critical-path/

Egan, G. (1994). *Working the shadow side: A guide to positive behind-the-scenes management.* Jossey-Bass.

Good, L. (2023, May 10). *Escalation process in project management guide.* Retrieved March 13, 2024 from https://project-management.com/a-guide-to-escalation-in-project-management/

Greene, A. (2023, August 06). *The dos and don'ts of managing up.* Retrieved January 25, 2024 from www.idealist.org/en/careers/managing-up

Herrity, J. (2022, October 01). *14 Tips to manage up at work (and why it's important).* Retrieved January 25, 2024 from www.indeed.com/career-advice/career-development/how-to-manage-up

Indeed Editorial Team. (2023, March 11). The 6 steps of project implementation (with tips). *Indeed.* Retrieved February 02, 2024 from www.indeed.com/career-advice/career-development/project-implementation

Jain, N. (2023, July 15). *What is innovation? Definition, types, examples and process.* https://ideascale.com/blog/what-is-innovation/

Kempton, L. (2024, February 21). *5 Tips for managing resistance to change.* Retrieved 29 March from www.prosci.com/resources/articles/tips-for-managing-resistance-to-change

Lewin, K. (1958). Group decision and social change. In E. E. Maccoby, T. M. Newcomb & E. Hartley (Eds.), *Readings in social psychology* (pp. 197–211). Holt, Rinehart.

Management Study Guide. (n.d.). *Contingency model of change management: Dunphy and Stace's model of change.* Retrieved January 24, 2024 from www.managementstudyguide.com/contingency-model-of-change-management.htm

Meredith, J. R., Shafer, S. M., & Mantel, S. J. (2021). *Project management: A managerial approach* (11 ed.). Wiley.

Partington, D. (1996). The project management of organizational change. *International Journal of Project Management, 14*(1), 13–21. https://doi.org/10.1016/0263-7863(95)00037-2

Pinto, J. K. (2000). Understanding the role of politics in successful project management. *International Journal of Project Management, 18*(2), 85–91. https://doi.org/10.1016/S0263-7863(98)00073-8

Project Management Institute. (2021). *A guide to the Project Management Body of Knowledge (PMBOK guide) and the standard for project management* (7 ed.). Newton Square.

Prosci. (n.d.). *Prosci methodology.* Retrieved February 13, 2024 from www.prosci.com/methodology-overview

Watt, A., Barron, M., & Barron, A. (2014). Project implementation overview. In A. Watt (Ed.), *Project Management* (2 ed.). BCcampus Open Education.

CHAPTER 9

Project closure and what comes next

DOI: 10.4324/9781003431701-10

This chapter addresses the final project closure **phase** (sometimes called **close out**). We focus on the practical tasks of project completion and close out, finalising evaluation, and ensuring important information about the processes, outputs and outcomes of the project is documented and communicated. We then turn to the transition from project to business as usual and the dilemmas involved in the premature closure of projects. Finally, we discuss the challenge of sustaining project outcomes and offer some thoughts on **project management** trends into the future.

Project closure

> Great is the art of beginning, but greater is the art of ending.
>
> *(Henry Wadsworth Longfellow)*

Sooner or later, all projects come to an end. For some, closure comes with a sense of celebration and achievement. For others, closure takes place prematurely in an atmosphere of high drama, resentment and blame. Projects can also drift along aimlessly until they are quietly killed off when no one is looking.

Sometimes projects that have been applauded on completion are found to be wanting when their outcomes are evaluated. Conversely, projects that appear to have failed can prove their worth at a much later stage. And for projects that set up and trial a new service or process, there is always the question of sustainability: will it continue when the project is finally over and there is no **project manager** in the driving seat? Regardless of how a project arrives at the end of its life, there are important final tasks that can ensure it ends in an optimal way for the project itself, the project manager, the project team and the organisation (Aziz, 2015).

Project closure is the final phase of the **project life cycle** and like any other part of the project, it requires a process to conclude all activities and to formally complete the project (or phase or contractual obligations; PMI, 2021). Typically project closure happens after the final handover of **deliverables** (Visual Paradigm, 2022) and includes all the activities that occur after the project has been delivered or the system has gone live. For some projects, entry into the closing phase may be subject to a **gateway review** that would specify what needs to be completed before the project can commence closure.

Why is project closure important?

> Project closing . . . is as impactful and significant as Initiation, Planning, Executing, and Monitoring and Controlling.
>
> *(Aziz, 2015)*

While it can be tempting to overlook closing phase activities and focus only on the completion of deliverables, project managers are encouraged to actively and strategically manage the closing phase to get the maximum benefit possible from the project and for the sake of projects to come. Effective project closure ensures that the project **objectives** and tasks are reviewed, loose ends are tied up, **stakeholder** acceptance and handover occurs and a plan is developed for all remaining activities to be completed.

There are many potential consequences for a project that is not effectively closed. Without closure there is an increased likelihood that formal acceptance may not be achieved, the project benefits may not be fully realised, the transition to operations may not be smooth and that **lessons learned** may not be captured. There is also a risk that the project team's work and credibility may be negatively perceived for matters that were not their responsibility.

What happens when projects are not effectively closed

There are at least two negative scenarios when project closure is not done properly including:

1. *The never-ending project*: where the project has fulfilled all the deliverables but the organisation still holds the project team accountable for maintaining and operating the ongoing activities rather than the intended operational departments. This may occur where there has been a lack of stakeholder acceptance, or contractor deliverables were not signed off, or because of insufficient handover and/or training or where the operational department or service is seen to lack the necessary workforce or skills.

2. *The orphan product*: where the transition to operations (business as usual) has not been accompanied by the necessary training, awareness or tools to enable effective support and maintenance of the product, or the operational group has not committed to their new responsibilities. The upshot is that the new product (or system, or protocol, or equipment) is unable to be effectively supported or used.

Source: Adapted from Aziz (2015)

When is a project finished?

A project is finished when the project objectives have been met, the planned deliverables have been accepted and the entire budget has been used or reallocated (MacNeil, 2022). More generally, a project is really finished when all the work has been completed, all agreed project management processes have been executed, and completion is formally recognised – that is, everyone agrees that it is completed (Aziz, 2015).

Of course, not all projects meet all their objectives and finish with handover of the deliverables and acceptance by stakeholders. Sometimes, project completion and closure can be rushed, inadequate or truncated due to competing priorities, a lack of budget or where management attention has moved on. And sometimes projects fail. These scenarios are examined later in this chapter.

Project closure steps and activities

A planned and comprehensive closing process should be conducted for all projects regardless of their size, nature or complexity. Individual closing activities and the order in which they are carried out may differ between projects but will typically include the processes listed here and outlined below.

- closure plan and strategy
- acceptance and signoff
- administration and paperwork
- final evaluation, post-implementation review and learning from the project experience
- the final report
- communication
- transition from project to operations (handover)
- transition of project team and resources
- celebration.

Adapted from Indeed Editorial Team (2022);
MacNeil (2022); Malsam (2022);
Mapue (n.d.); Nicholson (2023)

Closure plan and strategy

Before commencing closure tasks, developing a wrap up plan and checklist will ensure that all aspects of the project are covered (Mapue, n.d.). The first step is to identify all outstanding tasks that need to be reviewed and assigned by:

- reviewing the **project plan** to identify any in-scope work or deliverables yet to be completed, objectives or essential requirements that remain unmet and any ongoing risks or issues
- reviewing any existing plans for handover/transition to operations to identify any outstanding tasks or issues
- identifying any activities that need to continue (e.g. **benefits realisation** activities) after the project is completed and who will complete them.

There may be aspects of the project's deliverables that cannot be wrapped up at the time of completion. A key piece of equipment or software needed for the full operation of a new service might not yet be available, or the industrial implications of a change might have to be sorted out in a different timeframe. These issues need to be clearly identified in the closure plan, a process for resolving them agreed, and interim arrangements to work around the outstanding issues made.

When all the outstanding tasks are identified, a closure plan (and/or checklist) can be developed with responsibilities assigned and a timeline. Closure strategies can be included in the plan as needed, such as how stakeholder acceptance will be achieved or how project team resources will be released. There are many online project closure resources available including checklists, templates and step-by-step guides. See Template 9.1 and links to other resources at the end of this chapter.

Acceptance and signoff

Acceptance is the formal process of presenting deliverables to the **project sponsor** and/or the **steering committee**, and the person/team (also known as the business owner) who will take over responsibility for the ongoing operation of the project outcomes; and getting **sign-off** or formal acceptance. Deliverables and services provided by contractors or third-party providers may also need to be accepted and signed off at this time.

Acceptance of the project outcomes or deliverables by the authorised person or group is a key milestone, and acceptance certificates (commonly used for ICT system or software acceptance) or other forms of sign-off (e.g. recording in the relevant meeting minutes) may be required to document this formally. See Template 9.2 for an example of an acceptance certificate, or the resources link at the end of the chapter. Recognition of the work and clarity about acceptance (including any residual issues) are important for all who have contributed and for those who will work with the project's outcomes.

Administration and paperwork

Projects generate a lot of documents and essential paperwork that should be reviewed and updated during the closure phase. Consider adding the following to the closure plan or checklist:

- listing all documents that need sign off and approval from stakeholders
- finalising any project documentation such as certificates, assets, or reports
- closing all contracts with internal partners, vendors and any other contracted providers
- addressing all outstanding payments, ensuring all invoices, commissions, fees and bonuses are paid so that the project expenditure can be finalised and closed.

Adapted from Malsam (2022) and Nicholson (2023)

Template 9.1 Closure Checklist

Project Name:		Project Manager:	
Project Start Date:		Project End Date:	

Project Closure Checklist

Project Closure Steps	Project Closure Activities (examples)	Status	Artefacts Required	Completed?
Closure plan & strategy	Develop closure plan	e.g. Complete, Closing, Incomplete	e.g. Project charter, project plan	☐
	Identify all outstanding work, deliverables, essential requirements, objectives & risks/ issues			☐
	Identify any post- closure and ongoing tasks or deliverables e.g. benefits realisation			☐
Acceptance and signoff	Acceptance process and certificates			☐
	List all documents that need sign off and stakeholder approval			☐
Administration & paperwork	Finalise all project documentation e.g. certificates, assets, reports			☐
	Close all contracts with internal partners, vendors and any contracted providers			☐
	Arrange payment of all outstanding invoices, commissions, fees and bonuses			☐
	Finalise the project budget			☐
	Index and archive all project documents			☐
Final evaluation & final report	Findings from evaluation, post implementation review, stakeholder feedback and lessons learned			☐
	Develop final report			☐
Communication	Debrief, close out meeting, communication to project team, governance bodies and stakeholders			☐
Transition from project to operations (handover)	Enact handover/ transition and go-live plans, signoff of completion, handover meeting			☐
Transition of project team & resources	Transition of staff, close project office, redistribute resources			☐
Celebration	Celebrate efforts, achievements and project outcomes			☐

Template 9.1 Closure Checklist

Template 9.2 Project Acceptance

Project	
Project Name:	
Sponsor/Client:	
Submitted by:	
Submitted to:	
Date:	

Deliverable description	
	[Provide a brief description of the deliverable/s and any necessary comments]

☐	Project/deliverable Accepted	The Sponsor/Client agrees that the project deliverables have satisfied the acceptance criteria, and takes possession of the delivered product.

Approval Signatures			
Name	**Title**	**Signature**	**Date**

Template 9.2 Project Acceptance

The next step is to index and archive all documentation to ensure it is accessible in the future. As Malsam (2022) notes:

> Even if you never access it, there's a need to keep a paper trail of the work done on any project for other people in the organization. This might include legal teams, or HR teams, or even your successor. You never know when someone might have to go back and respond to a question or want to learn how an old issue was resolved.

Final evaluation, post-implementation review and learning from the project experience
Preparation for evaluation pays off as the project draws to a close and the needed analysis of results can be more easily completed. Increasingly, tailored methods of evaluation are being mandated, particularly for larger projects – post-implementation review (PIR) (also called Post Project Review) and benefits realisation studies being among the best known (see Chapter 6). Even if planning for evaluation was not done, the project plan provides an implicit basis for evaluation, and can be used for this purpose when necessary. In essence, this means that the project manager writes a simple evaluation plan based on the project's goals and objectives and uses available data as well as reflection and review activities.

Reflection and learning are always happening during projects. Project managers, team members and stakeholders are engaged in figuring out how to do something new, or how to do something in a new way – so their minds are engaged at least some of the time in problem-solving and assessment of options. In the closing phase, many project participants will welcome an opportunity to engage in reflection and discussion, and are likely to be doing it in staffrooms, cafes or bars anyway.

Some process questions can be answered with information that the project itself supplies:

- Did that approval happen on time?
- Was the report well received by the executive, sponsor and partners?
- Was the project plan modified during the course of the project?
- Did the vendor respond readily to **variance** requests?
- Did the steering committee meet regularly and make effective decisions?

For information about why things happened the way they did, other sources are usually needed, and the data or information is usually qualitative in nature:

- Were the stakeholders satisfied that they were effectively engaged, their views considered and given weight?
- If **co-design** was used, what did we learn about it?
- Were team meetings successful in coordinating the work, and why?
- Was the communication strategy successful, and why?
- Did any changes to the plan contribute to the project's successful completion?
- Were there any major difficulties that the project team encountered, and how were they overcome?

Methods of collecting qualitative data and information generally rely on asking people the right questions in ways that enable them to be as honest and constructive as possible with the minimum possible time and effort. Face-to-face communication generally (but not always, and not for every-one) yields richer results. People think as they speak, or as they listen to others' views, and the struggle to articulate their experience helps them to understand it better and inform the evaluator more reliably. On the other hand, anonymous but methodical collection of responses to questions by means of surveys can generate information that might be hard to obtain in person.

Recommendations and learnings gathered from the project manager, team and stakeholders can be captured in a **lessons learned log** through-out and after a project. Lessons learned logs capture both the positive and negative experiences of a project and give project managers the opportunity to learn from the actual experiences of others, while also demonstrating the organisation's commitment to project management excellence (see also Chapter 6). A template for a lessons learned log is provided in Template 6.1.

As the project draws to a close, project sponsors and managers often need to look beyond the immediate concrete project goal (essentially, did we make it happen?) and consider the larger question of whether the pro-ject's results will deliver the value in practice that inspired the creation of the project. Answers to this question vary greatly according to the type of project.

Many projects in health and community services are just the first step, the initiation and testing of an innovation intended to be taken up in ongoing operations or **program** delivery. So, if the project did achieve its immediate goals – the concept was proven, the trial was successful, or the information system is in and working – the more significant question becomes 'will it deliver the benefits we seek?' Sometimes, this question can be answered at least provisionally in the project's final report, but even so the real test comes in routine operations.

These long-term questions will have been included in a good evaluation plan, perhaps using PIR, but can't be answered in the closing phase of the project due to timing. Making sure that the business of answering them is identified as a future activity, and that responsibility is allocated, is one of the tasks at completion and handover.

If benefits realisation or PIR methods are being used for the project, an updated plan may need to be prepared by the project manager, perhaps with assistance from finance and information staff. It will update the origi-nal plan with information about progress towards achieving the intended benefits at the time of project closure, factors likely to affect success over the coming review period, and any needed changes to the method or targets (e.g. ways of measuring productivity gains, or the period over which they will be realised). This updated plan should also include details as to how – and by whom – monitoring will be undertaken and final assessment made. The updated plan is then part of the formal handover of the project. A process for the approval and implementation of any recommendations for change in the benefits realisation/PIR assessment will be needed.

The closing phase is also a good opportunity for the project manager to reflect and self-evaluate their performance during the project and update their resume. This evaluation may simply be reflecting on the progress of the project, how major issues or hurdles were handled, what might have been done differently and even personal lessons learned and skills developed. Alternatively, a more formal approach may be to request a performance review from the project sponsor or the project team.

The final report

The final report is an important element in closing a project and summing it up, either as part of acceptance and transition to operations (handover), or as part of the PIR. Usually written by the project manager, the final report details the overall project at the point of completion and is useful as:

- a historical record of the project and what it achieved
- an opportunity for reflection on the project as a whole
- a comparison of the project at completion with the plan
- a way of informing stakeholders of the status of any outstanding issues
- a record of recommendations for future projects and strategies for sustaining the outcomes of this project
- a summary of the project evaluation, and the learning from it, with the aim of promoting enhanced capability for subsequent projects (MacNeil, 2022).

A good final report is structured so that the reader can quickly get a clear overview, can easily find particular information of interest and doesn't get lost in the detail. While the size and structure of the report will depend on the nature of the project, the sections or headings shown in the final report (Template 9.3) provide a useful starting point.

The project report should not be structured as a chronological record of the project process (the 'what I did on my holidays' approach). Rather, it should be logically structured in a way that best meets the knowledge and decision-making needs of the readers. The right structure will also assist in avoiding repetition and enabling the reader to assess the quality and import of the information and data. Hopefully the result will be that readers agree with the team's conclusions and recommendations.

If the report needs to help those responsible for implementing or sustaining the project's outcomes, it should focus on the practical and operational aspects of effective implementation. This would usually include the conditions under which the outcomes work well, and the minimum requirements for effective ongoing operations.

Template 9.3 Final Report

COVER
Organisation name and logo
Name of project
Date of submission

Contents page

Executive summary

Maximum 2–3 pages giving an overview of project background, goals, methods, outcomes, achievements, recommendations or future implications

Introduction

Project background and purpose, rationale, the problem statement or opportunity, acknowledgements of those who made significant contributions

Project goals and methods

Drawn from the project plan – goal/s, objectives, scope, strategies, program Budget, resourcing, sponsor, team, project organisation, governance etc.

Outcomes and key achievements

Outline key achievements, deliverables and project outcomes including results of any impact evaluation

Risks/Issues

Any residual risks and issues arising from the project but not resolved by it

Learning from the project

Outline findings from post implementation review and final evaluation including lessons learned and stakeholder feedback

Recommendations and action

Covering acceptance, handover, further monitoring and assessment of longer-term outcomes or realisation of intended benefits

References

Published sources of evidence and internal documents cited in the report

Appendices (if needed)

Key project documents
Details of important project data and performance indicators not included in the body of the report

Template 9.3 Final Report

If the report needs to convince decision makers to adopt a proposed change or sustain a project outcome, the logic of its structure should be designed to lead the reader to agree with its proposals and conclusions. Or if the report is needed to meet the accountability requirements of a funding body (including corporate head office), the author needs to be aware of what their expectations are and strive to meet them.

A well-written report is a lot more convincing than one that leaves the reader to disentangle spelling errors, poor grammar and unclear meaning. Writing the contents page first is one way to focus on clear, logical structuring (Template 9.3 provides a starting list that can be varied to fit the project). Some writers find it useful to outline the report first, using dot points, while others prefer to draft whole sections or paragraphs and move them around later if necessary. For most people, there is no real substitute for drafting, reading (and preferably getting others to read) and redrafting.

The project report may need to conform to a house style for documents. The sources of ideas and assertions in the report should be acknowledged, something that is becoming more important as agencies pursue the goals of **evidence-based practice** and evidence-informed decision-making. There are many acceptable referencing styles, and the agency may have a preferred style. The most important thing is to use it consistently, including for information and documents found on the internet.

If there is a wealth of important detail, it should be organised into attachments so that the data are available for those who need it (perhaps in the form of a separate volume with limited circulation). If the report has a practical use after the life of the project, it may be worthwhile to budget for a professional editor – readability can be significantly improved at a fairly modest cost.

For some projects and some organisations, simpler documentation may be required, perhaps little more than a set of presentation slides. In any organisation, a clear, concise presentation is an effective way of communicating the project's outcomes and implications and is a valuable adjunct to the written report. It can be worthwhile doing this well, as a good presentation can be used repeatedly to ensure that a clear, consistent message about the project is communicated to all those affected or interested in its outcomes.

Communication

Communication is an essential component of the closure phase and there are several elements of a good approach. A debriefing process, that is an opportunity for people to discuss their experiences and impressions of the project, can be rewarding in itself and can also provide input to the evaluation and the final report. It can also help with refining the communication approach. Members of the steering committee and other key stakeholders, as well as the team, might appreciate both formal and informal opportunities to reflect, debrief and provide feedback.

A final close-out meeting with the steering committee and project team and vendor or contractor is a good way to present the final report and it enables debriefing and the tying up of any loose ends or issues. Final communications such as an email or newsletter may be a good way to close the loop with stakeholders, advise how any incomplete items will be tackled, mark the end of the project, outline any next steps and importantly, to express thanks to all who have contributed.

Consistent communication with the project team throughout the closure phase about final transition to operations and handover is important. They need to understand any debrief or feedback processes, how and when the team will be wound up and any next steps.

Finally, there needs to be a method of ensuring that suitable project information is distributed to stakeholders, and often the community, through the organisation's website and/or intranet and if relevant through lodging in library collections.

Transition from project to operations (handover)

Transition to operations (sometimes called transition to business as usual [BAU]) is the formal name for handover from the project to the person, team, or entity that will be running (or responsible for) the new process, service model, program, role, training or technology. Depending on what the project is delivering, the transition to operations may simply involve documentation and training for the team who will be carrying out the new process, plus a briefing for team management. For more complex projects such as introducing new technology or a new model of care, or a project with a large cohort of users, the planning for transition should begin in the planning phase (see Chapter 5) and depending on the project may involve a **go-live** (or cutover) that happens at the end of the implementation phase, or parallel running of old and new processes for a period of time.

Transition to operations is not a milestone but a handover process, with technical, decision and communication tasks, as this project story illustrates.

Project story: recognising handover in an outsourcing project

The laboratory staff of a large government health service had struggled against an outsourcing imperative, and their in-house bid (a proposal to keep the service in-house on new terms) had failed. Most of them had been offered jobs by the successful bidder, but there was a lot of sadness and some anger – particularly for the long-serving staff, some of whom had been with the organisation for many years and felt that they had always delivered excellent work.

Care had been taken throughout the project to offer support to the staff, to keep them regularly informed of progress, to facilitate access to independent financial advice, to maximise their opportunities for ongoing employment and to assist those who missed out. The People and Culture Department argued that this approach should be sustained to the end, and that there should be a farewell party for all the staff, whether they were leaving or transferring to the new employer. The general manager agreed but approached the occasion with dread.

The usual form was to be followed – food and drink, gifts – and a short speech was definitely part of the agenda. With her heart in her mouth, the general manager spoke of the good work and loyalty of the staff, as well as acknowledging that the policy requiring competitive tendering of diagnostic services was deeply unpopular and that the staff had been through a time of uncertainty and anxiety about their futures. She finished by expressing the good wishes of the health services community. The applause was muted, and the mood sombre, but it was clear that the staff appreciated this proper farewell with the usual courtesies extended. This formal, respectful recognition of the moment of transition may also have contributed a little to the good working relationships that were later experienced under the new contract.

Transition to operations involves the following activities and depending on scale can take between one and six months (Girdler, 2021):

- Gain acceptance and signoff of deliverables (see section above).
- Develop and enact a transition plan that identifies who will be supporting the system, how issues are to be resolved, how functioning and use of the new processes and/or technology is to be monitored, updating training documentation with 'live' scenarios and retraining if needed.
- Identify and if appropriate enable the tasking or transfer of core project staff (including subject matter experts) to provide assistance to the operational team.
- Get sign off from the business owner that handover is complete.

Transition of the project team and resources

The team will need to wind up, even if some members will go on to work on another project or become part of the ongoing operating team. The project office may need to be closed, and its equipment distributed to the appropriate areas. Individuals sometimes need assistance in the transition back to their old jobs, or in moving on to new ones either inside or outside of the organisation. Recognition of the transition, and practical assistance, can make it easier. Preparations for this process made in the early stages, and good management of team members, will pay off at this point.

Celebration

Finally, there is a need for celebration. The effort and commitment, as well as the achievements, of those who have contributed to a successful outcome need to be recognised. A special edition of the agency's newsletter, recording and celebrating the project's outcomes, might be released. A formal handover meeting might end with refreshments and thanks to all involved. The 'go-live' point for a new system delivered by the project can also be the occasion for celebration. Celebrations of success can be a good way of building or maintaining a positive climate and can consolidate the pride and satisfaction people feel in their work and their organisation.

When projects fail or need to be terminated

In our experience, the survivors of failed projects usually attribute failure to inadequacies in the planning, prioritising and resourcing of projects. A typical pathway starts with failure to define the goals and **scope** well enough, with the result that the project goes 'off track' and is then hard to stop. But there are many ways to fail, and many causes. The reasons for project failure can be seen as the mirror image of the predictors of success (see Chapters 1 and 2) and are outlined below.

Poor project design, preparation and planning

- requirements or specifications of the project result are not clear or are unrealistic
- requirements or specifications change so fundamentally that the underlying approach or contract cannot be successfully adapted to match
- lack of project planning, especially risk management
- other technical reasons.

Problems of leadership and governance

- inadequate human resources, tools, or material
- the project overruns its budget due to high costs, or it becomes clear that the results will not return the expected profit or cost-saving.

Lack of organisational support and stakeholder engagement

- lack of management support
- lack of customer, stakeholder or user engagement or support.

Changing environment or conditions

- the intended result or product becomes obsolete, is no longer needed
- force majeure (e.g. earthquake, pandemic disease, flooding)
- necessary conditions disappear
- the 'parent' organisation no longer exists or changes its strategy and the project does not support the new strategy.

Source: Adapted from Stoemmer (2022)

If a project hasn't succeeded or is limping along without a clear path to completion the best course of action may be to abandon or discontinue it. Projects can fail in many ways – escalation ('just one more extra mile to go') is a common one in major digital projects. Seismic shifts in the environment (e.g. the arrival of the COVID-19 pandemic) also cause many projects to be abandoned. In any time of upheaval innovation projects are halted or abandoned because of the way the upheaval disrupts teams, plans and decision-making, or because the project champions exit the organisation.

When the barriers are insurmountable, or when rescue efforts have failed, the only alternative is to terminate the project, discontinue the work and reassign the people who were working on it. Closing a project can also be a planned **contingency** – for example, when the findings in one stage of a project indicate a fatal flaw in its design or feasibility, and the decision not to proceed with further stages is the only option.

Terminating a project prior to its planned conclusion is difficult because it usually involves the curtailing of a previously held vision, the breaking up of a 'project family' and perhaps an admission of failure. Termination may simply mean that a project no longer continues in its current form. Meredith et al. (2021) examined the varieties of project termination, calling them extinction, addition, integration and starvation. *Extinction* means the project is stopped (whether successful or unsuccessful). *Addition* means that the project is incorporated into ongoing operations as a distinct unit or department in the organisation. *Integration* is where the project disappears but elements of it are distributed within the organisation, and *starvation* is where the project still exists but budget cuts mean that no progress is achieved. An example of a project made extinct is illustrated in this project story.

Project story: cancelled!

The project manager identified warning signs in the early days of a project that aimed to upgrade an existing intensive care unit (ICU) information system. Though the system was well out of date (about three major versions behind), and the software vendor had advised that they no longer supported the old version, the new ICU management team had shown little interest in the upgrade project. The medical director (the project sponsor) had escalated the risk regarding the critical software being unsupported and requested that the ICT project manager urgently work with the ICU staff to develop the **business case** for a system upgrade.

In drafting the business case, the project manager discovered that there was little support for the existing ICU system, with ICU management actively investigating systems to replace it. They felt that upgrading the current system was a waste of time, effort and money.

The project manager completed and submitted the business case (with the information that ICU had provided), but also advised that there had been lack of stakeholder buy-in. The project sponsor agreed that a new system was desirable, but believed that there was not enough money, and informed the ICU staff that the upgrade of the current system was going ahead.

The upgrade project was therefore put in motion – the business case was signed off and a software vendor was engaged. It was not until the project team was being established, with the secondment of ICU staff, that ICU management moved from passive to active resistance. One after another, the ICU manager assigned people to the project who were variously not interested, unavailable, had little knowledge of the current system or were paid significantly more than was estimated in the business case. Then there was the issue of releasing them from the ICU roster, which involved a delay of up to six weeks.

The CEO became concerned about resulting variations to the project plan and timelines and lobbying by ICU management further destabilised support. The CEO was also aware that an alternative pathway had opened up, because ICU functionality was in scope for a planned new statewide EMR. The straw that broke the camel's back was a forecast overrun on the budget. The chief finance officer stepped in (with the support of the CEO) and announced that the project would be cancelled forthwith. The project manager disbanded the team, informed the vendor, and thanked them all for their efforts.

Termination is not necessarily the same thing as failure, but poor management of the process can make things worse. While it is never easy, once the decision is made it should be done quickly to minimise further waste of resources and disruption to the organisation. It is almost always a good idea to develop and articulate a clear statement of reasons for termination, and proactively communicate this message to all concerned, without delay and as consistently as possible. This tactic will not stop rumours, but it will at least ensure that they are not circulated in a vacuum. The rights and interests of the staff involved need to be protected with clear and prompt action.

One exit method for a project that is limping to a dead end is simply to declare it finished: adopt a modified goal that has been achieved and cut the losses, with as much dignity as possible. Recommendations for follow-up activity might be made, and evaluation might enable the team and organisation to learn from the experience. The team should be thanked for their efforts and then resettled, with perhaps an informal gathering and opportunity to debrief.

Sustaining project outcomes

Sustaining the outcomes of successful projects can be difficult when the project team disperses and funding is exhausted. One of the reasons for this lies in the way funding is secured and dreams are pursued. When resources are scarce, organisations sometimes enact their pursuit of better or bigger services using small dollops of project funding in order to make a start. Then they are likely to face the problem of a long journey, requiring ongoing support and resources they don't have. The question of sustainability should be addressed at the concept stage, and dispassionate decisions are needed at that point. While there are good reasons for taking big risks very occasionally, to do so routinely is to dissipate energy, reputation, capacity and support.

There are many aspects of sustainability that the project itself cannot influence – emerging organisational budget problems, for example. But the project method can make a difference in at least one way: by maximising the engagement of those who will be responsible for ongoing operations. If members of the future operational team are involved in the project concept, design, planning and implementation, they are more likely to be enthusiastic implementers of the outcomes.

Where the project is someone else's good idea or is operated in a way that excludes or frustrates the receiving team sustainability is more likely to be a rocky road. This has implications for the way in which PMOs or other central project units conduct their work. It is also important that there is skilled engagement with stakeholders, particularly those with legitimate interests in the detailed working arrangements that the project will later seek to hand over to them.

We have also discussed the use of projects as seduction: persuading others to act by showing how a good idea can work in practice. If such a project succeeds, its existence changes the balance of probabilities (by increasing the intangible costs of not proceeding with something that works) when ongoing resources are being divided up.

A successful project can also work to improve the chances of a supportive policy decision being made. It is easier for governments or health authorities to make policy supporting innovative services, or interventions in social problems, if they can point to the results of a successful trial. The success of needle exchange programs in reducing the rate of HIV infection among intravenous drug users is an example of this – the idea of handing out equipment for use in an illegal activity is otherwise hard to justify.

While there are many excellent examples of this strategy – 'show it can work and then get the money (or the policy change)' – embarking on this course is a significant risk. It should be done knowingly, for very good reasons, and as an exception not the rule.

Projects and project management into the future

The future of project management is full of opportunity.

(PMI, 2023)

As noted in Chapter 2, the current context within which all projects are undertaken is one of increasing complexity where disruptive forces such as labour shortages, supply chain problems, resource scarcity, spiralling costs, cyber threats, the pace of change and the increasing importance of environmental, social and governance (ESG) strategies are all impacting on projects and project performance (AIPM & KPMG, 2022). Many of these issues will continue to challenge projects and project managers together with the ongoing 'trickling' impacts of the pandemic (Simplilearn, 2023) and the growing impacts of climate change. Project management practices will always need to be innovative, agile and flexible, and project managers will need strong interpersonal and leadership skills (PMI, 2023).

The future trends described in the literature and by our research participants roughly fall into three categories – technology and the project environment, embedding of project approaches in organisational strategy and general management, and project management and workforce trends.

As the digitisation of health and community care services and agencies continues, the use of new technologies will expand including cloud computing, cyber security, artificial intelligence (AI), machine learning, data analytics and the growing use of devices and wearables by staff, patients and clients (Boutel, 2023; Patra, 2023; PMI, 2023). The impacts on project management practices are likely to include increasing adoption of AI in all its forms (expert systems, machine learning and deep learning [Association for Project Management, n.d.]) to automate data-intense project tasks such as decision support, estimating, resource scheduling, data visualisation and risk analysis (Patra, 2023).

Whilst it is not predicted that AI will replace the essential work of a project manager, it will significantly influence how services and products, capabilities, systems and solutions get built and delivered (PMI, 2023). More advanced project management software will be used to manage data, resources, scheduling, budgets and project dashboards, and there will be an increasing focus on data analytics for data-driven project management. People will continue to experiment with methods and tools (Patra, 2023).

It seems likely that project approaches will be an increasing element of organisational strategy with implications for general managers and project managers. Project management and the rise of ESG initiatives will go hand in hand, and project leaders will need to embrace culturally responsive leadership to support diversity, equity and inclusion (PMI, 2023). These developments, along with increasing climate risk and climate change impacts, will require an increased focus on effective change management to ensure sustainable outcomes.

For project managers, interpersonal and leadership skills or 'soft skills' (called power skills by PMI) and the ability to work in teams will be a priority, and there will be increased demand for emotionally intelligent leaders (AIPM & KPMG, 2022, Jenkins, 2023; Patra, 2023; PMI, 2023). At the same time, it seems likely that technical skills in 'future focused' areas including digital integration, testing, software development, architecture, data literacy, and databases will be in demand (Patra, 2023).

Project management skills, experience and careers will deepen and may become more specialised. More people will identify as project management professionals with the qualifications, credentials and experience to back that up. But at the same time, managers and professional staff in health and community services are likely to need project management knowhow as it continues to grow as an embedded part of their roles. Other workforce practices like remote working will also have an impact (Boutel, 2023; Jenkins, 2023; Simplilearn, 2023). Labour shortages seem likely to continue and will affect the project management sector globally (AIPM & KPMG, 2022; Boutel, 2023).

Conclusion

Throughout this book, we have emphasised the need for genuine organisational commitment to the projects that are taken on, for a well-developed and feasible project plan, and for adequate resources and a high-performing project team. We hope it is clear that project management in a complex industry is not just a set of competencies that can be taught from a manual but rather requires flexibility, understanding and good judgement.

Good judgement is not something that can be learned from a textbook; good judgement comes from experience and a willingness to reflect and learn from that experience. As Smyth, Legge and Stanton (2006, p. 15) point out, 'Where managers have real choices they cannot *know* the right answer; they have to rely on their judgment (and this means taking risks).'

However, taking risks can be tempered through reflection on practice – on what worked and what did not – and the ability to recognise the patterns or similarities in past experiences that might help to guide the project team in dealing with a current dilemma. The more we reflect and learn from our personal practice, the greater chance we have of making improved decisions when faced with complex situations.

When the first edition of this book was published, we expressed three hopes about the future in project management. The first was greater uptake of project approaches by organisations that face innovation and implementation challenges. As we finish this fourth edition, it is clear that this hope has been realised, and the sector is now a much more sophisticated, mature and effective user of projects. General managers routinely rely on project management approaches and know-how in their work.

The second was that more leaders and managers might accept the discipline of project management in their own approaches to managing change and development. We have seen significant progress in this area, with greater clarity and openness about goals and methods of change, willingness to support skill development, better understanding that 'the devil is in the detail', and greater knowledge of and respect for the real work of project teams.

The third was that using project management would mean that organisations were better able to achieve their goals and meet the needs of their stakeholders. This remains the major purpose of this book, and its success is partly in the hands of the reader.

Summary
- Project closure is an important step in the project life cycle and needs to be actively managed. This phase includes acceptance and handover of the project outcomes and deliverables to the authorised person or group.
- Activities in project closure also include a final meeting and the submission of a final report. Recognising and celebrating the efforts and achievements of those involved in the project, and planning for life after the project, are important.
- Some evaluation activities may need to be completed after project closure, for methods like post-implementation review and benefits realisation, or outcome evaluation generally.
- Projects can fail for a variety of reasons and may require termination. While closing a failed project can be difficult, once failure is clear, closure should be prompt and decisive.
- Sustaining the outcomes of a project can be difficult but is more likely where members of the future operational team are involved in the project concept, design, planning and implementation.
- Project complexity has become the norm and projects will increasingly involve more technology which will require project managers to upskill and reskill in new areas.

- Projects and project management are becoming part of the normal repertoire of general managers and are an increasingly important element of organisational strategy.

Readings and resources
Close phase checklists and templates
Project closure: https://www.projectmanagementdocs.com/project-closure/

Project acceptance template: https://www.projectmanagementdocs.com/template/project-closure/project-acceptance/

Post implementation review template: https://www.projectmanagementdocs.com/template/project-closure/post-project-review/

Lessons learned questions: https://www.projectcubicle.com/lessons-learned-template-questions/

On handover and transition from project to operations
How to transition from project to operation: https://projectskillsmentor.com/project-skills/how-how-to-effectively-transition-from-project-to-operations

Project handover process: https://www.youtube.com/watch?v=OLibddcR3Yg

On the future of PM
The future factors and trends in project management: https://www.linkedin.com/pulse/future-factors-trends-project-management-virtual-spaceaiglobal

2025 vision: the future of PMOs: https://www.projectmanagement.com/blog-post/11473/2025-vision--the-future-of-pmos#_=_

Future of project management: future trends and skills: https://www.knowledgehut.com/blog/project-management/future-of-project-management

References
Association for Project Management. (n.d.). *What is artificial intelligence in project management?* Retrieved February 02, 2024 from www.apm.org.uk/resources/what-is-project-management/what-is-ai-in-project-management/

Australian Institute of Project Management and KPMG. (2022). *The state of project management in Australia 2022: Leading projects through volatility.* https://info.aipm.com.au/hubfs/Reports%20and%20major%20content%20assets/The%20State%20of%20PM%202022%20Report%20FINAL.pdf

Aziz, E. E. (2015, October 10). *Project closing: The small process group with big impact* [Conference paper]. PMI Global Congress 2015, London, England. www.pmi.org/learning/library/importance-of-closing-process-group-9949

Boutel, M. (2023, December 21). *Project management trends to watch in 2024.* Retrieved January 29, 2024 from www.pm-partners.com.au/insights/project-management-trends-to-watch-in-2024/

Girdler, A. (2021, September 9). All the basics you need to know about the project handover process [Post]. *LinkedIn.* www.linkedin.com/pulse/all-basics-you-need-know-project-handover-process-girdler-cet-pmp

Indeed Editorial Team. (2022, June 25). What is a project closeout? Definition, steps and tips. *Indeed.* Retrieved January 06, 2024 from www.indeed.com/career-advice/career-development/project-closeout

Jenkins, C. (2023, April 25). The impact of the pandemic on project management. Retrieved January 29, 2024 from www.forbes.com/sites/forbescoachescouncil/2023/04/25/the-impact-of-the-pandemic-on-project-management/?sh=4b85168124f5

MacNeil, C. (2022, December 20). Project closure: 8 steps to finish projects confidently. *Asana.* https://asana.com/resources/project-closure

Malsam, W. (2022, February 15). 5 Steps to project closure (checklist included). *Project Manager.* Retrieved January 06, 2024 from www.projectmanager.com/blog/project-closure

Mapue, J. (n.d.). *The ultimate project close out checklist.* Retrieved January 02, 2024 from www.goskills.com/Project-Management/Resources/Project-close-out-checklist

Meredith, J. R., Shafer, S. M., & Mantel, S. J. (2021). *Project management: A managerial approach* (11 ed.). Wiley.

Nicholson, R. (2023, April 11). Project closure checklist: 8 steps to project peace of mind (+ free template). *ResourceGuru.* https://resourceguruapp.com/blog/project-closure-checklist

Patra, A. (2023, January 23). *12 Project management trends emerging in 2023.* www.replicon.com/blog/project-management-trends/

Project Management Institute. (2021). *A guide to the Project Management Body of Knowledge (PMBOK guide) and the standard for project management* (7 ed.). Newton Square.

Project Management Institute. (2023). *5 Predictions for the future of project management.* Retrieved January 29, 2024 from www.pmi.org/learning/publications/pm-network/digital-exclusives/5-predictions-for-the-future-of-project-management

Simplilearn. (2023, April 26). *How COVID-19 pandemic will impact the future of project management.* Retrieved January 29, 2024 from www.simplilearn.com/how-covid-19-pandemic-impacts-the-future-of-project-management-article

Smyth, A., Legge, D., & Stanton, P. (2006). Learning management, (and managing your learning). In M. G. Harris & Associates (Eds.), *Managing health services* (2 ed., p. 15). Elsevier.

Stoemmer, P. (2022, March 16). *Project termination.* www.project-management-knowhow.com/project_termination.html

Visual Paradigm. (2022, March 8). *5 Phases of project management [PMBOK version].* Retrieved March 13, 2024 from https://guides.visual-paradigm.com/5-phases-of-project-management-pmbok-version/

Index